Money Matters

MONEY MATTERS

ANSWERS TO YOUR FINANCIAL QUESTIONS

LARRY BURKETT

THOMAS NELSON PUBLISHERS
Nashville

A Division of Thomas Nelson, Inc.
www.ThomasNelson.com

Published in Nashville, Tennessee, by Thomas Nelson, Inc.

Scripture taken from the NEW AMERICAN STANDARD BIBLE ®, Copyright The Lockman Foundation 1960, 1962, 1963, 1968, 1971, 1972, 1973, 1975, 1995. Used by permission. (www.Lockman.org)

Edited by Adeline Griffith, Crown Financial Ministries

Library of Congress Cataloging-in-Publication Data

Burkett, Larry.
    Money matters : answers to your financial questions / Larry Burkett.
        p. cm.
    ISBN 0-7852-6609-7
    1. Finance, Personal—Religious aspects—Christianity. 2. Finance, Personal—Biblical teaching.
I. Title.

HG179 .B83854 2001
332.024—dc21

2001045032

Printed in the United States of America

01 02 03 04 05 BVG 5 4 3 2 1

CONTENTS

INTRODUCTION

I WOULD LIKE TO THANK YOU FOR CHOOSING to read this book. Essentially, it's made up of questions I've been asked, over the last fifteen years, on our daily *Money Matters* radio program. During this time, I think I've heard basically every question on money that can be asked—from a biblical perspective.

To the best of my ability, I've tried to answer these questions honestly and, when possible, to quote the Scripture that deals with the specific question. As you might imagine, in most instances my answers are based on my limited knowledge of some complicated economic issues presented in a short time frame (a thirty-minute radio program). Therefore, as you read this book you'll often see the phrase "in my opinion," and it means exactly that.

I'd like to back up a bit and tell you how I came to be a teacher on biblical principles of handling money. I believe this book actually began about thirty years ago—when I became a Christian. Obviously, becoming a Christian at thirty-two years of age meant that many of my thought patterns, opinions, and objectives in life had been settled long before I accepted Christ.

My wife, Judy, had accepted the Lord about three years before I did, through the influence of Campus Crusade for Christ and their door-to-door evangelism. She subsequently joined a Baptist church in Florida, and during the next two and one-half years I had a steady parade of Baptists through my home (including her pastor)—all sharing Christ with me.

Unfortunately, my personal opinions had been well established prior to that, and I was not interested in becoming a Christian and told them so pretty vehemently. I wouldn't go to church and I wouldn't change my life, so my wife asked if I would attend a Tuesday evening Bible study with her. The only reason I agreed to go was the fact that I had just finished all my college education and was looking for something in which I could get involved. Also, the Bible study was being taught by a businessman I knew and respected. So I joined this couples' Bible study, and for about five months I proceeded to argue with everything the teacher said.

One of the mistakes he made was telling us what scriptures he was going to cover the next week. I would go home and study those scriptures and come up with a good argument for why they couldn't possibly mean what they said. Then I'd go back the next week and dispute what he was teaching.

After a few weeks of this, he asked if I would meet him for breakfast one morning. I accepted his invitation and fully expected that he, like many of the other members of Judy's church, was going to present Christ to me (again). So, I was ready to explain (again) why I didn't need Christ. I believed there was a God, but I had no need for a personal God. Besides, I couldn't comprehend the fact that God would care one way or the other about human beings; it seemed to me that we were just a bother to Him.

I met my teacher/friend that morning, and as we ate breakfast he commented that I was a disruptive influence in the study group. My ready defense was that I was there to learn and that the way I learned was by confronting what was being presented. Furthermore, I thought that if someone believed what he said he should be able to defend his position. He then said something to me that really made an impact.

The conversation at breakfast went something like this.

"Larry, obviously you've been studying the Bible. Am I right?"

"Sure. You assign the scriptures and I read them."

"And then you come back and argue about them."

"Well, I take the position that if you believe what you say you should be able to defend it."

He stopped eating and looked directly at me. "Let me tell you what your problem is. When you read the Bible you're looking for errors, and if that's the only reason you're reading it you won't learn the truth." He continued, "I'd like to ask you to do two things. Number one, just sit down and read through the book of John and ask God to show you the truth as you read. After you read through the book of John, if God doesn't show you anything meaningful, then put the Bible down. It's not for you, because if you're seeking the truth God promises to show it to you."

Then he told me the second thing he wanted me to do. "Please don't ever come back to my Bible study, unless you become a Christian, because you're entirely too disruptive. I'm not teaching that class just for your benefit; I'm there to help others learn."

As I thought about what he said, at first it irritated me (just a little bit), but then it made a lot of sense. Most of the other Christians I had met (the majority of whom were my wife's friends) had encouraged me to accept Christ. That didn't get through to me, but what he said did.

This man couldn't possibly have known what I was going through, but I was sincerely searching for truth. College had always been a life goal of mine; but, after getting two degrees I concluded that most of what I'd learned in school really didn't help solve my problems.

At the time, I was running a department with General Electric at Cape Canaveral and had just started a business venture with some friends, which led me down the road to another new career. I was pretty disheartened about life in general.

Even though I was making more money than I'd ever made before, somehow it didn't seem to make me any happier. Since I had come from a poor family, I had always believed that money would be the answer. It wasn't that I was going to spend the money; I was sure that just having it would make me feel better. But it didn't.

So I was drifting, believing in nothing in particular. There were some things that I didn't believe in, and I had put Christianity among them. But there was nothing that held my attention or interest.

So I went home that evening, sat down with my Bible, and asked of God as honestly as I could, "If there's something in here that I'm supposed to know, please show me." Later that night, I accepted Christ as my Savior. I made a promise to God that, to the best of my ability, I have kept for the last thirty-two years: "God, You know that I'm an ignorant person. I don't know much about the Bible and what I know is probably wrong, but I promise You this: if You will show me the truth and help me to understand it, I will do it, no matter what." And that's all God asks of any of us. He doesn't ask for our ability; He asks for our availability.

As the psalmist says, *"I love the LORD, because He hears my voice and my supplications. Because He has inclined His ear to me, therefore I shall call upon Him as long as I live"* (Psalm 116:1–2).

Fortunately, Judy's pastor was a spiritually astute man who understood clearly what he was dealing with in my case. He had been to my home several times over the previous months. My last recollection of him was one evening, sitting in my living room, discussing religion. Obviously, I was arguing about everything he said, assuring him that I thought Christianity was for people who needed a crutch—and assuring him that I didn't need one. I remember that he got so mad he stormed out of my home, promising never to return.

The Sunday after I accepted Christ I went to church with Judy (I still hadn't told anyone about my experience). After the service the pastor asked, "Would anyone here like to make a public confession of your faith?" I got up and walked down the aisle. You could have knocked both Judy and the pastor over with a feather.

I went through the church's new member process, and then I

was assigned to a new members' class for about twelve weeks. During this time I went through an orientation of what a church is, why people go to church, and what Baptists believe—their doctrine. But, more than that, I learned what it really means to be a Christian. I found out how much I didn't know and what I needed to learn, and I did a lot of studying during that three-month period.

As soon as I finished the new members' class, our pastor did something that was most beneficial to me: He assigned me to teach the next new members' class. So I had an opportunity to teach what I had just learned. And, it was probably the best thing that anyone could have done for me, because it forced me to get into the Bible, talk to people, ask questions, and discover how much I didn't know.

When that new members' class ended, my pastor asked if I would like to join him and some other men in an early morning Bible study. Of course I immediately said yes, because I was anxious to learn. So I spent the next several months in an intensive Bible study, looking at the Bible itself, how it was constructed, how to interpret it, and how to study it.

During this time, as I read through the Bible in my personal study time, one of the things that greatly impressed me was how many scriptures there are that deal with the area of money. Because of my educational background, I was attracted to the wisdom and simplicity of what the Bible had to say about money management. I mentioned that many times during the Bible study.

As couples who were having financial problems would come into our church, some of the associate pastors asked me to help counsel these people. I guess, after getting to know me a little, they realized that I was inherently cheap and thought that maybe it would rub off on some of the people having money problems. And since most of these couples basically needed to get on a budget and learn to manage their money better, the task fell to me.

I can remember being amazed by the first couple I ever counseled, because they were making about twice as much as I was at that time, and yet they were deeply in debt. Back then, a large amount of debt would have been $2,000 in credit cards, and this couple owed about $10,000. Clearly, they made a significant amount of money—more than enough to be able to manage it well and stay out of debt—and yet they were going further into debt every month.

As I talked to them, I realized several things: These habits had been developed over a long period of time, they both had come from fairly wealthy families, but they had no concept of how to handle money. I also realized that whatever I could talk them into somebody else could talk them out of. In other words, no matter what I said, someone selling a new boat, car, or swimming pool could turn them in that direction.

So I shared with them some of the biblical principles about money that I had been studying from the book of Proverbs. In fact, during the time I was counseling them (probably the better part of six months), I outlined a short Bible study for them that dealt with their debt problems. Actually, debt was not their real problem; debt was only a symptom. Their problems were poor training and indulgence.

When my pastor heard about what I was doing, he asked if I would agree to teach a study based on God's principles of handling money. I said, "You know, I've never thought about it, but let me pray about it and I'll get back to you." Actually, I never did teach that class, but it did get me to thinking about the area of biblical principles and money.

I recall sitting in a men's Bible study, where we were discussing a variety of biblical topics. Little did I know when I went to that study that each person also had to teach, so when my turn came I decided to teach them the biblical principles of handling money, according to the book of Proverbs.

During the course of my teaching, I made an offhand statement to the group: "You know, I've found over a hundred scriptures that deal with the topic of money in the Bible."

One of the older men in the group stopped me and said, "Larry,

I don't believe there are a hundred scriptures dealing with the subject of money. I don't think money is that important to God."

Well, I'm a pragmatist about almost everything, and I believe that if you say it you ought to be able to prove it. So I bought a new Bible, started in the book of Genesis, and worked my way through the Bible with a yellow marker. Every time I saw a scripture that dealt specifically with the area of money I highlighted it. Then I gave that Bible to my secretary and asked her to type the scripture references.

After several passes through the Bible, I found that I had identified almost 700 direct scriptures that dealt specifically with the subject of money. (By the way, if you include the scriptures that have at least an inference to money or related objects, there are approximately 2,000 scriptures that deal with money.)

Over the next year, I spent my spare time organizing those scriptures. Usually what I would do in my own devotion time was ask myself questions like, "Okay, what does the Bible say about borrowing?" Then I would review all the scriptures dealing with money, looking for those that dealt specifically with borrowing. I would highlight them and label those scriptures "borrowing."

Without realizing it, I had started a topical concordance of finances. I still have the three notebooks that I compiled those many years ago, and I still use them in my study. They outline God's principles of handling money, and they form the foundation for all the answers I give on the subject of money.

How I happened to get into ministry work is an even more convoluted path. I was running a small company at the time and trying to determine what the Lord wanted me to do. Even though I knew that was not where the Lord wanted me to invest the rest of my life, I had no idea what I was supposed to do.

I attended a Campus Crusade for Christ Lay Institute for Evangelism at Lake Eustis in Florida, close to where I was living. I had become good friends with the businessman who had told me not to come back to his Bible study, and he was teaching at that particular conference. At dinner that evening he sat next to Bill

Bright, the head of Campus Crusade for Christ. As Dr. Bright discussed Campus Crusade's need to have a financial ministry, he mentioned to my friend that they were looking for people with financial backgrounds.

My friend said, "Well, I know someone with a financial background who's looking for something to do."

The next time I saw Dr. Bright he said, "God has told me that you should be on our staff."

And I thought, *Marvelous! How about that?* I'd been looking for something—a direction—and God provided it through Dr. Bright. What I didn't realize until later, after becoming good friends with Dr. Bright, is that he believes that God has told him that *everybody* should be on his staff.

However, it was the right thing for me, at the right time, and God used Bill Bright to change my direction. As a result, I resigned my position and joined the staff of Campus Crusade for Christ. I stayed for only about six months. During that time I realized that they really didn't know what I was supposed to be doing, and I certainly didn't know what I was supposed to be doing, but it probably *wasn't* fund-raising.

So, I left the staff of Campus Crusade and took my family on a vacation—a long-needed vacation. I'd never taken one before in my life, and we traveled for about six weeks that summer, just looking at America. When I got back home, I found several messages from Dr. Bright. When I talked to him, he asked why I'd left.

I said, "Well, primarily because what you need me to do—fund-raising—I can't do."

Dr. Bright asked, "What is it that God wants you to do?"

I responded, "I'm not really sure, but I believe it's to teach God's people the biblical principles of handling money."

To Dr. Bright's credit, he's open to whatever the Lord is telling somebody to do, so he asked, "Why don't you come back on staff and do it with Campus Crusade for Christ?"

I went back on the Crusade staff for an additional three years, during which time I helped some of my fellow staff members who were having financial problems. As a result, I began to get invitations to teach Sunday school classes or Bible studies. It was then that I began to hone my skills in answering financial questions totally from a biblical perspective.

The whole thing probably came together for me in 1975 when I was asked to come to the Dallas Theological Seminary in Dallas, Texas, and address the graduating class. I shared the simple truths of stewardship from God's Word—that we are stewards over all the material things that God puts in our possession—and I stressed the necessity of being good money managers. *"It is required of stewards that one be found trustworthy"* (1 Corinthians 4:2).

I also gave them a foundational truth found in Luke 16:10–11: *"He who is faithful in a very little thing is faithful also in much; and he who is unrighteous in a very little thing is unrighteous also in much. If therefore you have not been faithful in the use of unrighteous [wealth], who will entrust the true riches to you?"*

After I had addressed the students, Dr. Howard Hendrix, a professor in Dallas, asked if I would like to come to one of their informal meetings—what they called a brown bag luncheon, where they just sit around and discuss various topics. And I heartily agreed to do it.

During that meeting I was sitting in the midst of some of the greatest Bible scholars in America—men with earned doctorates in Bible and Greek and Hebrew and many other disciplines—and I listened as they asked me questions about what the Bible said about handling money. During that time I thought to myself, *Boy, it really is true: in the land of the blind a one-eyed man can become king.* But I also realized how little God's people understood about the area of money, and it set me on the path that God has allowed me to follow ever since.

From that humble beginning I began to travel across the country, teaching seminars. At one time, when I was doing live seminars, I would travel thirty times a year! I'm not a great traveler and, as a result, I began to look for a better way to do what I felt God had called me to do.

In 1981 I received a call from Dr. James Dobson, founder of Focus on the Family. He'd heard that I was going to be in the California area doing a conference, and he asked if I would come by the studios of Focus on the Family and do a couple of radio programs (this was back when he did a daily fifteen-minute program). I agreed, and a few weeks later we sat down to do just that. However, I think we ended up doing ten or twelve that day.

Over the next several months, as those programs were released on Dr. Dobson's radio network, I began to get calls from station managers around the country, asking if I had anything else that they could air, which I didn't. Dean Simple, the station manager at a Moody affiliate in Chattanooga, Tennessee, kept calling. In fact, at one point he offered to rent studio time in Atlanta if I would do some recordings that he could air. Faced with what seemed to be God pushing me along, I agreed. I went to Atlanta and recorded some (really awful) five-minute programs.

Dean began to air the programs on his station and distributed them to other Moody affiliates, who then sent them to other stations, and within about a year our programs were being aired on nearly 240 stations. The radio ministry has expanded ever since, and today we're on approximately 2,000 outlets with our English program and about 600 outlets with our Spanish version of the *Money Matters* program.

Money Matters is a thirty-minute program, aired Monday through Friday. Listeners from all over the country have the opportunity to call in and ask questions about finances, many of which are in this book.

I love doing radio for several reasons. It's totally interactive and extemporaneous, and I like that format very much. Also, it allows me to hear what's going on in the lives of God's people. I know what they're thinking; I know what they're feeling; I know what their financial problems are; and it gives me a great opportunity to find out what's going on in the (real) economy. And most of all I like being able to share God's timeless truths.

We sorted through some 1,600 different questions that were

asked over the last two years and came up with the most frequently asked questions. Obviously you need to be aware that no answer, either by radio, by book, or in person, can be perfect. The best I can do is respond to the specific question being asked. Many times the way a question is asked, even the nuance of what a person is saying, makes a huge difference in the response.

For instance, if somebody asks, "Do you think a Christian should tithe?" I would answer by saying, "Yes, I do." But if that person asked, "Why do you think a Christian should tithe?" I might respond, "Because we are told, *'Bring the whole tithe into the storehouse, so that there may be food in My house . . . says the* LORD *of hosts'"* (Malachi 3:10).

But if someone asks, "Why does the New Testament not speak of tithing?" that question would elicit an entirely different answer. So what I've tried to do is take each question in context and answer it as straightforwardly as possible.

Also bear in mind that, as we sorted through these questions and answers and put them into categories, many times a question would not only have multiple answers, it might also fit into multiple categories. For instance, somebody might ask, "Do you think it's okay if I tithe to my local church when I don't agree with the denomination and how they're using my money?" There are numerous questions hidden within that question, as well as numerous answers. In that situation, we categorized them the best we could. That particular question would go under the topic of giving.

Somebody else might ask, "Do you think it's okay to borrow money to tithe?" That question addresses two categories: one is the issue of borrowing; another is the issue of tithing. I would primarily categorize that as a question on borrowing; therefore, it would show up in the category entitled "Debt and Credit." The point I'm making is that it is very difficult to split those categories perfectly.

Another thing: there is often a conflict with the question that's asked and whether I can answer it biblically or whether it requires an opinion. For example, someone might ask, "Do you think it is biblical to save money?" In that case I would say, "Yes" and give them a Scripture reference: *"Go to the ant, O sluggard, observe her ways and be wise, which, having no chief, officer or ruler, prepares her food in the summer, and gathers her provision in the harvest"* (Proverbs 6:6–8).

But the question also might be asked, "Do you think it's biblical to save money, and if so, where's the best place to invest my children's education money?" That entails two separate issues: Do you think it is biblical to save money? And, Where is the best place to invest? The first can be answered from a totally scriptural position; the second requires an opinion. In these answers I state very clearly, "In my opinion."

Since I'm trying not to repeat questions, you may find that you'll have to look through several categories to determine your particular question and whether it's been answered here. I trust you'll find the answer you need.

When I do a radio program, I struggle with an issue that the apostle James spoke of: *doing* versus *hearing*. Many people who call in basically know the answers to the questions they are asking, but they just don't know exactly where or how to start. (This may be true for you.)

What I try to do is to bring the person back to the basics and tell them, "Let's not deal with the symptoms, let's deal with the problem." If you're deeply in debt, can't pay your bills, owe a lot on your credit cards, and you want to get a consolidation loan on your home, you're dealing with a *symptom*. The symptom is debt.

In order to solve that symptom, you must deal with the *problem*, and the problem can be a variety of things—all the way from ignorance (just not knowing what to do), to disobedience, covetousness, or greed. It could be any one or all of those things, so we must identify the problem and deal with it.

Therefore I struggled in writing this book (as I do on the radio), because I want to help people *do* something. This is not a why-to book, "Why should I do something?" This is a how-to book, "How can I do what God wants me to do?" Many people, when they call, are looking for easy solutions to some very difficult situations. And in most instances there are no easy solutions.

Whatever time it took to get you into a problem, it's probably going to take more than that to get you out. If you've borrowed money to the point that you can't make the payments on your bills, it's not going to be easy to reverse that situation. You didn't get in that situation in one month, and you won't get out of it in one month. If accumulating excessive debt took three or four years, and often it does, it may take four or five years to get out of debt.

There are many people who don't want to pay that price. They're shopping around for easy solutions, so they call a radio program, looking either for a miracle—which I don't have—or looking for a handout—which I also don't have. All I have are biblical answers to worldly situations.

Any situation can be solved, and many times God does intercede on the behalf of His people, but more often God will let them work their way out of the problem the way they worked their way in.

A lot of people get discouraged when they find out that their problems don't go away quickly. In other words, they make the commitment to get on a budget, work on it for a while, and then find out the next month that they still don't have enough money to pay their bills. So, they get discouraged and quit. That's a shame, because they're on the right track; they just didn't try it long enough.

Again, many of these problems are not going to just disappear. If you're in debt and working hard to get out, the minimum amount of time to make your budget work will probably be a year. And it will look very discouraging along the way when you find out it doesn't work immediately, but don't give up. It will work and God will help.

What I found when I was counseling was that God seldom, if ever, puts similar people together in a marriage. If He did, one would be unnecessary. Opposites normally attract. So usually one spouse will be a spender and one will be a saver. One will be a worrier and the other will seem to never have a care. One will get up late and the other early. One will be sloppy and the other neat. And it goes on and on.

By putting opposites together, God makes one whole person, which is exactly what His Word says in the Old Testament: *"For this reason a man shall leave his father and his mother, and be joined to his wife; and they shall become one flesh"* (Genesis 2:24).

One person. But because people are opposites, they're going to approach their problems differently.

One spouse is going to be worried and want to deal with the problem, but the other one won't want to be bothered and may want to just ignore it. I would say, more often than not, it's the wife who is concerned with the situation and wants to solve it. The husband may be concerned about it, but he just wants to avoid the issue.

Then there are the husbands who are more than willing to deal with problems, as long as it doesn't cost them anything. But you know what? If you're making payments on a bass boat and that's keeping you from being able to balance your budget, the bass boat (or whatever) has to go. But again, remember that opposites do attract and what may frighten one may not bother the other. You don't want to give up because you don't agree. Keep in mind that you are opposites and don't overreact.

Most important, if you're married, it takes two people to work on problems. No one person can be stuck with this burden and expect the problems to go away. Both husband and wife must work together. And remember, in general (and this is a broad generalization), many women worry too much, and many men spend too much.

I found in my counseling that although, in large part, people categorize women as the spenders, many times that's not true. Under impulse, women will often spend too much on food and clothes. Under the same impulse, her husband will go out and buy a new boat, a motor home, or an airplane. We men may not spend as often, but when we do we buy big-ticket items, and we tend to get very attached to them.

As you might imagine, the most frequently asked questions are going to shift periodically, according to the economy. If this book were being written in 1999, the most frequently asked question would be, "Where should I invest my money?" or "Where can I maximize the return on my 401(k) or my IRA?"

However, this book is being written in 2001, and the majority of the questions being asked now are, "What does the economy look like? Is it slowing down? Do you think I might lose my job? What can I do about all the credit card debt that I have?" In our society debt is a plague. It is the number one tool that Satan is using to destroy families and to disenfranchise Christians—literally, to defeat them.

That's true at all ages—all the way down to the teenage years now, because young people are being saddled with more and more debt. Most young couples today tell me that debt is the number one problem they have. Current statistics tell us that about one-half of all new marriages (first marriages) are going to dissolve within the first six years.

About 80 percent of those couples who are divorced also say that most of the problems they had were financial. It's my opinion that they weren't having financial problems; they were having financial *symptoms.*

The real problem probably was ignorance, indulgence, or a whole variety of other issues. The symptom was the debt that built up. It's time we really took this in hand and tried to solve the problems that manifest themselves in the form of debt. I trust this book will be a first step in answering the questions that you have.

I will always remember one of the really good professors I had in college. Whenever he would address his class, he would go to the blackboard and, in big, bold, chalk letters, the first thing he would write is "KISS," which means "Keep It Simple, Stupid." He was talking to himself, reminding himself that, whatever you teach, keep it as simple as you can; don't complicate it. And then he would often write on the board this statement: "Answer the questions that people are asking." He was addressing students in that case; and, in my case, it's my readers.

So this book is an attempt to do just that. It is an attempt on my part, number one, to keep it simple and, number two, to answer the questions people are asking. I trust you will find it beneficial. If we can help you, contact Crown Financial Ministries. The information on how to do so is in item 7.0 in the Appendix.

1
AUTOMOBILES

THE PURCHASE OF AN AUTOMOBILE IS the second largest expense that most families will incur in their lifetimes. In reality, if you take the cumulative total of automobiles purchased during the life span of most people, it may well be the largest single expense that most of them incur. And that's especially true when you factor in the associated costs of maintenance, gasoline, insurance, and other expenses. It's important for most families to understand the consequences of making good financial decisions about automobiles.

I believe I can say without fear of contradiction that the vast majority of American families are living well beyond their automobile budgets. They buy new cars when they really can afford only used cars; they finance their cars without any expectations of ever owning a

> **Our motorcar is our supreme form of privacy when away from home.**
> MARSHALL MCLUHAN

car debt free; and most of them are more concerned with the monthly payments than they are with the retail cost of their cars.

Also, in my opinion, car leases are the worst deals available for nonbusiness car buyers.

QUESTION:

Is it a good idea to lease an automobile?

We're getting ready to buy a new automobile. My husband is a salesman and needs a good car in order to do his day-to-day routine. Unfortunately, we don't have enough money saved to buy an automobile for cash; neither do we have enough money to make a down payment on a vehicle. Do you think that a lease is a good alternative for families like us?

ANSWER:

In my opinion, because of the depreciation on the automobile as soon as you drive it off the lot, buying a brand-new car, by whatever means, is not a good deal for the majority of people. Typically, a new automobile will depreciate between 15 and 25 percent of its initial value, depending on the type of car and the retail price, just as a result of titling the vehicle. That's a lot of depreciation for most people when you figure that a $30,000 automobile may lose as much as $7,000 to $8,000 of its value just as a result of your purchase. That doesn't seem like a good deal to me.

Further, the difficulty with buying new automobiles is simply compounded in a lease. This is because the dealer and the manufacturer are going to make a profit on each automobile, whether you buy it outright for cash, buy it with a loan, or lease it. The difficulty I see with leasing an automobile is that you usually are paying maximum retail price for the vehicle and financing it at high market rates. And, in the end, you *still don't own it.*

Unfortunately, most people are not even concerned with what a vehicle costs them. All they're concerned about is the monthly payments; and the same is true if they lease. When an automobile is leased, the contract carries with it penalties for excessive mileage—mileage in excess of what was agreed to in the contract, which is usually around 15,000 miles per year. Many families today will put more than 15,000 miles a year on a vehicle, so when they return the car, after the lease period, they owe mileage penalties. They also may owe wear penalties—that's a penalty to cover the excessive amount of wear and tear on the automobile (in the leaseholder's opinion).

Another thing to remember is that signing a lease is just as binding as signing a contract to buy a car. If you want to get out of the lease early, you'll owe early payoff penalties on the vehicle, plus whatever wear and tear is assessed.

One caution I offer to anyone who is already driving a leased vehicle: Don't allow any other person, friend or otherwise, to assume your lease. Your name is still on that contract, and if that person doesn't pay, you're going to pay. If the car has been abused, you'll be stuck with the bill for the wear and tear as well.

Bottom line, I don't believe that leased automobiles are an especially good deal. In fact, for most individuals outside of the business environment, leases are a very bad deal. Normally, I don't recommend leasing a car.

God's Word says, *"Which one of you, when he wants to build a tower, does not first sit down and calculate the cost, to see if he has enough to complete it?"* (Luke 14:28). Most people don't consider the total cost.

QUESTION:

Is it better to keep an old car and repair it or trade for a new one?

My husband and I drive two old cars, one with 150,000 miles and the other with over 180,000 miles. At what point should we decide that it's no longer profitable to keep these old cars and trade them in for new ones? I've heard you say many times that the cheapest vehicle to drive is the one you're driving, but is that always true? Don't cars eventually wear out?

ANSWER:

Yes, you're absolutely right. There is a point at which it's a losing proposition to try to maintain an old automobile. That's particularly true with a car that has in excess of 200,000 miles, because often at that stage metal fatigue sets in and the car begins to disintegrate.

In general, though, the cheapest car to drive *is* the one you are driving. Of course, that will depend on the specific car you own (some cars are just better than others), how much mileage it has, and your use of the automobile. If you just drive your vehicle around town, a breakdown might not be a major catastrophe. However, if you drive it long distances and use it to make a living, that's something else.

Let me mention another point: If you're trading in an old vehicle, generally you're better off to sell it on your own or give it to a nonprofit organization (and write it off on your income tax) than you are trading it in. Usually, if you trade in an old automobile, the dealer will appear to give you something for it but actually will mark up the price of the vehicle you are buying to compensate for it. After all, the dealer has the same problem trying to sell an old used car that you have.

I caution most young families not to buy new cars. Buy an older car, perhaps one to two years old with a reasonable amount of mileage on it. A two-year-old car with reasonable mileage, in my opinion, would be about 20,000 miles; a one-year-old car, about 10,000 to 12,000 miles. There are very good buys in what are called program cars (some call them demos). These are nearly new cars that have been driven by employees of the dealership. They usually put between 8,000 and 12,000 miles on the vehicles and then resell them. Often you'll get a significant discount on these vehicles (see item 1.2 in the Appendix).

QUESTION:

What do I do with a car that has payments that are too high for us to afford?

About a year ago, we bought a brand-new automobile because our old one was pretty much worn out. We now realize that the payments, almost $190 a month, are far too high for us to afford. However, when we checked the value of the car, we found that we still owe more than the car is worth. What options do we have? Should we take the money out of our 401(k) to pay it off? Do we have the option to just give the car back and buy another used car?

ANSWER:

No, you can't just give the car back. You have a contract. Your purchase contract may not be with a dealer; it may be with a third-party financier, and the financier doesn't want your car back. If he does get it back, he's going to sell it at a discount and sue you for the difference.

> **Automobile: the down payment on a finance company.**
>
> MORTON THOMPSON

In most instances, you're far better off trying to sell the automobile yourself, with the lender's permission, and surrendering the sales price to the lender. Then you'll have to sign a note for the deficiency (the difference between what you sold the car for and what you still owe on it). But normally, you're going to lose less if you sell the car yourself.

You also asked if you should use your 401(k) to pay off your car. Remember that when you prematurely withdraw money from your retirement account, prior to 59½ years of age, you do pay some stiff penalties: a 10 percent penalty on the early withdrawal of the money, plus federal tax and state income taxes. That's a large expense to pay for a vehicle. I can't tell you that you should never use retirement funds, but look for other options first—perhaps a loan from the 401(k) would serve you better.

Unless selling the car and signing a note for the difference would jeopardize your finances, I would not recommend using the 401(k) as an option. You really don't solve your problem; you just shift it to a new location for a while. Also remember that when you dispose of a car prematurely, even with the lender's permission, it will go on your credit record for up to seven years, so this is not a thing to take lightly. *"Better is a little with the fear of the LORD, than great treasure and turmoil with it"* (Proverbs 15:16).

QUESTION:

How much should we pay for the new car we are planning to buy?

ANSWER:

If you'll look at the Percentage Guide table in the Appendix (see item 17.0), you'll notice that you should spend no more than 15 percent of your Net Spendable Income (that's your income after paying taxes and tithes) on your automobile. Note that the percentage includes the expenses to cover the loan payments, insurance, maintenance, fuel—everything that goes into your vehicle, including its eventual replacement.

It's very important to select a car you can afford and not be dazzled by the attraction of new ones. The vast majority of American families earning less than $50,000 a year cannot afford to buy a new car—ever! You should buy a good used vehicle—one you have very carefully selected that will meet your needs.

When I buy an automobile, I first check very thoroughly the model I want. The resources I recommend are *Consumer Reports* magazine, as well as one of the national auto-trade Web sites. Some of these Web sites are listed in item 1.2 in the Appendix. It's very important that you stay within your budget and select a car you can afford.

"Without consultation, plans are frustrated, but with many counselors they succeed" (Proverbs 15:22).

One of the ways to find a good used car is to ask your friends and family if they have one for sale. Many times they do and just haven't mentioned it. If you can't find one among your friends and family, go to your local newspaper and try to buy from an individual. That way, you can talk to the owner, see the car, and drive it before you make a decision to buy. Plus, in most states, there's no sales tax on private owner sales.

In my opinion, the last place to shop for an automobile is at a dealership, unless you know the dealer personally. It's not that most dealerships are dishonest; they aren't. But remember that they buy these cars at used car auctions and rarely know the total history of the automobile, so you won't know what you're getting.

QUESTION:

Should we borrow against our home equity loan to pay off the car we purchased that was too expensive?

ANSWER:

I have to admit that sometimes this is not a bad idea, because quite often you can get a better home equity loan than you can a car loan. And remember also that, in most instances, if you itemize your deductions the home equity loan is deductible on your income tax. So, effectively, you end up paying less for the automobile.

However, remember this: When you borrow against your home, particularly on a home equity or a second mortgage, the payments can be extended for a longer period of time, meaning that although you're paying less interest initially, over the long run you may be paying more in absolute dollars.

> **Car sickness: the feeling you get each month when the payment is due.**
> ANONYMOUS

Also, before you consolidate any loans, I recommend that you get on a good budget and stay on it for six to nine months—to prove to yourself that you can discipline yourself not to overspend. You need a well-balanced budget that ensures that you have enough money in your budget for repairs and the eventual replacement of the vehicle.

Remember, you want to solve the *problem*. The *symptom* is the fact that you have car payments in excess of what you can really afford; the problem is that you bought something you couldn't afford. Make all future decisions about buying cars based on your budget—not on slick advertisements.

"He who loves pleasure will become a poor man; he who loves wine and oil [expensive automobiles] *will not become rich"* (Proverbs 21:17).

QUESTION:

What kind of automobile insurance do I need?

My car now has about 100,000 miles on it, and I question whether I need the comprehensive and collision as well as the liability insurance.

Answer:

Obviously, liability insurance is an absolute must, but I believe you're at the breakpoint where collision and comprehensive may not be necessary. However, even a car with 100,000 miles on it needs the collision insurance unless you have enough cash in the bank to fix it in the event of a major accident. Remember, it's not much cheaper to replace a fender on a five-year-old automobile than it is on a one-year-old automobile; the costs are essentially the same.

You might say, "Well, I can drive the older car even though it's banged up." And that's probably true to some degree; however, some of the banging may be so severe that you wouldn't want to drive it around. It might even be dangerous. Liability is a *must;* it's not for your protection, it's for the protection of the people you might hit.

"The prudent sees the evil and hides himself, but the naive go on, and are punished for it" (Proverbs 22:3).

Collision covers the damage on your automobile; comprehensive covers things like glass breakage. In my opinion, comprehensive is probably one of the better buys in automobile insurance. You could do without it, but for what it pays, it's usually worth the cost.

Remember also that if your medical insurance policy excludes automobile injuries, you need to carry some kind of hospitalization health plan on your automobile policy. Before you buy any insurance on your vehicle, shop thoroughly.

When you buy a car, avoid buying your insurance through the dealer or through the lender. Shop for your own insurance. You can use the Web and shop one of the insurance evaluation Web sites listed in item 1.3 in the Appendix.

QUESTION:

What do I do if an insurance company will not replace my automobile even though I was hit by somebody else and that person was at fault?

ANSWER:

This is a very common occurrence. When someone hits you and his or her insurance won't pay to replace your automobile, generally the insurance company has used the average wholesale value of your car to determine its value. Your car may have been in much better shape than an "average" wholesale car, and you do have a right to contest the company's decision.

However, if after you negotiate with the insurance company in good faith they still won't pay, you need to consider whether the difference in what you think your car is worth and what the company says it's worth is significant enough to go to court over. Because, ultimately, that's probably what you'll have to do.

In most states, you can sue in Small Claims Court if the amount is $5,000 or less. My observation is that sometimes you win and sometimes you lose. If you're sure you're right and you think you can prove that your vehicle is worth more than the insurance company's evaluation, go for it!

It will help to get a statement of the condition of your vehicle from the mechanic who works on it and from friends who are familiar with it. Also, check one of the automobile pricing Web sites, find an equivalent automobile, and see if you could replace the vehicle for what you're being offered. If not, you may have to take the company to court.

It's best to appeal to the insurance company first. Many times you'll find they're bluffing—often right up to the point that you're ready to file the case in court. They'll tell you they won't pay; but then they'll negotiate at the last moment. You should have an absolute price you're willing to accept, and if they won't meet that price be willing to take them to court.

"Wisdom is protection just as money is protection. But the advantage of knowledge is that wisdom preserves the lives of its possessors" (Ecclesiastes 7:12).

QUESTION:

What do I do about a mechanic who ripped me off?

I recently took my automobile to a local mechanic who told me initially that my repairs would cost around $150, but when I got my car back the bill was almost $700. Also, I feel that he replaced many parts that were not defective. Do I have any rights in this case?

ANSWER:

Yes, you do have rights. First, if possible, you need to get the actual parts that were taken off your automobile to determine if they were defective. In retrospect, whenever you're doing business with a mechanic and you agree on a price, you need to have a written agreement that if the price of his work exceeds the estimate by some percentage—say, 10 percent—he's required to contact you personally and get your approval. But, who thinks about that first? Right?

Since that opportunity is already past, chalk that up to experience. Be persistent, and try to negotiate a lower price if at all possible. Many times that isn't possible, in which case be prepared to take this mechanic to Small Claims Court. There the judge will listen to each of you and make a decision. You need to have pretty conclusive evidence, though, that he actually replaced parts that were not defective and that you were not having that particular problem, before the judge will agree with you. No matter what, though, you need to file a complaint with the Better Business Bureau. Maybe you can help the next victim.

"Wisdom is better than jewels; and all desirable things can not compare with her" (Proverbs 8:11).

Question:

Do I have the right to take a Christian automobile mechanic to court if I believe he cheated me?

I feel violated.

Answer:

The apostle Paul said, *"Does any one of you, when he has a case against his neighbor, dare to go to law before the unrighteous, and not before the saints? . . . Actually, then, it is already a defeat for you, that you have lawsuits with one another. Why not rather be wronged? Why not rather be defrauded?"* (1 Corinthians 6:1, 7).

We are instructed that we should not take our brother to court and that it is better to be defrauded than to go to court. However, that doesn't leave you without options if you feel you've been cheated by a Christian in any field, including an auto mechanic. You should go to that person and confront him, and have very clear evidence that you were cheated. Allow him to tell you his side of the story; he does have that right.

If you still feel you were cheated, you should ask if he would be willing to go to arbitration with one of the Christian Conciliation services. If he refuses, you still have a right to take your case to his pastor; and, if you have witnesses, you should take them with you at that point. If the church is doing its biblical duty, the pastor should be willing to listen to your case and then confront the offender with you.

Actually, I've been through this many times and have found that very few churches are willing to follow the biblical edicts, and seldom will the accused repent (or pay). Essentially, if the person is not honest, a biblical admonition probably isn't going to dissuade the offender either. But you do have the biblical right to do it, and if I were in your place I would pursue it. Until we do this, cheaters will never repent.

"Set your mind on the things above, not on the things that are on earth" (Colossians 3:2).

2
BUDGETING

WE ALL HAVE A BUDGET IN ONE FASHION or another. For some people, it means they spend until all the money for that month is gone, but they determine not to overspend. That plan seems to work until the car breaks down or they lose a job for a while. Then they rationalize the use of debt as a necessity they couldn't avoid.

Some people spend all they make and rely on credit cards to fund the monthly deficits. They realize they have a problem but rationalize that they just don't make enough money to get by.

A smaller segment of the population makes enough money to be sloppy and get away with it. They may overspend, buying expensive indulgences, but they can cut back and pay their way out without much pain. However, they also are the ones who wonder how they can earn so much but never seem to have any money.

The goal for those who want to be good stewards is to live by a plan that balances their earnings with their spending—in other words, a *budget*.

A budget is a simple plan that divides the available income (after taxes and tithes) into the common categories of spending (Housing, Auto, Food, and the like—see the Percentage Guide for Family Income table in Appendix item 17.0, which lists all the budget categories). Spending has to include what doesn't come due every month (clothing, vacations, car repairs, and so on).

QUESTION:

How can we get started on a budget and get ourselves out of debt?

My husband and I have been struggling to get on a budget and have tried several times, but they never seem to work for us.

ANSWER:

There is really no easy answer except to do it. The reason most people's budgets don't work is because they continue to spend more money than they make on a month-by-month basis. If this is your problem, you'll need to solve that first. No budget will work until you commit to living on no more than you make.

Go through each budget category shown in our Percentage Guide table (see Appendix, item 17.0) and compare it to your own spending. For instance, if the Housing category (which includes payments, taxes, utilities, maintenance) for your income allocates 35 percent of your income and your budget is consuming, let's say, 60 percent on Housing, your budget won't work. The logical solution to that problem is to sell your house, move into a less expensive one, and get your budget percentage back in line. There's really no other way it will work.

A second problem that many people run into is that they set up their budget properly as recommended, and then they find out the first month that it doesn't work because they allocated $25 to car repairs, but they had a $150 car bill. The only way that most budgets will work is over the long term. Remember that you didn't get into debt in one month, and you're not going to get out of debt in one month.

But if you'll stick to the budget, it will work. At first, you might have to get that $150 for car repair by robbing every other category. However, if you'll stick to the plan and start paying those categories back, within about one year you'll find that you have the surpluses to meet emergencies in the various categories.

When you start your budget, you have to tailor it to your family; our guidelines are only recommendations. The bottom line with any budget is that when you add all of your percentages, the total cannot exceed 100 percent.

> **Whether you think you can or think you can't, you are right.**
>
> HENRY FORD

You must also be realistic. Many people try to make their budget work by allocating zero for things like Entertainment/Recreation, Clothing, Miscellaneous, or some other category. This won't work. Not one couple has ever shown up for counseling naked; therefore, I knew they had to have money in their budget for clothing. And yet many budgets allocate nothing for clothing. It may mean that you have to modify your buying habits for clothes, but you do have to have something in every budget category.

Many people say, "We never take a vacation." But most people do, and if you don't allocate money for it, your budget simply won't work. So, be realistic.

QUESTION:

How can we keep our Housing budget at 40 percent on a $100,000 salary?

I've gotten a copy of your budget, as you recommended on your radio program. I have reviewed the various categories, and there simply is not enough money to go around. For instance, we live in California and housing out here is very expensive.

Answer:

We didn't make up these budget percentages; they represent the average of what it actually costs to live. If in California you need a higher percentage—let's say 50 percent—you simply have to cut back in other budget categories to make up the difference. But if you continue to violate multiple categories, you'll never be able to balance your budget.

I was doing a radio program in California several years ago when a caller took great exception to the percentage I had allocated for Housing. She said, "Forty percent is not enough for housing in California."

So I asked, "Well, how much do you need?"

And she said, "Well, I need about 60 percent."

My response was, "Okay. You've got it." Then I asked, "What do you think about the Automobile percentage?"

She said, "Fifteen percent is not enough."

I asked, "Well, how much do you need?"

She said, "Twenty-five percent."

We went through every budget category, and when I added them she needed 140 percent of her monthly income! Unfortunately, that wasn't a possibility. So, the principle of budgeting is that the total of all budget categories must not exceed 100 percent.

Question:

How do I budget if I only receive disability payments?

I don't really make enough money to budget.

Answer:

Let me assure you that if you make any money at all, you make enough money to budget. What you may be saying is, "I don't make enough income to meet all of my expenses," but that's only true if you're not willing to adjust your lifestyle.

You may not have an adequate income, based on where you're living and what you're spending, but God would not have provided you with that income unless He knew that it's exactly what you need. Perhaps He wants to use your situation to get other Christians involved in helping to meet your needs. Your responsibility is to manage what you do have properly and let your needs above that be known to others.

People who are making less income actually have an even greater need to budget, because if they don't budget, and budget well, they can get themselves into debt beyond their ability to get out again.

Unfortunately, creditors are only too eager to extend credit beyond your ability to pay it back. That doesn't make any sense, but that's the way it is.

QUESTION:

Now that our budget is working and we have some money saved, where's the best place to put the savings and how do I allocate it?

ANSWER:

Since you need to keep it readily available, I recommend that you set up a money market account at your local bank or a brokerage firm. money market accounts will pay the most interest, and the money is available as needed. For instance, if you have your money in a checking account, you're probably making 1 to 2 percent on it; if you have it in a savings account, you may be making 3 to 4 percent; but if you put it in a money market account, you could be making 5 to 6 percent. Most money market accounts will allow you to write checks on the money in your account.

As far as allocating the savings, remember that the money is there for a purpose, and your Savings Account Allocation form in the Appendix (see item 17.0) reflects that purpose. Let's assume, arbitrarily, that you have $1,000 in a money market account, but $100 is for clothing, $100 for travel, $100 is for miscellaneous, and so on. In other words, the money is allocated, and when you look at the Savings Account form it should reflect that you have $100 available to spend on clothing, miscellaneous, and so forth. Therefore, this money is budgeted and allocated like any other category. The money can stay in one account, but it has to be allocated by use.

QUESTION:

How can we stay on a budget when our income has been reduced by almost half?

My husband lost his job where he'd been making almost $60,000 a year. He's now employed, but he's only making $38,000 per year. We realize we need to make some changes, but we're not sure where to start. It seems so overwhelming.

ANSWER:

There's no easy way to do this except to be realistic. One of the difficulties I find with many people whose income has been reduced—and that's always a possibility in our volatile economy—is that they aren't willing to face the facts. The fact is, they don't make as much money as they used to make; therefore, the second fact is, they can't spend as much money as they used to spend.

You have to take a realistic approach to where you are financially. Look at every category—Housing, Automobile, Food, Entertainment/Recreation, and the others—and bring those percentages down until you can live within the available income (and remember the total can be no more than 100 percent). It may mean selling your home or scaling down the cars. It also may mean not taking a vacation for a period of time and no private schools for your children; but that's what reality is all about.

And remember, whatever you're making, there are probably millions of other people out there making even less and living on it.

QUESTION:

Why do I end up at the end of the month without enough money when I have a budget?

I've been working on my budget now for several months and, on paper, when I plot our income and spending, it looks okay, but at the end of the month I don't have enough money to meet all our needs. I don't understand what my problem is.

ANSWER:

In practical truth, you have made out what I call the idealistic budget. You've programmed everything based on income, but you're not controlling your spending. You have to let the budget control what you're spending.

For instance, let's say you are using the envelope method of budgeting. You have an Entertainment/Recreation monthly budget of $200, and you get paid twice per month. That means that in each pay period you would put $100 into your Entertainment/

Recreation envelope. When you go out for entertainment, you take your envelope with you and you pay for whatever you do (eating out, movies) out of the envelope and put the change back in. This way you know exactly what you have left. But when you look in the envelope and it's empty, then you must stop spending in that category until you get paid again.

That principle works with every category of budgeting. It's not complicated; it is what's called self-discipline.

QUESTION:

How can we afford to buy gifts?

I've been working at getting my family on your budget now for a few months, but I get very frustrated. I can't see how we'll ever be able to buy gifts for Christmas, birthdays, or any other occasion. That really bothers me because I'm a person who loves to give.

ANSWER:

Gifts fall into your Miscellaneous expense category, and the only way you can afford to be able to buy gifts is to budget them. In other words, you'll have to set an amount for gifts and stick to it.

But there are some ways you can save money. Let's assume, for instance, that you can afford $100 a month, $1,200 a year, for all gifts—Christmas, birthdays, anniversaries, everything. That's not a lot of money, and it can be spent on a very few gifts, so you have to discipline yourself not to spend more than you've budgeted for gifts.

One idea is, rather than giving everybody gifts, limit your gift buying to your immediate family and send your relatives nice cards for Christmas, birthdays, and anniversaries. And, by observation, I've found that a lot of the things we buy for others they hide away, throw away, or give to someone else, so don't be too concerned.

There are many ways to save money. One is to take advantage of the off-season sales. For instance, a store that's going out of business might have gift items on sale that you can buy and keep for later. My wife often buys gifts throughout the year and stores them for special anniversaries, birthdays, and the like. You can save a lot of money by shopping sales and closeouts.

No budget will work unless you discipline yourself to spend only what you allocate, and that's very difficult for most parents, especially around Christmastime. You need to feel peace about your decision and not feel guilty if you can't buy your children all the popular gifts everyone else is buying. In my opinion, the majority of Americans go way overboard in gift buying anyway. We should all try to bring our families back to the right balance.

Buy your gifts carefully, allocate your money, stick to your plan, and shop bargains whenever possible. Discipline is the key. Remember that Proverbs 13:18 says, *"Poverty and shame will come to him who neglects discipline."*

QUESTION:

Can you give me some scriptural reasons why we should budget?

My husband listens to you, and he says that we need a budget, but I don't see the purpose. I manage our money very well, I don't spend more than we make, and I think a budget is far too restrictive.

ANSWER:

"The mind of a man plans his way, but the LORD directs his steps" (Proverbs 16:9). God expects us to be participants in planning

our budget, not observers. The purpose of budgeting is to free your mind of financial worries; it is not supposed to be a self-inflicted punishment.

I'm not trying to make your life miserable. All I can do is offer some good counsel to Christians, the majority of whom don't manage money very well. You should be free from worrying about whether your annual insurance is paid on time, whether you put money aside for the taxes on your house, and whether you have enough money to educate your children when it's time for college.

If those areas are not problems for you, then you're among the fortunate few in America. Even when you live within your income, you can still be spending too much money.

I never go into debt—never have, never will. But from time to time I find myself spending a lot more money than I need to spend and more than I probably should spend. So my

> **It seems as though the second half of a man's life is made up of nothing but the habits he has accumulated during the first half.**
>
> FYODOR DOSTOYEVSKY

budget is for the purpose of monitoring my self-discipline.

If you're not willing to live on a budget, you won't be able to help your kids get on a budget either. And what happens if your children aren't able to make the kind of money that your husband is making? They're in danger of overspending, debt, depression, and perhaps divorce. That's what is happening with a lot of young couples today.

Scriptural guidelines for budgeting can be found throughout

God's Word. For instance, *"Know well the condition of your flocks, and pay attention to your herds; for riches are not forever"* (Proverbs 27:23). If you don't happen to have any flocks and herds, probably God is saying to know well the condition of your clothing allowance, housing budget, and your food budget.

Another positive aspect is that a budget can help you and your husband develop better communication. If he wants to live on a budget, he obviously sees a need to do so. He wants to be a better steward of the money God has provided the two of you. And you, as his helpmate, should be willing to sit down with him, discuss this, and then come to some reasonable compromise.

Your budget probably won't need to control your spending to the exact dollar every month, nor should it, but there should be some reasonable way for you to work this out together. All a budget can do is show how much money you're making and help you decide where you're going to spend it. That's neither complicated nor confining—except within the limits of your income and God's will.

I believe that everybody needs a budget. Ten percent of our population make enough money to be sloppy and get away with it; 10 percent are so cheap they'll probably never overspend; but the other 80 percent, among whom may be your children, will get themselves into deep trouble. Remember, financial problems are the number one cause of family conflicts in America today.

QUESTION:

Now that we're close to accomplishing our financial goals, what do we do next?

We've been living on your budget now for the better part of three years and we've paid off our credit cards, we're nearly ready to pay off our car, and we've got a plan to pay off our home in about six years. We even have some surplus money now. The next question is, Now what do we do? It seems like we've been concentrating on budgeting for so long, we're not sure what the next step is.

Answer:

There are several things that you can be doing. Number one, because the interest you were paying on the loans is now available, you can increase your giving.

Next, you can plan long term for the future. If you have children, start thinking about their college education funds and start looking for places to invest that money. I recommend good-quality mutual funds because, over the long run, they tend to reflect the overall economy. But, in order to get there, you need to start a long-term savings plan.

I would set aside a specific amount of money. If you can put it into your company's retirement plan, all the better, particularly if they match some of your contributions. If you don't have another plan, save the money until you have enough to open an IRA. Then invest in good-quality mutual funds through your IRA.

I congratulate you on reaching one of your goals: to get out of debt and stop paying all that interest in consumer loans. The next goals are to start saving money, invest for the future, and give more. Beyond that, I'd suggest that you take what you've learned and teach other young couples in your church. There are always those who need to know what you've learned.

Question:

How do I budget my husband's income when it is so irregular, and how much of his travel expenses should be included in our family budget?

My husband is a trucker, he's rarely home, and his income is irregular (when he's working certain times of the year his income is high; other times it's very low).

ANSWER:

First, you need to keep two entirely separate budgets. If your husband is a self-employed contractor (truck driver), you need to set aside the taxes (in a separate account) and pay them on a quarterly basis. You also need a budget just for the business. The money that's left after all the business expenses have been paid becomes income to the family—or profit—so, you also need a second budget for your family.

Since the income is variable, I would recommend that you do the following. Figure how much he makes annually, divide that by twelve, and that becomes your monthly income. Set up a savings account or a money market account and deposit all the family funds into that account. From that account, you'll pay the personal taxes that are due; then the amount left over becomes your monthly budget.

Let's assume that your estimated income is $24,000 per year, or $2,000 per month. All money earned (after business expenses) goes into the savings account; then once a month you withdraw $2,000 to pay your household expenses. That's the only way you'll be able to make this budget work.

You have to take your variable income and make it appear to be a more regular income. That means that during the high-income months you store the money so that during the low-income months you can draw from that pool. The vast majority of the people who have a variable income—commission or otherwise—end up spending all the money during the higher-income months, because they treat it like a windfall profit. Then during the bad times they don't have any reserves and go into debt. You don't want that to happen to you.

QUESTION:

If my husband takes the new job he's been offered, he'll make less money, so how can I tell if the new income will be enough to live on?

The new job will pay a slightly lower salary than what he has been making, but it would allow him to stay closer to home and not have to drive so much, and it would allow us more time together.

ANSWER:

The first thing you want to do is make out a realistic budget, based on the new salary. If the old job required a lot of driving and car expense, very possibly that savings will help to keep your budget in balance. Take his total salary, divide it into the appropriate categories (according to the Percentage Guide), and determine if you have enough money to maintain your current level of spending. If you can't, you'll need to pare down some of the categories so you can make it.

Overall, you'll need to decide if the added family time is worth the financial sacrifice. Think about twenty years from now, when the kids are grown and gone. Then it will be easier to decide.

QUESTION:

Can you help us figure out how to pay for our daughter's care?

Our disabled daughter's care costs about $600 a month—far above what our insurance will pay. We really don't have that much money in our household budget. Somehow we've been able to meet expenses over the last couple of years, but as I look at the next fourteen or fifteen years, the life expectancy of our daughter, I just wonder how we are going to be able to make it.

Answer:

It sounds like the only way you'll be able to make it is with God's help. God knows your needs; this is not a situation you created. You need to commit this to prayer, tell your friends and your family, and trust that God is going to provide the resources when you need them. *"He is a shield to those who take refuge in Him"* (Proverbs 30:5). And remember, many times it won't come from a predetermined source.

I implore you to avoid the use of credit cards to pay for her expenses. There are many Christians who will help if they are made aware of your needs. That is certainly true if they know that you have a disabled child, but the same people probably wouldn't help you pay off your credit cards.

So you need to rely on the Lord and on the Lord's people and let them know your needs. Most Christians I've met in your situation are reticent to tell anybody else about it, because they feel like they're begging. But let me put it to you this way: If you knew of people in your community who had a situation like yours and, even though they were managing their money well, they couldn't provide the care their children needed, would you help them? Certainly you would, and let me assure you that there are many others who will help if they just know about your needs. Don't presume they know unless you tell them.

Question:

How do I convince my husband that we should start living on a budget?

I've been listening to your program for several years now, and I am convicted to get on a budget, but I don't think our budget is going to work. We always spend more than we make, and it seems like every time we get a raise the money is consumed before we even get it. My husband is not interested in working on a budget with me. He says it's too depressing. Any ideas?

ANSWER:

The reason it's depressing to your husband is because he's not facing reality. The time to start a budget is now! Don't wait until you get out of debt, because without a budget you probably aren't going to get out of debt. I'd suggest asking your husband (as sweetly as you can), "I really would like to get on a budget, but I can't do it without your help. Will you work with me?"

If he says yes, then all you need to get started are the materials mentioned in the Appendix. We also have many volunteer counselors—perhaps we have one in your area (see item 2.2 in the Appendix).

If he says no, you have to be willing to be blunt and turn the finances over to him. Be honest and tell him the truth—that you can't handle the pressure and it is really his responsibility. Explain that you're more than willing to help but that you can't do it alone. That's the only way you're going to be able to deal with this problem. Remember, in a marriage, it takes both of you working on the problem or else it won't be solved. To attempt to handle this alone will result in a lot of frustration.

"Two are better than one because they have a good return for their labor. For if either of them falls, the one will lift up his companion. But woe to the one who falls when there is not another to lift him up" (Ecclesiastes 4:9–10).

QUESTION:

How can we get out of debt and stay out?

I've heard your radio broadcast many times, and many of the things you say I agree with; however, in our family we live paycheck to paycheck. We never have any accumulated surplus, and we live on credit cards. If we get a large bonus or something, we get ourselves nearly out of debt, but then we just get right back in again. Any suggestions?

ANSWER:

There is no alternative but to get on a good financial plan—for a family, it's called a budget. First, you need to take a realistic look at what you're spending versus what you're making and then decide how to make the two compatible. If you can't increase your income, and most people can't, then you must decrease your spending. And that requires some difficult choices.

Sometimes it means selling a home. Sometimes it means getting by with a single car—not very convenient today. Sometimes it means not taking vacations for a period of time or else taking short trips. Other times it means shopping in thrift shops for your kids' clothes and shopping in discount stores for gifts. That's not a lot of fun, and it's humbling for most people, but sometimes that's what it takes to make a budget work. If you're willing to sacrifice, a budget will work, regardless of your income.

I've counseled with people who made $200,000 a year, others who made $100,000, some who made $50,000, and others who made only $20,000. Most of them said the same thing initially: They didn't make enough money. If the income of the couple with $20,000 had suddenly been raised to $100,000, they would have thought they were wealthy, but if they didn't change their habits, within a couple of years they would be spending it all. It's a matter of facing the problems realistically and deciding that you really want to solve them.

QUESTION:

What's the difference between what you call your savings plan and an emergency plan?

ANSWER:

Within the budget there are several categories of savings. For instance, the Automobile category has a savings category for car repairs, tire replacement—those types of things. Within the Clothing category there is savings for seasonal clothing. When those monies are saved, they're allocated to a specific category.

However, in addition, I recommend that a budget include an emergency savings account, which is a surplus of money that's available for unforeseen contingencies. For instance, if you lost your job, you would have that money to fall back on. I recommend saving about six months' income, if possible, but not less than three months'.

In addition, you should have a category of savings that could be called Long-Term Savings for the Future, such as money put aside for your children's college education or perhaps retirement.

So, in essence, a well-managed budget would have three categories of savings: one for individual categories of spending within your budget—Housing, Clothing, Food, Automobile, and so forth. The second would be emergency savings for unplanned contingencies. And the third would be for long-term planned events. *"Divide your portion to seven, or even to eight, for you do not know what misfortune may occur on the earth"* (Ecclesiastes 11:2).

QUESTION:

Do you think it would be beneficial to us to take out a loan, for instance a home equity loan, to fund the categories you talk about so that our budget will work?

We got your budget workbook and we are starting to get on a budget, but we don't have any surplus funds to put into the categories.

ANSWER:

No, in my opinion, that's not a good idea. It's too easy to fall back on credit whenever you have a problem. Let's assume that to pre-fund the categories would require $1,200 and you borrowed that much money. That would make your budget work from the *first month*.

The budget now looks good on paper, but it's too easy. The next time something comes up and you spend the surpluses, you'd be tempted to borrow some more.

Instead, I recommend that you work out the budget process over a longer period of time. Almost certainly, your budget won't work the first month. But if you'll keep funding it properly month by month, within six to eight months you'll see it begin to work; and within one year or so it will work well.

As a general rule, I don't recommend that you borrow to get a budget started.

QUESTION:

What can we do if we don't have enough money to meet our month-to-month bills and also pay our creditors?

We've started your budget, but our difficulty is that we've cut back as much as we can, and we still don't have enough money to go around. If we don't pay the creditors, obviously we're going to get into financial trouble. In fact, we have some credit card companies threatening to sue us right now. What are our alternatives?

Answer:

First, you need to be sure that your budget is realistic. If you think you've trimmed it as far as it can be trimmed and you can't get it down any further, get some help. It probably can be reduced more. Also, perhaps you can contact your creditors and work out an alternative payment plan that doesn't require as much money per month. Some of them will work with you, but many of them, I suspect, will not. Therefore, you'll need some outside help.

I recommend using one of the credit counseling companies—like Consumer Credit Counseling Service—and have them help you work out a plan with your creditors. They almost always can help you not only reduce the payments but also reduce the interest as well. See item 2.3 in the Appendix. We work with a group in Atlanta that handles the entire nation via telephone for us, and it works very well.

But stick to your plan, pay what you can, and don't give up. You're doing the right thing, and God is still in control.

"Commit your works to the LORD, and your plans will be established. The LORD has made everything for its own purpose" (Proverbs 16:3–4).

Question:

Can you help me figure out a way to tithe?

I'm a single parent, and I really do appreciate all the emphasis you put in your program on helping single parents. I'm doing the best I can. I work two full-time jobs, but I don't make enough money to pay all the bills and still tithe. After paying for childcare and all the other things I have to provide, there just simply is not enough money. I want to tithe to the Lord, and I feel very badly that I don't seem to be able to do so.

Answer:

Let me say in advance that God is not an accountant. He doesn't care about the money we give, except that it's the outside indicator of what is going on inside our hearts. Having said that, I also believe that God wants us to trust Him and believe in Him. It's easy to say that we believe in God; it's another thing to actually trust Him.

As a single parent, the way you tithe is to take one-tenth of your income and give it to God—the same as anyone else who tithes. Then budget the rest, believing that God will meet your needs. Remember that He said, *"Bring the whole tithe into the storehouse, so that there may be food in My house, and test Me now in this . . . if I will not open for you the windows of heaven and pour out for you a blessing until it overflows"* (Malachi 3:10). God is totally trustworthy, and He will meet your needs.

Second, you need to let the Christians around you know what your real needs are. I've talked to literally thousands of Christians about the plight of single parents during my teaching career; and, without fail, I ask them a very direct question: "If you knew there was a single mother in your church who was working hard—even working two to three jobs—managing her money the best she could, but she just didn't make enough money to take care of all her needs, including clothes for her children or being able to send her kids to camp from time to time—the normal things that most families are able to do—would you help her?"

Without exception, I've never had a person respond, "No, I wouldn't help." To the contrary, I've had people say, "I would feel offended if someone didn't let me know about her needs." Every person I have asked has said that he or she would help.

I believe that is also true in your community. Your responsibility is to let your needs be known. God's responsibility is to convict His people to help you.

QUESTION:

Now that we are totally debt free, what do we do?

We've been following your budget now for almost ten years. We started by paying off our credit cards. Then we paid off our automobiles and made a commitment to pay cash for them from that point on, which we do. As of last month, we paid off our house and we're totally debt free. What now?

ANSWER:

Now the fun part begins. Take some of the money you were spending on interest and put it into God's kingdom and watch how God can multiply that money.

Now you start the next phase of life. Pray about how God can use you now that you're debt free. What has He freed you to do? I've talked to many people who've been freed up to do mission work, others who've been freed to give to send others. At the very least, find a single mom in your church and help her.

There's something else that God wants for you. Remember that being debt free is not the end of the plan; it's the beginning of what God wants to use you for. Look and see how God can use you now that you're not only financially free, but totally free spiritually as well.

"The mind of man plans his way, but the LORD directs his steps" (Proverbs 16:9).

QUESTION:

Should our budget be a source of strife?

My husband and I began a budget several months ago, but it seems like whatever we do, we do to the extreme. My husband is so committed to this budget that he allows me no flexibility whatsoever. We've eliminated all Entertainment/Recreation, all Clothing, and even sold my car. Now he's seriously considering selling our home and moving into a mobile home, even though I believe we'll be okay where we are. He says that we're not saving enough for the future.

ANSWER:

The best counsel that I can give has been given by God in Genesis 2:24, where God said He created a husband and a wife to be one person. That means that any budget worked out in a family has to work for both people, not just one. A common mistake in budgeting is to try to overcorrect, based on the dominant person's personality. These kinds of budgets work well on paper, but they don't work very well in real life. I suggest that your husband needs to reach a better balance.

I saw this principle demonstrated some time ago when I was counseling a financial analyst and his wife. He could analyze a company's financial report, but he didn't know how to balance his own checkbook. After our second counseling session, I gave them a task of developing a budget to control their Miscellaneous spending (that's the category that eats up your money and you can never remember where it went).

In their case, they were overspending nearly $300 a month on a variety of miscellaneous things, such as boats and trips. When they returned, about two months later, I asked the husband, "How do you like your plan so far?"

His response was, "This is great. We now have our spending under control. We've stopped going any further into debt. In fact, we're paying off some debt and we have a little savings."

Then I asked his wife, "How do you like your plan so far?"

She replied, "This is absolutely the worst thing that has ever happened in my life."

"Why is that?" I asked.

"I thought you told me this would be a plan that would work for both of us."

I responded, "Absolutely."

"Well," she said, "let me tell you something. He's decided that my hair appointment is miscellaneous, our kids are miscellaneous, my car is miscellaneous, our house is miscellaneous." She went on to name the things that he had trimmed out of their budget. "But," she said, "his boat is not miscellaneous. And when the motor broke and we had to spend $200 on it, he said it was a necessity."

Obviously, that husband had made out a budget that worked very well for one person. Unfortunately, there was another person in the marriage, and therefore the budget had to work for both of them. I shared a scriptural reference that I thought would help their situation perfectly: *The way of a fool is right in his own eyes, but a wise man is he who listens to counsel*" (Proverbs 12:15). The primary counselor of any husband is his wife. The primary counselor of any wife is her husband.

I recommend that you work through a third party—a counselor—and get the situation under control. No budget should create the strife you two are having.

QUESTION:

Is it okay to increase our food budget to 25 percent, instead of 15?

We're a family of six and our food cost is about 25 percent, but I don't know how to reduce this category of spending.

ANSWER:

Remember that the budget percentages I use are only guidelines that represent the average family, and the average family consists of four people, not six. If you require more money for food, that's fine. Just be sure that you take that percentage out of some of the other categories and don't go into debt for it. Remember, you only have 100 percent to spend.

Also, think about ways to reduce your food cost, and I'm sure with a family of six you're good at stretching your food budget. Plan menus for the month and use the menus to make out your shopping list. The average family eats about seventeen to twenty different kinds of meals per month, so it doesn't mean that you need hundreds of menus; you probably need only about twenty. When you go food shopping, buy only what's on your shopping list.

Another idea to reduce your food budget is, don't go to the store hungry. Most people who do buy more than they need. Also, don't take your husband grocery shopping, because husbands love junk food. Don't take your children for the same reason.

You might consider joining a food co-op—a group of families that get together and buy food in larger quantities and then divide it. This cuts down on each family's costs.

If you don't already, use manufacturers' food coupons. I interviewed a lady one time with a family of seven people who fed her entire family on less than $100 per month. She did it by using coupons—lots of coupons! It takes time and effort, but it is well worth it. *"Food is for the stomach, and the stomach is for food"* (1 Corinthians 6:13). Our bodies were created to need food, and the food you choose can have a significant impact on your budget and your family's health. Plan well, shop well, and pray a lot. You have to be very creative to keep your food budget under control.

QUESTION:

Can budgets be too detailed?

I'm the budgeter in our family, and my husband is getting very discouraged with it. He says he feels like he's caught in a vise.

Being a detail person, it takes me about three hours per pay period to maintain our budget, and I've allocated all of our spending down to the last dollar per month for each of us. I'm concerned that maybe I've gotten our budget too intense.

ANSWER:

Considering the details of your budget, I would say that it is too detailed for Arthur Anderson and Company (auditors). It's interesting how God puts opposites together; one will be a "detailist" and the other will be a "generalist." You've done a very good job developing a spreadsheet for your personal finances; however, it probably is driving your husband crazy. I'm pretty detailed myself, and it would drive me crazy.

> **A budget is just a method of worrying before you spend money, as well as afterward.**
>
> ANONYMOUS

You don't need to allocate spending down to a dollar. For example, if your husband is allocated $50 a month for spending money, that should be his and he shouldn't be accountable to you for how it is spent. Nor are you accountable to him for how your $50 is spent. And you don't need to track every category down to the last penny to have a good budget.

My suggestion is, bring your husband into the budgeting process, get his opinions, and back off a little bit. That doesn't mean to be careless in budgeting and accounting, because you do need to be detailed, but you don't need to plot everything out for a five-year period of time, which is what you've evidently done in your spreadsheet.

Yes, you can be too detailed, just as you can be too sloppy in record keeping; therefore, try to reach a practical balance. God is most blessed when, by working together, a husband and wife offset each other's extremes.

"The wise woman builds her house, but the foolish tears it down with her own hands" (Proverbs 14:1).

3
BUSINESS

MANY BOOKS HAVE BEEN WRITTEN ON THE ethics of business. In fact, I wrote one several years ago dealing with the biblical principles of business, *Business by the Book.*

This question and answer book is not a forum for discussing all of what God has to say about business ethics. So, I'll just answer some of the more common questions I'm asked.

> **Make yourself an honest man, and then you may be sure that there is one rascal less in the world.**
>
> THOMAS CARLYLE

For those who are serious about applying God's Word to their work and careers, I encourage you to get a copy of *Business by the Book* or the associated tapes. You can learn some of the simple but profound truths from the Source of all truth.

Clarence Demmings put many of these basic principles into Japanese society after World War II and helped to create one of the most profitable industrial countries of the twentieth century.

God's Word is still as applicable in our high-tech society as it was when Joseph established the world's first commodity market in Egypt.

QUESTION:

What do you think about my working at home?

I am a stay-at-home mom, and I find that our budget is short about $200 a month. I would like to start a home business. I've read in magazine ads that there are companies that will pay me for stuffing envelopes, but I have to pay them a $500 sign-up fee. Is this advisable?

ANSWER:

In the vast majority of cases, any offer that requires you to pay up front is a scam, and I recommend that you stay away from all such "deals." If a legitimate business wants to hire you as a stay-at-home employee, it provides the necessary materials, you provide the labor, and they pay you for your efforts. You should not have to pay any money up front.

I suspect the company that you're referring to is selling people the idea of getting into a home business. There are legitimate enterprises that hire people to do specific tasks at home; generally, though, it is not stuffing envelopes. Again, remember this rule: If you have to pay, it's a good deal for the company, a bad deal for you.

QUESTION:

What is a good way to earn money at home?

We're a young couple with a new baby. I was an office administrator for a doctor prior to having the baby. Now I'd really like to be able to stay home, so I'm looking for ways to earn money. I was thinking about medical transcription. Do you think that's a good idea and, if so, how would I get into it?

ANSWER:

The obvious answer is that it's better to make a business out of something you know than something you don't. Since you were an office administrator for a doctor, then you probably understand medical transcription and also patient billing. My suggestion is to go to some local doctors, including the doctor you worked for, and ask if they would be willing to pay you to do this at home.

Generally speaking, I would think the area of billing patients should be a good opportunity, because many medical practices hire outside agencies to do this anyway. However, I caution you to stay away from companies that offer to help you get into this business for a fee. Some of them are legitimate; the majority are not.

Before you make the decision, do a little research and find out if there is a demand for your services. In the current economy, with faxes and the Internet, there should be no reason why you couldn't do this kind of work at home and fit it into your schedule.

QUESTION:

What do you think about changing careers?

I don't like what I do; at present I'm a full-time secretary for a major corporation. I feel like I have more talent than is being used, but it's hard to give up my job because of the benefits. Do you have any suggestions?

Answer:

Obviously, God has blessed you with certain abilities, and you need to work in an area where you can fully utilize them. I recommend that you take a career guidance test (you'll find information about the one offered by Crown Financial Ministries in item 5.0 in the Appendix). This will help you understand what you're best equipped to do. Then you should start looking for a job in that career field. If you need additional training, go to night school.

Under no circumstances would I recommend that people stay in jobs that frustrate them and don't utilize their abilities—just for the benefits. It would be a miserable thing to spend your life thinking, *I can't wait to retire and do what I want.* Most people are not capable of doing what they want after retirement, and to stay in dead-end jobs is a waste of the talents God has given them. Don't be foolish and quit without a plan; but don't be fearful either.

Question:

Should we commingle my husband's self-employed business expenses with our personal expenses?

I never know exactly how much money we are making; nor do I know how much money we have for my budget, since our business and personal finances are held in the same account. Do you have any ideas?

Answer:

Yes. You need to separate your husband's expenses from your personal expenses as quickly as possible. For the business, I recommend that you select a good business computer program (you'll find some listed in items 4.1 and 4.2 in the Appendix). If you don't have a computer, I recommend one of the manual systems. But no matter what, separate the personal and business expenses.

For the business, you need to know how much income is generated and how much expense is involved, including your husband's travel—even if he uses the family automobile. What's left over should be the profit that's available for your family budget. In most instances, that will not be a fixed amount per month. Since it is a variable amount, you'll need to go on a variable-income budget.

The way you do that is very simple. Calculate what you expect to be the minimum (not the maximum) annual income your husband will generate. That becomes the basis for your monthly budget. Let's assume that, based on past experience, you anticipate that he will make a net income (after business expenses) of $36,000 a year, but it varies month by month. Set up a separate savings account into which you will deposit all family income. From that savings account you'll pay yourself a total income (before taxes) of $3,000 per month.

During the high-income months, the money in the savings account will accumulate, and during the low-income months you'll draw from it. But under no circumstances should you live on the income as it is being generated; it will frustrate your budget attempt, because it will fluctuate so widely.

Also, bear in mind that you do have to pay taxes on his income, which include Social Security and federal and state income taxes, if applicable. You need to set that money aside in a separate account. Your household budget should show you exactly where your money is going each month. Our computerized budget program, *Money Matters Deluxe*, is listed in item 2.2 in the Appendix.

QUESTION:

Should we go into debt to start a business?

My husband was laid off recently and can't find another job. He'd like to go into business for himself and start a plumbing repair company, but we don't have the money to start the business. He thinks that we should borrow against the house. I feel hesitant about this. Could you give us some counsel?

ANSWER:

It is very important for your husband not to go into business simply because he can't find another job. There are two key elements that make the majority of small businesses fail: a lack of capital—not having enough money to operate on until the business is developed—and a lack of management. Not everyone can manage a business.

Your husband needs to talk to somebody in the plumbing repair business to find out the particulars. In my opinion, it would be better for him to work for someone in that business for a couple of years to learn the ins and outs of the business. This will give him a good foundation for starting his own business. Plan ahead, though, because most small businesses don't generate enough income to live on for the first year. Without sufficient cash reserve, the majority of small businesses fail and leave their owners deeply in debt.

Personally, I don't recommend borrowing against your home, unless there's a high probability of success and you can handle the stress. It would be far better to work for somebody else, even at a lesser salary, than to go into business and lose your home and the business, which often happens.

QUESTION:

What do you think about multilevel sales?

I've been approached by some people in our church about selling a product. The plan they presented is called a multilevel sales product: I buy the product from them and sign up other people to sell for me. Is this honest? Is it a good idea for a Christian to do this?

ANSWER:

It's not how a product is sold that makes it a good or a bad product or an honest or dishonest business; it is the people who are involved with it. Multilevel marketing has been around for a long time; actually it has been around longer than retailing has. The traveling peddlers who sold products out of a wagon were, in fact, multilevel marketers. They bought their products from others at one price, marked them up, and sold them elsewhere at a higher price.

So it's not the marketing system that causes problems; rather, it's the ethics of some of the people who sell the products. All too often multilevel selling becomes a phenomenon that takes on a life of its own. Not everyone can succeed at sales, and not every product is worth selling to your friends. Clearly, there are many excellent multilevel sales companies and millions of people have made successful full- and part-time careers from the sale of their products.

There should be some conditions for becoming involved in multilevel marketing: Do you believe in the product manufacturer? Do you believe in the product, and do you use it yourself? Would you be willing to use it even if you couldn't sell it to somebody else? If you can answer yes to all three of these questions, then proceed.

However, I repeat that not everyone has a talent for sales; therefore, not everybody should try it. And also bear in mind that not every friend is a prospect for a sale. In fact, if you treat all your friends as prospects you could end up having very few friends. But if you can keep a good balance, I believe there is nothing wrong with multilevel marketing. Actually, it's a good way for many stay-at-home moms to make additional money to supplement their family's income.

QUESTION:

What do you think we should do about our family business that's in trouble?

My husband, his two brothers, and his father are all employed in the business, but at this point my husband and I are feeding almost $1,000 a month into the business. We can only continue to do this a few more months and then we will be totally out of money. What should we do?

ANSWER:

There's a time in any business when it's time to quit. I can't tell you that this is the time, but you and your husband should seek some counsel quickly. If the business is losing money steadily and there's no realistic prospect of turning it around, it would be better to shut it down now rather than later. Unfortunately, many people continue to operate a business far beyond the time when it should be shut down.

Your husband should talk to his brothers and father and be totally honest with them. It's very difficult for people in a family business to make these kinds of decisions because of the emotional aspect, but there's a time when any business should be closed if it is losing money. I'm sure none of you want to plunge your family into debt. Don't wait until the pit is too deep to climb out.

> You may spend years striving and pushing to get more out of life, but all you gain is a sense of being burned out.
>
> CHARLES STANLEY

There's a group of volunteers known as SCORE (Service Core of Retired Executives) that may have a chapter in your area. If they do, they can be a good resource (see item 4.3 in the Appendix).

QUESTION:

What should I do to prepare for starting a small business on my own?

I'm still working for a large company, but I plan to retire in about five years and would like to have something to do then. I'm mechanically adept, so I was thinking about starting some kind of a home repair or perhaps a house-wiring electrical business. Does this sound like a good idea? Also, about how much money does it take to get a new business started?

ANSWER:

There is no exact answer to how much money it takes to get a small business started. In your case, you have the ideal circumstance of being employed by someone else, so you still have a steady income. You also have the advantage of time to help you prepare well.

If you're going to start a home repair or electrical maintenance business, I'd suggest that you go to either a local trade school or a community college and take some associated courses. You'll also learn the building codes for your area and the licensing requirements—almost everything that you need to know to start a small business.

In most cases, the business you've chosen doesn't require a large amount of capital. You'll need tools, but if you already have those you have a head start. And there's a small cost to do some advertising and have business cards printed. But, on the plus side, if you're doing small-scale home remodeling or repairs, you probably won't lack opportunities; it's very difficult to find people who will do these small jobs. I encourage you to continue in the direction you're going. I think it's a great idea for your retirement years.

QUESTION:

How would I tithe on a home-based business (or any other business) if I don't anticipate making a 10 percent profit?

ANSWER:

The principle of tithing scripturally is a simple one: Put God first in your life and reflect that through your finances. If you can't tithe 10 percent of your gross income on your business, and most businesses can't, tithe what you can. I believe the principle taught in God's Word is that you can tithe only on what belongs to you. In other words, it would be the profits from your business.

Obviously, you can't tithe on what you owe your employees; that's their money. And you can't tithe on what you owe your creditors; that belongs to them. You can tithe only on what is yours, but don't get hung up on a percentage. I believe that God wants us to give a tenth, but He is going to bless your heart attitude.

QUESTION:

What do you think about the vending machine business?

I've been approached by someone who would like for me to take over his vending machine and territory, but it will require a sizable investment.

ANSWER:

I caution you about going into the vending machine business for several reasons. It's highly competitive, location is the lifeblood of any vending machine business, and most good territories are not available. Also bear in mind that in many large cities the vending machine business is dominated by organized crime. If you're required to pay a sizable amount of money to get into the business, my recommendation is, don't do it. It is a very, very difficult business in which to make a living.

QUESTION:

How do I go about selling a business, and how do I establish an asking price?

I have a business I've owned for the better part of ten years. It doesn't make a large amount of money—about $10,000 per year after my salary. I'd like to sell the business and retire.

ANSWER:

There is no one method for selling a business or for determining its value. Let's discuss pricing first. Often a small business is priced based on earnings (in your case $10,000 per year after your salary). I would advertise the business to show this profit, including your salary. Let's assume arbitrarily that your salary is $40,000 per year; therefore, this would be a business that makes an annual profit of $50,000. A price of four to five times the earnings would be in line.

For advice, my recommendation would be to contact an association that's involved in your type of business. For instance, if you're in the real estate business, contact a real estate association. Normally they will have excellent information on how to value a business.

How do you sell a business? You advertise it, and there are a variety of ways to do that. Try the cheaper ways first: local newspaper, local trade magazines—perhaps even post ads in business-related stores around town. If you want to expand the search for a buyer, you could place an ad in the regional *Wall Street Journal* or perhaps an association magazine.

If that doesn't work, go through a small-business broker; you normally can find them in the Yellow Pages or your regional *Wall Street Journal.* Another area that has proved to be useful is the Internet. There are several Web sites that host businesses for sale.

Also be sure to tell all your friends and your family; you might find a buyer within your own circles.

QUESTION:

How would I evaluate the value of my home-based business so that I can sell it?

For several years I have been doing transcripts and other academic work on a computer and have built a pretty good clientele at the local college near my home. I am now thinking about getting out of the business. How do I establish a value for what I do?

ANSWER:

In your case, valuing the business is relatively simple. You simply take the amount of money you make (including your salary) and advertise. For example, "Have a business for sale that makes $25,000 per year." Pick a value you feel comfortable with and try it. Small home-based businesses can sell for anywhere from two to five times their earnings. The bottom line is, find a willing, able buyer who will pay what you want. And don't finance it yourself. Cash up front only!

I would recommend advertising in your local area newspapers or in a swap shop. Many times radio stations give free advertising for businesses for sale. And also advertise at the college or university. Very possibly you will find a buyer in your local community.

QUESTION:

Am I bound to a deal if someone else reneges?

As a Christian businessperson, I make many contracts with people who simply don't keep their word.

ANSWER:

It's an indictment of our generation that most people (Christians included) don't understand what a vow is—a pledge to keep our word, literally our honor. Once a Christian makes a vow, it's a binding contract and must be fulfilled regardless of the cost. Therefore, don't agree to a contract (a vow) unless you understand the total agreement. The psalmist says, *"Make vows to the LORD your God and fulfill them"* (Psalm 76:11).

You can make a unilateral vow, which means you promise to do something regardless of what the other party does, or you can make a bilateral vow in which you promise to do something *if* the other person does his or her part. You need to be sure that you understand exactly what the guidelines are in any contract you agree to. If you promise to do something—no matter what—you must do it.

Vows seem to be conditional today. Many people feel that a contract made under one set of circumstances can be broken if the circumstances change.

In past generations, vows were a commitment of honor. When an honorable person shook hands, it was a deal. Even if it required all he or she owned, an honest person would fulfill the vow. God's Word says, *"A good name is to be more desired than great riches, favor is better than silver and gold"* (Proverbs 22:1). The outside indicator of an honorable person is a good name. I encourage you to keep your word, regardless of what others do.

> **You can be deprived of your money, your job, and your home by someone else, but remember that no one can ever take away your honor.**
>
> WILLIAM LYON PHELPS

I also recommend that your contracts be bilateral. That way you only have to do something if the other party does his or her part.

QUESTION:

What do you think about the validity of Christians in ministry recruiting others to be salespeople and distributors?

I'm a Christian in full-time ministry, and over the years I think I've been approached with every multilevel product sales scheme that exists.

Answer:

First, we have to differentiate between pyramid selling and multilevel sales. In the former, an individual buys the right to bring somebody into an organization and receives a commission or finder's fee as a result of recruiting. In other words, no product is sold—only a recruitment. With rare exception, this system is illegal because the recruitment fee is considered a security and is governed by the individual state's security laws. Those who get involved normally are not licensed securities dealers.

In multilevel sales, several people in a marketing chain make a percentage on the sales of those below them. Multilevel selling is a widely accepted marketing system. In fact, virtually every product sold in America is multilevel. The manufacturer produces a product and marks it up to the wholesaler. The wholesaler marks it up to the retailer. The retailer marks it up and sells it to the consumer.

Often the difference in the multilevel selling you presented is that a participant not only makes a percentage of sales but also has the right to earn commissions on the sales of people he or she has brought into the business. All of this is legitimate if the product is of good quality and the intent is to sell a product and not just recruit more salespeople.

The difficulty in multilevel sales is the attitude of those who get involved. Sometimes greed and materialism take over. If Christians want to engage in this activity, some fundamental principles should be observed: (1) They should care more about other people than themselves, (2) they must be sure that their sales techniques are honest, and (3) they should not proselytize solely in their churches, Bible studies, or other Christian networks. These people are brothers and sisters in the Lord, not sales prospects.

When products are to be sold exclusively within Christian circles, be suspicious—doubly so if a minister is involved. It's too easy to abuse a pastoral relationship this way. The apostle Paul said, *"Those who want to get rich fall into temptation and a snare and many fool-ish and harmful desires which plunge men into ruin and destruction"* (1 Timothy 6:9).

QUESTION:

Would I be better off selling my business or keeping it?

My husband died approximately eighteen months ago and left me his sales company. The company did very well when my husband was alive and it is still very profitable. The manager we had running the company is still running it and would now like to buy it. Should I sell it to him?

ANSWER:

You should get some businesspeople to help you evaluate your options. You also need to get good, independent counsel to evaluate the business's worth. I recommend that you contact SCORE (Service Core of Retired Executives; see item 4.3 in the Appendix). Often you can find a retired Christian businessperson who will help.

Normally, it would be better for a widow not to sell her husband's business immediately if she has the ability to run it herself. But if you weren't involved in the business (especially a sales company) on a day-to-day basis, it's probably better to sell it. Again, I recommend that you gather a support group of Christian businesspeople from your church, in addition to someone from SCORE, to help you evaluate this decision.

Here's one caution: If you wait too long to sell a sales-oriented business, a key employee might start his or her own company using your customer base. This can seriously undermine the value of the company.

However, a word of encouragement from God's Word will help to balance any fears about the future of your business. The Word says, *"The LORD protects the strangers; He supports the fatherless and the widow, but He thwarts the way of the wicked"* (Psalm 146:9).

You can turn to God and claim that promise, because God knows exactly what your needs are, and He can intercede to protect your interests.

4

DEBT AND CREDIT

THE MAJORITY OF FINANCIAL QUESTIONS I'm asked daily deal with the subject of debt and credit. Unfortunately, many of these are tragically similar. Young couples (and older ones too) are caught up in the debt spiral. Often they owe nearly one-third of their total incomes in interest alone. The problem is so acute that our radio broadcast producers sort through more than 100,000 calls each month, trying to find questions that don't deal with debt alone.

Thirty years ago credit card debt was fairly new. Twenty years ago it was more common but limited largely to the upper-income, more affluent families. Today it's like a plague spreading through our land with no one—young, old, educated, or illiterate—immune.

Just as the stock market went euphoric (nuts) in the '90s, so did consumer debt. College campuses now allow credit card companies to recruit their students—just as employers do. The result is a new market for high-interest consumer debt, and college students carrying thousands of dollars in credit card debt.

It can be said that capitalism removed from biblical ethics becomes a cancer on society. Looking at consumer debt today, I can believe it.

QUESTION:

What's the secret for staying out of debt?

We are almost out of debt again. I say "again" because this is the fourth time that we've worked our way totally out of debt and then gotten back into it again. It seems like once the pressure is off we go back to spending.

ANSWER:

The only way you're going to solve this problem is through personal discipline. Let me give you an idea of a plan that has worked for many people. Fill out an Impulse Buying Sheet that will control all nonbudget spending.

> **Some people [spend] half their ingenuity to get into debt, and the other half to avoid paying it.**
>
> GEORGE D. PRENTICE

These are the rules. For anything you want to buy that isn't already in your budget and costs more than $10, you get three additional prices and wait thirty days before you buy it (or whatever period of time feels comfortable to you). That will give you time to shop for a better price, and often it allows enough time for that impulse to pass. As soon as the impulse passes, you probably won't even buy that item.

What's happened in your situation, I expect, is that you've gotten yourself into a habit of living beyond your means, so you overspend, go on a crash budget, then overspend again because you're tired of the crash budget. Crash budgets, like crash diets, seldom work. Balance and moderation usually do.

The only way to break this cycle is through self-discipline. There is no secret to it.

QUESTION:

Do you think we should go bankrupt?

About six months ago my husband lost his job. Prior to that we seemed to be doing fine. Although we did have some credit card debt and some other consumer bills, we didn't have a lot. But over the last six months we have accumulated a huge amount of debt in credit cards and personal loans. It seems like every time I get a call now it's a creditor after us. I don't know what to do. My husband thinks that we should go bankrupt and just start all over again. I don't have peace about doing that, especially after listening to your program.

ANSWER:

Six months ago you should have let the people who care about you know about your needs instead of relying on those credit cards.

Remember, God wants us to trust Him. It's one thing to say we trust God, but it's another thing entirely to actually trust Him. Money is the one objective way we can see God move in our lives, but so many times we just don't respond properly.

I encourage you and your husband not to go bankrupt. That is *not* the answer. Remember what God's Word

> There are but two ways of paying debt: increase of industry of raising income, increase of thrift in laying out.
>
> THOMAS CARLYLE

says, *"The wicked borrows and does not pay back"* (Psalm 37:21). You owe the money, so you should pay it back. Hopefully yours is a temporary situation.

As soon as your husband is employed, start working on your debts. I recommend one of the counseling agencies, like Consumer Credit Counseling Service (see item 2.3 in the Appendix), and try to work out a payment schedule. If it takes you ten years, it takes you ten years. God can still bless you in the meantime, but don't give up. If you quit, Satan wins.

"Evil men do not understand justice, but those who seek the LORD understand all things. Better is the poor who walks in his integrity" (Proverbs 28:5–6).

QUESTION:

Since we owe so much, we can't pay on every bill. What are our options?

> **It is hard to pay for bread that has been eaten.**
>
> DUTCH PROVERB

Most of our debt is in credit cards—about $15,000—but we're also behind in our equity loan and two car payments. Do you think that we should try for another equity loan or refinance all of our debt to try to get caught up?

ANSWER:

The important thing to remember (and something I can't stress enough) is that debt is a *symptom*. The amount of money you owe is a symptom, not a problem. The symptom will keep returning if you don't correct the problem. If I'm counseling people who have the symptom of too much debt and they're thinking about consolidating, my prerequisite is for them to live six months with no new credit and charge nothing whatsoever.

Commit to a very strict budget so you know where your money is going and exactly how much you can pay your creditors. Then I suggest that you work through one of the credit management organizations, like Consumer Credit Counseling Services (you'll find their number and Web site in item 2.3 in the Appendix). They will negotiate with the creditors to reduce the interest rates and alter the payments to fit your budget.

I would not recommend consolidating the loans again—at least not until you have been on a budget a minimum of six to nine months or, even better, a year. You need to demonstrate self-discipline first. *"Like a city that is broken into and without walls is a man who has no control over his spirit"* (Proverbs 25:28).

The common question is, "Well, what do we do if we have an emergency—like the tires wearing out or the car breaking down?" The answer is that you need to pray, trust the Lord, and learn to do without until you can commit to no more borrowing. Until you do, you will never solve this problem.

It's important to understand why the debt occurred in the first place. Many people say, "Well, I lost my job," or "I had a sick child," but remember, there are hundreds of thousands of other families out there who lose their jobs or have sick children, and they don't go into debt. Some of them have families or friends who help, and others simply do without rather than overspend. So it's important to *solve the problem*, which usually is a violation of the basic biblical principles for handling money.

QUESTION:

Where do we start when we owe so much?

We have about $25,000 in credit card debt, and we make about $50,000 a year, but we never seem to get ahead, and we argue all the time. I feel like my husband won't face reality, but he says that he has tried budgeting before and it doesn't work and, besides that, he can't be bothered with these things because he has to earn a living. I tried to get us on a budget, but we have two car payments and private school costs, and we are saving nothing toward retirement.

Answer:

First, you need to pray together about this problem. There's no way you're going to solve this situation unless both of you work on it together. I suggest that you sit down together and list all the debts. Do not exclude anything, including old debts that you haven't paid on, family loans, everything.

> **Loans and debts make worry and frets.**
>
> Unknown origin

If you can't do that without fighting, my recommendation is to schedule an appointment with a marriage counselor. Ask your pastor if there is someone in the church who can work with you. If not, Crown has several thousand trained financial counselors around the country. You'll find our phone number and Web site listed in item 7.0 in the Appendix.

If you're serious about getting yourselves out of debt, keep a diary of what you're spending, by category (Housing, Auto, Food, Clothing, and so forth), for at least one month. A lot of your monthly income can be consumed in the variable expenses that don't necessarily show up in your checkbook every month (miscellaneous items).

You also have to face reality. The private school, one of your cars, perhaps even your home, are all luxuries; they are not necessities. I understand the argument Christians use about Christian schools. I also understand the discussion about the kind of home you live in and the kind of cars you drive. But until you're willing to face the reality that some of those don't fit your income, your budget isn't going to work.

Then, together, you need to make out a budget. It probably won't work the first month. It may not work the first five or six months; but, if you'll stick to it, it will be working a year from the time you started. Initially, some categories—like Automobile(s), Entertainment (vacations) and Miscellaneous (gifts, haircuts, and so on)—won't have money in them.

It may mean relying on the help of friends, family—even your church. This is where many people fail—because of pride. The thing I try to remind people of in this situation is that others will help if you'll just ask. If you would help a friend in your situation (and most would), others will too.

"Take hold of instruction; do not let go. Guard her, for she is your life" (Proverbs 4:13).

QUESTION:

What can we do about the foreclosure on our house?

We are way behind on most of our debts, and as result we haven't been making our house payments regularly. In fact, we're about four months behind and have gotten a notice from the mortgage company that they're going to foreclose on our home. We think that bankruptcy is the only way out. Do you have any other options?

ANSWER:

Bankruptcy is never the only way out. Generally, it's the result of ignoring the problem for too long a period of time. There are two types of bankruptcies for families: Chapter 7, which totally eliminates all the debt and liquidates most of your assets; and Chapter 13, which is called a reorganization, under which the courts will force the creditors to accept the payment you're capable of making.

The court also can put a hold on the foreclosure of your home. That's a very drastic step, and once you do it one time, generally you won't have a second option.

If the home is too expensive for you, face that realistically. My recommendation is to avoid bankruptcy if you can. Once you file for bankruptcy, it will stay on your credit record for ten years. From that point, you probably won't get a legitimate lender to work with you again (a legitimate company means a mortgage company that charges reasonable rates or a credit card company with reasonable interest rates).

As a Christian, you need to remember that the money you borrow is a moral obligation. And even if you decide to go through bankruptcy, which is not my recommendation, you still need to repay the money you owe. Nothing is impossible. I've heard from many couples who were in your situation and yet made the commitment to pay their creditors and not claim bankruptcy. I can't tell you that it worked out every time, but in many cases it did, even though it took them years to work their way back financially.

The most important thing to do in this situation is to pray. You need the Lord's help. God's Word says, *"Cast your burden upon the* LORD, *and He will sustain you; He will never allow the righteous to be shaken"* (Psalm 55:22).

QUESTION:

How do we pay off our debt?

Even though we owe a lot, we think that it's within our income ability to pay it. Some of the debts are delinquent, but some are so far past due that probably the creditors have written them off;

they don't contact us anymore. We have a good income and we do have some surplus now, but where should we start? Is it better to invest some of the money for the long term or to pay off all our debt?

Answer:

I wouldn't worry about long-term investing at this point. One of the principles I share is to never do one thing to the exclusion of everything else. First, if you don't have any personal savings, I recommend that you take some of the surplus and set it aside for emergencies—the amount depends on your income. I'd say that if you have a $50,000 income, you should set aside $4,000 or $5,000 in a cash reserve. That way you're not dependent on credit anymore; you can rely on your own money.

But other than that, it's preferable to pay off your debts before any long-term investing. Listed in the Appendix (item 8.0) you'll find the materials needed to make out a debt elimination plan. I recommend that you pay on the high-interest loans first; however, there are some exceptions. If you have several small bills, even at lower interest rates, it may be better to concentrate on paying those. It's encouraging to see some of the bills being paid off, and it allows more money to pay on the other debts.

Another thing to keep in mind is, don't sacrifice everything else in your budget. For instance, don't totally eliminate your Entertainment/Recreation budget (or your travel budget) or your Clothing budget. You need to maintain a reasonable balance in each category.

"Be strong, and let your heart take courage" (Psalm 27:14). You didn't get into this situation overnight, and you're not going to get out of it overnight; therefore, you need to have a balanced perspective toward budgeting. Write down your goals, when you want to achieve them, and then review them about every six months to remind yourself why you're doing this.

QUESTION:

Would it be better to use a recent inheritance to pay off our loans or should we invest the money?

We have school loans totaling $135,000 for my education and for my husband's. He's in his medical residency and thinks it would be better to invest the money since he'll be making a lot more money once he starts his practice.

ANSWER:

First, answer the question "Am I going to manage my finances God's way?" Since your husband chose the medical profession, he should earn enough money to pay back your school loans. But you don't want to get trapped into the mind-set that debt doesn't matter and that it's more profitable to invest than to pay your debts.

What if God calls you to go to the mission field? If you owe money, you would be ineligible according to most missionary groups. I've known several physicians who were called to become missionaries while in medical school. But they had borrowed so much money for their educations that they had to go to work to pay the loans. By the time the debts were paid, their zeal for mission work had cooled. So be careful. Debt is one of Satan's favorite methods for steering you right out of God's plan.

"Do not withhold good from those to whom it is due, when it is in your power to do it" (Proverbs 3:27). If you don't make a commitment to pay these loans back in a timely fashion, it may affect your attitude about debt for the future as you make more money. The old principle I've observed with many couples is: More money in means more money out. Don't get trapped into our society's debt-forever mentality.

QUESTION:

Do we need to claim bankruptcy?

We owe about $40,000 in credit cards and other debts, and our income is $25,000. My wife just had a baby and we believe that she should stay home. Is this a sin, and will God punish us for it? I'm a pastor and I feel very strongly that we should not file for bankruptcy, but I can't see any way to handle this pressure or ever pay back these debts.

ANSWER:

In many instances, bankruptcy is simply a quick fix for bad habits. People (usually good people) get under pressure as a result of their overspending, so they file for bankruptcy, which liquidates the debt. But since they haven't dealt with the problem that got them there, they go right back to their old habits and within two years they are back in debt again. Under the bankruptcy law, you can file bankruptcy only once every seven years, so creditors are prompt to lend more (at very high rates).

Unfortunately the pressures return, arguments ensue, and quite often the next step is divorce—or in some instances suicide. Bear in mind that if you don't solve the problems that got you there in the first place, they will return.

Put yourself on a budget. When you're sure you're living within your income, including paying on the debt, then be totally honest with your congregation about your situation and ask them to pray with you about it.

"Submit to them; for they keep watch over your souls, as those who will give an account. Let them do this with joy and not with grief, for this would be unprofitable for you" (Hebrews 13:17).

Bear in mind that if you claim bankruptcy your reputation is going to be damaged. Word of the default will get around, as it always does, and because you are a pastor the church will take the heat. I believe there are only two reasons for a Christian to resort to bankruptcy: one, the health of one of the family members (perhaps mental health, as a result of the pressure); and, two, a few creditors have filed suit and are getting a disproportionate amount of money, making it impossible to pay back the other creditors.

QUESTION:

Do I have to pay a bill for something I didn't charge on my credit card?

I'm sure it came as a result of an online purchase through the Internet. Is it dangerous to give my credit card number on the Web, and is there a way to protect myself?

ANSWER:

One of the first things you need to verify when ordering from the Internet is that the site is secure. A note stating it is a secure site will be displayed, so you can *know* it's secure. Next, be sure you keep very good records of what you order.

If you find that your credit card number has been stolen, contact the credit card company, cancel your credit card, and notify the company of these charges. You are not responsible for charges you didn't authorize. Notify the credit card company in writing, and when the bill comes pay only the valid charges. The false charges will be investigated and removed from your bill. However, check your statement for several months to be sure the bill doesn't show up later.

You should have a personal identification number (PIN) for every credit card you have. This will keep anyone else from using your card at an ATM.

QUESTION:

What can I do about charges that show up on my bill for merchandise I returned some time ago?

The card company is threatening to sue me.

ANSWER:

You're protected by the Consumer Credit Protection Act. You can get a copy from the Consumer Affairs office of your state government, or it is available on the Internet (see item 6.3 in the Appendix). But, no matter what, subtract the disputed amount from your bill total and do not pay it. Include a note of explanation about the disputed charges and send it to the credit card company by registered mail, so you know that the company received it. For at least one year, keep your bill of sale on everything you charge on that credit card.

In most cases, the credit card company will clear these disputed charges without difficulty, but with a few you probably should expect two to three months of hassle. If they still don't clear your account, you have a right to contact the credit reporting agency, notify them of this dispute, and have a letter attached to your credit file.

Then you might need to pursue the credit card company in Small Claims Court. In general, most major credit card companies are very good about clearing these erroneous charges, but not all of them.

QUESTION:

Can companies that advertise they can fix bad credit reports actually do it?

I have a bad credit report, and when I applied for a home mortgage loan I was turned down. My credit report shows several slow pays and two no pays. They are accurate, but I would like to know how to fix my credit report. Is that possible?

Answer:

Remember this: When a deal sounds too good to be true, it generally is. And this deal sounds too good. There is basically no way to fix your credit report, except to pay the bills and get a note or a letter from the satisfied creditor, which is attached to your credit report. I know of no other way except to wait for the reporting statute to expire. Generally speaking, bad credit reports (with the exceptions of bankruptcies and a couple of others) will be reported for seven years.

Bankruptcies can be reported for up to ten years, at which time they must be removed. But again, the best way to clear up your account is to pay the money you owe and then ask your creditors to notify the credit reporting agencies. One notification should come to you and one to the credit reporting agency. If the information doesn't get into your account, you should contact the credit reporting agencies. You'll find a list of them and their Web sites in the Appendix (item 6.4).

The bottom line is that, essentially, you need to reestablish good credit by paying your bills. There's no company out there that can do that for you. All they can do is take your money.

Question:

Do I owe a credit card debt even though I never signed anything?

My husband left last year and we are now divorced, but I find that my name is still on his credit cards, and he has charged a large amount. I never really signed anything, even though my name was on the credit card.

ANSWER:

The difficulty is that you may have created an implied contract. You should consult an attorney about this. In my opinion, the credit card company erred, because you should have been required to sign the application. If they can't produce a signed application for the card, in most states you probably aren't legally responsible for the indebtedness. However, if you were using the card and charging merchandise on it, you may be held responsible.

The divorce court can assign all the debt on your joint credit cards to your husband if it decides to do so. However, the credit card company can still hold each of you responsible, and your failure to pay will be reported on your credit account if you charged on the cards and signed for merchandise. However, if you never signed the cards and never charged anything on them, you probably aren't responsible for the debt.

QUESTION:

How do I fix a bad credit report when the information on it is not mine?

ANSWER:

First, request a current copy of your credit report. If you are ever turned down for credit, by law you can get one free copy. If not, you can purchase one from the credit reporting agency; generally the cost of credit reports ranges from $3 to $20. The items you protest should be noted in writing to the credit reporting agency and to the creditors that claim you owe money. If the creditors cannot produce signed bills, you are not responsible.

Currently there are three credit reporting agencies, and you need to contact all three of them (see item 6.4 in the Appendix). To be assured that your account is cleared, you need to submit your protest in writing and register the letters to each of the agencies, as well as to the creditors. If your account isn't cleared in a timely fashion (six months), you'll need to contact an attorney to pursue this. You might also try contacting the Consumer Affairs Department of your state or the Federal Trade Commission in Washington, D.C. (Good luck with getting the FTC to respond.)

QUESTION:

Is there any way to avoid paying 22 percent interest on my credit card debt?

I owe about $12,000 on six cards at very high interest. Is there a better way to pay this back?

ANSWER:

A lot is going to depend on your credit rating. If you still have a good credit rating, you can transfer some or all of this debt to credit cards with lower interest rates. In other words, you can consolidate these credit card bills into a lower interest rate credit card. However, as I have said over and over, unless you solve the problem, the symptom will come back.

The symptom is that you have a lot of high-interest debt, but that's not the problem. The problem is that you're spending money you don't have, buying things that you can't afford, and not paying your bills on time. So, you need to clear that up first.

The good news is that there are some cards that have low initial interest rates and you can transfer your debt to those cards (once you get yourself on a good budget).

QUESTION:

Am I held liable because I co-signed for my nephew's car and he wrecked it?

The insurance won't cover the cost, so what are my options?

ANSWER:

Well, unfortunately, as the Scripture says, *"A man lacking in sense pledges, and becomes guarantor* [surety] *in the presence of his neighbor"* (Proverbs 17:18). And that includes our relatives as well as our friends. The purpose of having a cosigner on a note is so that if one person doesn't pay the debt, the other one will. So, you are liable. About the only thing you can do in this case is to recover the car, sell it for as much as you can get, and then pay the debt yourself.

You do have the right to sue your nephew, although that probably is not the best idea. If he didn't pay the debt, he probably wouldn't pay whatever court assignment you might get. But you do need to confront your nephew and his family and let them know that this is his responsibility. Hopefully, this can be a learning experience for both of you.

There's an old saying that the definition of a distant friend is a close friend who owes you money, and that's also true in families. Your nephew probably will avoid you now because he owes you money, and you'll stay away from him for the same reason. This is a hard lesson, but unfortunately you are responsible for his debt.

The Bible says, *"Do not be among those who give pledges, among those who become guarantors for debts"* (Proverbs 22:26).

The principle to be learned is, don't co-sign for anyone else's debt. In a broad sense, when you co-sign for someone, you're allowing that person to buy things he or she probably can't afford.

QUESTION:

Would it be better to set up a payment plan with the Internal Revenue Service to pay the $20,000 in taxes I owe due to a business failure or try to finance this debt elsewhere?

Also, is it unethical or unscriptural to file for bankruptcy?

ANSWER:

Almost always, if you can borrow the money someplace other than the Internal Revenue Service, you should do so. In general, the interest rates the IRS charges are some of the highest in the economy. Also, sometimes the IRS will negotiate a lower overall debt if you're able to pay the debt in full. In other words, if you were able to borrow, say $15,000, and you went to the IRS with an offer in compromise, it's possible they would accept the $15,000 as total payment (instead of the $20,000).

One additional point: If you borrow the money against your home, the interest is generally deductible on your taxes, effectively dropping the interest rate. But bear in mind that although borrowing against your home may be the best financial decision, it may not be the best thing to do. Most women don't like additional loans against their homes.

You also asked if it is unbiblical or unethical to go bankrupt. First of all, with few exceptions, you can't claim bankruptcy against the Internal Revenue Service. And if you borrowed the money from someone else to pay the IRS in contemplation of going bankrupt, that is unbiblical and probably illegal as well. I would not encourage bankruptcy.

QUESTION:

If it is okay for me to borrow to build a home, why is it unbiblical for me to borrow to build a church?

Answer:

It is not unbiblical to borrow money for a home, a church, or otherwise. However, virtually every reference to borrowing is a warning. There are three specific cautions about borrowing in God's Word: First, all borrowing should be short-term; second, borrowers should not sign surety (borrowing beyond the limits of secured collateral); and, third, borrowing should be uncommon (versus what we see today). (See Deuteronomy 15:1–11; Proverbs 1:15; 22:7.)

We are not *prohibited* from borrowing; neither is the church. However, it is not a positive witness for churches to borrow money when so many of God's people are deeply in debt. On average, Christians pay 400 to 500 percent more in interest per year than they give to God's work.

The church should be leading people out of debt—not into it. There are no examples in Scripture of God ever telling people to do something and then directing them to borrow the money to do it. However, I repeat, borrowing is not a sin, unless you define *sin* as "missing the mark."

The question I always ask in relation to church borrowing is, "Do we *believe* God, or do we just *say we believe* God?" It doesn't cost us anything to say it; it does cost something if we believe it. It is also my conviction that if we trust God, God will provide for those things that He wants done, including the building of churches.

The apostle Paul said, *"My God shall supply all your needs according to His riches in glory in Christ Jesus"* (Philippians 4:19).

Question:

What can I do about a collection company that's calling my home about a debt that isn't mine?

It's either a case of mistaken I.D. or somebody is charging against my account.

ANSWER:

First, request a copy of the bill in question from the collection agency so you can verify the charges and the signature. If you find this is not your bill, then notify the collection agency in writing, and you'll also have to contact the credit reporting agency.

If the collection agency won't stop, by law you have a right to demand that they not call you at your office or your home in the evenings. You're protected by the Fair Credit Protection Act. If they still won't stop, you'll probably have to take them to court.

However, if you find that it is your bill, you must pay it. If it isn't your bill, you need to be sure that the bogus bill doesn't go on your credit report, because it will hurt your credit for up to seven years. Try the consumer affairs department of your state. Often they can help.

QUESTION:

Can I get a credit card with a $500 limit for my son?

He is a college student, and I would like to give him a credit card that he could use only for emergencies. But how can I be sure that he will stay out of debt? A lot of his friends have credit cards, and I have heard some real horror stories about how much they have charged.

ANSWER:

The only way you can be sure your son can't get into debt is to give him a debit card (a card that is guaranteed by a savings account at your bank). Even if you get a credit card with a specific limit, often the credit card company will allow these kids to charge above the minimum. In other words, if they have good credit and are paying on the first $500, the credit card company likely will extend the limit well above the initial amount.

The worst story I've come across was about a sophomore in college who had twelve cards with a total of about $78,000 debt, and his parents didn't know it, although they had signed for the first card. Once he was able to get credit, he was able to get a *lot more* credit. You need to be very careful that if you co-sign for your son's debt you're sure that your liability is limited to only the first $500. Unless the contract is extremely clear, you may have unlimited liability, and many credit card contracts are very difficult to understand.

Credit card debt is much too accessible for young people. In my opinion, if you're going to help your son you should use a debit card, because it is easier to control. I recommend that if you do allow him to have a credit card (and I think there is nothing wrong with that if he's been trained to use it properly), you need to have a signed agreement with your son.

Remember that credit cards are not the problem; the misuse of them is the problem. Your intentions are good, but I caution you to be careful about extending credit to a college student. *"Every man's way is right in his own eyes, but the LORD weighs the hearts"* (Proverbs 21:2).

QUESTION:

What do we do about medical bills from our premature baby?

We are being pressured by our hospital to sign a promissory note against our home, and the doctor has turned us over to a collection agency. Do we have any options?

ANSWER:

Unfortunately, you have allowed this to continue longer than you should have. You should have faced these obligations early on. You need to contact the doctor and the hospital and be totally honest with them. In fact, if possible, you need to have a budget in hand, to show them exactly what you can pay. If they won't work out a repayment plan with you, you need to contact one of the credit agencies, like Consumer Credit Counseling. You can find their Web site in the Appendix (item 6.1).

Start paying on the bills, even if it's only $10 a month. It is their right to refuse your payment and take you to court, but they're not going to gain anything. If they know your financial situation and know that you're being honest, they will realize they have nothing to gain.

In some states, collection agencies can take you to court and get a garnishment (or attachment) against your salary. If that happens and you literally can't pay your bills, I recommend that you file a Chapter 13 reorganization bankruptcy and have the court manage the money. I have found, in general, that the bankruptcy court will be more fair with you than the typical Small Claims Court judge will.

Remember to trust the Lord in this. The cost of medical care is very expensive, as is the cost of a premature baby. The Lord knows your need, so pray about it, trust Him, tell your friends and family, and then do the best you can. That's all God asks of us. He will take care of you. And, one last thing: Don't worry!

"This is the confidence which we have before Him, that, if we ask anything according to His will, He hears us. And if we know that He hears us in whatever we ask, we know that we have the requests which we have asked from Him" (1 John 5:14–15).

QUESTION:

What does the term "surety" mean?

I've heard you use the term often in discussing finances.

ANSWER:

God's Word says, *"He who is guarantor* [surety] *for a stranger will surely suffer for it, but he who hates being a guarantor is secure"*

(Proverbs 11:15). Surety means personally guaranteeing an obligation. Co-signing a note for another person is an example of surety. When somebody borrows money and you sign the note, if that person doesn't pay, you have to. That's called surety.

Almost everybody who borrows money today signs surety. For instance, if you borrow on an automobile, you sign surety. The lender knows that the automobile is rarely worth what you owe on it, so the loan agreement guarantees any deficiency if you have to sell the car or give it back to the lender. Thus, you are in surety.

About the only way you can avoid surety is to have collateral that can be surrendered in total payment of a debt. For instance, if you borrowed to buy a piece of land that cost $100,000, and you put down $10,000, an exculpatory contract (nonsurety) would stipulate, "If I can't pay for this, I'll let you keep the money I paid in, give you the land back, and be free and clear from all liability." In my opinion, that's only way you can absolutely avoid surety.

QUESTION:

If people in our congregation borrow money to give to the church building program, is that any different from the church itself borrowing to build?

Some fund-raisers recommended this.

ANSWER:

Remember that borrowing is not prohibited scripturally, but if you violate a principle that God has shown you it is still disobedience. Bottom line, there's no scriptural prohibition against either an individual or a church borrowing, so you have to decide what God wants *you* to do.

In our generation, when so many people are in debt, I believe it is wrong for the church to borrow money, because it teaches Christians to borrow more and more.

If a fund-raiser came to my church and recommended that the people of the church borrow the money to build a church, as opposed to the church borrowing the money (because it is more scriptural), I would say, "Nonsense." The church is made up of God's people and when God's people borrow, the church borrows. That makes no biblical sense whatsoever.

QUESTION:

What is overdraft protection?

We've just opened our first checking account and our banker offered a service called automatic overdraft protection. He said that if we ever overdraw our checking account, the bank will cover the deficiency. Sounds like a good idea to me, but I know it must have some drawbacks.

ANSWER:

In my opinion, automatic overdraft protection presents two distinct dangers. Number one, it encourages people not to keep their checking accounts balanced, because they know they have this overdraft protection. And, number two, an overdraft is an automatic loan. It comes out of a credit account, and you're going to be charged a fee plus interest in most banks for using it.

I believe the automatic overdraft is one of the worst banking services ever offered and one of the quickest sources of debt for undisciplined couples who don't balance their checkbooks. *"Understanding is a fountain of life to him who has it, but the discipline of fools is folly"* (Proverbs 16:22).

QUESTION:

Is there a difference between personal debt and business debt, and how can anyone operate a major business in America without using credit?

ANSWER:

Obviously, debt is debt, and it really doesn't matter whether it's business or personal. Unfortunately, both businesses and individuals assume they can't buy anything without debt anymore, which is not true.

In business, one way to avoid debt is to bring in money from investors. In other words, sell equity in the business. That was the most common method used to fund businesses before World War II. Keep in mind that the Bible doesn't teach that you can't borrow money, either individually or in business; it simply teaches that when you do, you assume a liability and some risk.

"The wicked borrows and does not pay back, but the righteous is gracious and gives" (Psalm 37:21).

I have counseled many couples who have had businesses fail, and they found out that the business debt translated into personal debt. So be very careful about borrowing, even for a business. If you borrow for a business, be sure that you have a good business plan and that you're borrowing to expand the business, not to keep a dying business alive.

QUESTION:

I can see no way to climb out of the hole I'm in.

I'm a Christian who has filed for bankruptcy and, unfortunately, I have lost everything—my business, my possessions, and even my family. How can I ever be a witness for the Lord while I still owe all this money that I can never pay back? Do you think there's hope for me?

Answer:

God's Word tells us that *"if we confess our sins, He is faithful and righteous to forgive us our sins and to cleanse us from all unright-eousness"* (1 John 1:9). That's all God ever asks. He can use any-one, whether that person is in or out of debt, married or divorced, or convicted of murder. God has a plan for everyone who has truly repented.

Although you might not see the solution right now, I can give you this promise: God is still at work. Exactly what He will do for you, I don't know, but I've seen God work many times when there seemed to be no visible answer. So I encour-age you to remember that God is in control. You can't do any-thing about the past; you can only do something about the future. If you place your faith in God and in His Word, you'll be able to start paying back your creditors. In the meantime, don't give up hope.

"Let Your lovingkindness, O LORD, be upon us, according as we have hoped in You" (Psalm 33:22).

Question:

Do you think the Bible teaches that we shouldn't borrow money?

I found a passage in Romans 13:8 that says, *"Owe nothing to anyone except to love one another; for he who loves his neighbor has fulfilled the law."*

Answer:

To interpret Romans 13:8 correctly, you must read Romans 13:1–7. It's my opinion that the apostle Paul was not referring to money in the verse you mentioned. He was literally saying, "Don't let anyone do something for you unless you are willing to do more for them."

If Paul had been telling us that Christians should never borrow money, he would have made it absolutely clear and would have clarified that in many other places, which he did not do. Paul would not have relied on a single Scripture verse to overturn all the teaching in God's Word covering the subject of debt. The Old Testament (which was Paul's only testament) has dozens of references to the dangers of debt, the advantages of not having debt, and how to pay debt. After much review, I have concluded that Paul was not referencing money in this particular passage.

Question:

Is an automobile lease the same thing as an automobile loan?

Answer:

In reality, a lease is no less binding than a loan. When you sign for a lease, it is a contingent liability and an obligation to pay that you must meet. For instance, if you lease a car and then you can't make the payments and have to give the car back, you'll owe the difference between the sale value of the automobile and your remaining lease. It's called a deficiency agreement. Once the lease contract is signed, you have a binding obligation to pay; therefore, you are in surety for that loan. (You can read more about vehicle leasing in item 1.0 in the Appendix.)

QUESTION:

Is it true that any debt, mortgage or otherwise, that exceeds six years is forbidden biblically?

ANSWER:

I don't believe that borrowing for any debt beyond six years (the "year of remission," discussed in the book of Deuteronomy) is forbidden; rather, it is discouraged. According to Deuteronomy 15:1, the year of remission came every seventh year, and during that year all the debts were to be released, particularly the debts that one Jew owed to another. Therefore, the longest debt discussed in the Old Testament was seven years.

However, it's important to remember that the responsibility to release the debt was always the lender's, not the borrower's. In other words, if somebody *owed* you money, even another Jew, you would have to release that obligation. But, if you *borrowed* money from someone, including another Jew, you didn't have the right not to pay, even if the year of remission was at hand.

So the biblical principle is to encourage God's people to think about short-term borrowing, not long-term borrowing. And bear in mind that this was not a law; it was a biblical *principle*.

The book of Hezekiah deals clearly with the principle of remission and debt forgiveness.

QUESTION:

Should we get a fixed loan for our thirty-year mortgage, or is an adjustable rate mortgage better?

We're looking at a new mortgage for our home and can't decide the best way to go.

Answer:

The key principle of an adjustable rate mortgage (ARM) is that it is adjustable; it can go down, but it also can go up. If you get an ARM at a lower rate than a fixed rate loan, you need to make absolutely sure that you can make the maximum payment, if you have to. Logically, if the fixed rate loan is about 2 percent higher than the ARM and the ARM can only increase by 2.5 percent, then the most you would have to risk is one-half of 1 percent, and it's probably worth that risk.

However, many couples have taken on ARMs that don't have caps, and some of these mortgages can go up 4, 5, even 6 percent or more. In my opinion, they are ticking time bombs. I recommend that when rates are down ARM loans be converted as quickly as possible to either a fixed rate loan or at least an ARM with a cap.

"A prudent man sees evil and hides himself, the naive proceed and pay the penalty" (Proverbs 27:12).

Question:

Could you give us your opinion of credit cards?

We were recently married, and we continually get credit card applications mailed to us. I would like to have one, but my husband says that credit cards are evil and that a Christian shouldn't borrow money and, therefore, we can't use credit cards.

Answer:

As far as I know, credit cards are not biblically prohibited; nor are they evil. The problem is not credit cards; the problem is the misuse of credit cards.

The problem starts when children see their parents using credit cards to buy everything. As a consequence, when they have the ability to get their own credit cards, they use them to buy things they can't afford. I personally find that even though credit cards are not essential, they are a great convenience.

Let me give you and your husband some simple guidelines that will help you avoid credit card difficulty. Ask your husband to read this, then pray about it, and try to reach a more balanced perspective.

First, you should live on a budget and the two of you should make a simple vow never to use your credit cards to buy anything that is not in your budget that month.

Second, pay the balance you owe on your credit cards every month, with no exception. This means you will never pay any interest.

And third, the first month you aren't able to pay off your credit cards, destroy them. If you'll do this, you won't have a problem with credit cards, but you can enjoy their convenience.

QUESTION:

If I owe $200 per month on my car but I can afford the payments, is this considered debt?

> **Happy is the man without sickness. Rich is the man with no debts.**
>
> CHINESE PROVERB

ANSWER:

Well, unfortunately it's not so simple to define what debt is or is not. In our generation, when you borrow money, people say that you're in debt. But if you're able to make the payments, you really aren't in debt; what you have is an obligation to pay.

Unfortunately, a great many Americans qualify as being in debt, because they aren't able to make all the monthly payments on the money they have borrowed.

In my opinion, *debt* should be defined as "an obligation to pay without the ability to meet the payments."

"To a person who is good in His sight He has given wisdom and knowledge and joy" (Ecclesiastes 2:26).

QUESTION:

Do you think we should still have a savings plan while we owe money to someone else, or is this unbiblical?

We're working on trying to get out of debt, and we live on a budget. We're also working on a repayment schedule with our creditors because we don't have enough money to pay them what we owe them month by month. We try to save at least $100 a month for emergencies, but is this cheating our creditors?

ANSWER:

I believe that every family needs a savings account. Then you can rely on your own money when something breaks down or you have an emergency, rather than relying on someone else's money and going further into debt. If you don't have any savings and your automobile breaks down or your washing machine quits, then you're probably going to fall back on credit cards and, ultimately, that's going to put you deeper in debt. So, yes, I believe you should be saving money.

Many times I've helped couples contact creditors and negotiate lower payments. Often, when creditors looked at budgets that included money set aside for savings, they would ask: "Why should I take less money when they have money in savings?"

My response was, "Because they have made a commitment to

get themselves out of debt. As long as they don't generate any more debt, then you can be assured that they're going to pay you what they promised." Once I explained this, most of the creditors didn't object to savings. So, I believe you should be saving, even though you are in debt. The purpose, primarily, is so you can use your money for emergencies, not someone else's.

5
EDUCATIONAL AND VOCATIONAL DECISIONS

FOR MANY FAMILIES, PARTICULARLY Christian families, education represents a sizable and increasing component of their budgets. More people are concerned about not only the costs of their children's college educations but also how to send them to private schools during the younger years.

> **Education is essential to change, for education creates both new wants and the ability to satisfy them.**
>
> HENRY STEELE COMMAGER

Unfortunately, few families can actually afford the costs of private schooling, but rather than face this reality they pay for the private schools and fund the deficits by accumulating debt.

I certainly don't want to condemn anyone for wanting to escape the crumbling public education system in many areas. But it's important to put the burden where it belongs—on God. If He wants the children in private schools He will provide, and God never provides through loans (at least not according to His Word).

Additionally, families that contact me have questions about college students using credit cards, having cars, and borrowing tens of thousands of dollars to go to school. I trust this chapter will help to answer some of your questions about finances for education.

QUESTION:

What would you suggest in the way of investments for my child's education?

He is only four, but we would like to start putting money aside for his college education. We have about $100 a month to invest.

ANSWER:

Since you have fourteen or fifteen years before he will be ready for college, you'll want to invest that money with an eye to the long-term future of the economy. By that I mean you have to take some risks with the money. Don't park it in a fixed earnings account, because the cost of education is going up faster than the earnings on your money in most cases.

In my opinion, you should invest in something like mutual funds. If it were me, I probably would choose a mutual fund with a good growth record, perhaps an index fund. An index fund is a composite of the stock market, such as the NASDAQ, Dow Jones, Standard and Poors, utilities, and so on. Index funds reflect the average of what's happening in that industry.

In my opinion, index funds are one of the best ways to invest for the long term. You can find a list of index funds by checking any good financial publication—the *Wall Street Journal*, *Money* magazine, *Worth* magazine, or any one of the financial magazines you'll find listed in item 9.1 in the Appendix.

QUESTION:

Since we live in an area where I really don't like the schools, do you think it would be better to send our child to a private school, like a Christian school, or to relocate to a better school district?

ANSWER:

That's a very difficult question to answer. You need to evaluate the schools yourself and make the choice that you believe is best for your children. A private Christian school is a good choice, if you have the resources to afford it.

> **Education has for its object the formation of character.**
>
> HERBERT SPENCER

Under no circumstances would I put my child (or grandchild) in a school that I believed to be inferior or unsafe. I would sacrifice (financially) whatever is necessary to pay for his or her education. Relocating into a better school district is an option, but often it is a very expensive option that isn't open to everyone.

Another alternative, for some families at least, is homeschooling. Even though this is an option, it isn't the right one for every family. Above all else though, make the decision that you believe is the best for your child. What he or she learns during these formative years is going to affect the rest of his or her life.

QUESTION:

Do you think college students should be given cars and credit cards?

We have an eighteen-year-old daughter about to go off to college for the first time and we wondered if we should buy her an automobile and if we should give her a credit card for emergencies.

ANSWER:

The answer to that depends completely on your daughter, her personality, and how well you've trained her so far. If she's going to a school where a car is a necessity, that's one thing. Otherwise, in my opinion, most college students are better off without a car; it's a distraction. Time that should be spent on studying is often spent on partying.

In terms of the credit card, you need to be very careful there also. I recall a friend whose daughter went to school in another state. He and his wife bought her a brand-new convertible and gave her a credit card with no specific limit. She was very popular for about two quarters—until they began to get the bills. The card had an average of $10,000 per quarter charged on it. She was lending her brand-new automobile and the credit card to her friends, who often drove hundreds of miles to visit other friends. They had a great time on her father's money.

There must be some limitations, and you have to know your daughter. If she really needs a car, my recommendation would be to find a car that fits her needs but not necessarily a new car. And if you give her a credit card, establish very specific rules for how it can be used, and have her sign the rules that you both agree to. If she doesn't abide by the rules, then you simply recover the car and the credit card.

QUESTION:

Should we save money for my daughter's college education, even though we are deeply in debt with credit cards?

My husband and I don't agree. Since my daughter is only ten, I think we should pay off our credit cards, rather than save money for her college education; but he thinks we should be saving now.

ANSWER:

I believe that you have to deal with first things first. It's not going to do any good to start saving money for your daughter's college if you're deeply in debt with credit cards. Ultimately, you have to work on the highest priority first, and that is your credit card debt. My recommendation is to concentrate on paying down the debt and then start saving for college.

When it's time for her to go to college, if you don't have enough money, you'll need to consider some alternatives. One option might be for her to attend a local community college for a year or two while you're saving money to pay for the last two years. It may not be the best plan for her social life, but it certainly would be the best plan for your finances.

In my opinion, you have an obligation to your creditors to pay them back, even prior to saving money for college.

QUESTION:

Do you think it is a good idea for children to work their way through college or should parents pay for all of it?

ANSWER:

This is not generally an either/or situation. If you have the money to pay your children's way through college, you might not be doing them the greatest service to simply pay for everything they want. It may be to their long-term benefit for you to require something of your children—perhaps even working part-time, or at least during the summer breaks—to help pay for some of their own expenses.

It's been my observation that people appreciate things more if they have to pay for them out of their own money than they do if someone else has paid for them. But remember that all children are different and the same advice will never apply to everybody. In principle, it's my conviction that children should work for what they get, to some degree anyway, not only while they're in college but even in high school, to a lesser degree, if at all possible.

> **The world does not pay for what a person knows. But it pays for what a person does with what he knows.**
>
> LAURENCE LEE

There are a lot of kids in college today simply because their parents are footing the bill, and they're having a good time on their parents' money. If they had to pay for even a part of their own costs, many of them probably would and should drop out.

Personally, as was common in my generation, I worked my way through college, and I don't really regret the experience. I did learn to appreciate my education, and I was still able to keep up with all the other students. Because of that, when I graduated I had a lot more job opportunities, because I also had some work experience.

Proverbs 16:26 says, *"A worker's appetite works for him."* If your children earn at least a part of their own way, their education is going to seem more precious to them. Some children probably will not appreciate that initially, but they will look back on it later with a sense of accomplishment.

"The hand of the diligent will rule, but the slack hand will be put to forced labor" (Proverbs 12:24).

QUESTION:

What do you think of prepaid college trusts, and do you think it is a good idea to put money into these trusts for your children?

My mother and father have put some money into an education trust for our children and they have asked for my advice.

ANSWER:

In general, education trusts are a good idea. If you use the money for education, there is no income tax to be paid on the earnings, which is a great asset. If the money is put into trust for one child and he or she elects not to go to college, you can redirect that money to another child.

However, if the funds are used for something other than college education, they will be taxable upon withdrawal.

I believe they are very good plans. You will find more information on the Web about education trusts (see item 9.2 in the Appendix).

QUESTION:

Where would we find information on scholarships?

Our daughter is about to go off to college this next summer and, unfortunately, we don't have the funds to help her.

Answer:

If you have access to the Web, you can find a lot of information about scholarships. There are a couple of good Web sites listed in the Appendix (see item 9.3). Also, there's an excellent book on applying for scholarships listed there. I suggest you get a copy of the book at your local bookstore.

However, you need to be realistic: If you haven't saved any money for your daughter's college education and she's going off to school this next fall, being able to find, apply for, and receive the scholarships she will need in just a few months is probably unrealistic. Therefore, you might suggest that your daughter attend a local community college for a year or so, while you are applying for the scholarships. It is better to do this well in advance and not wait until the last moment.

Question:

Do you think student loans are okay for a family to help their children go through college?

Our son and daughter are both going off to college in the next two years. We don't have the funds to pay their way all the way through college, though we do have enough for about one year for both of them. Should we resort to loans?

Answer:

First, let me say that the Bible doesn't say that you can't borrow money, and a loan is a loan. If you're going to borrow money for anything, in my opinion, student loans are probably one of the better things to borrow for. At least you're buying into an appreciating asset, a college education.

However, you need to be very careful. Statistics tell us that about one-half of all college loans are not used for college purposes; they are used for automobiles, travel, vacations, televisions, and stereos. Therefore, many students come out of college owing a lot of unnecessary money. In most cases, it's going to be the equivalent of buying a brand-new Lexus and not getting to drive it.

It will take most college graduates from eight to ten years to pay off their student loans, so you should limit the use of these student loans just as you would any other loan. Make it clear to your children that you're going to sign for the loans but that they're going to be responsible to pay them back.

Also, to be sure that the money is used properly, have them submit a budget to you of how they're going to use the money. Then, periodically, at least once a quarter, verify that they're using the money properly. But, bottom line, there is nothing any more wrong with student loans than with borrowing for an automobile. Both can be an asset or a liability, depending on how they're used.

QUESTION:

Can you tell me something about student loans?

My husband and I both have student loans. I have been paying on mine regularly since I graduated and they are down to where they'll be paid off in about two years; it will have taken me just under ten years to pay them off. My husband, who graduated the same year I did, still owes about 75 percent of his student loans. He's been very erratic in paying, and there are many penalties attached. He thinks that after ten years the statute of limitations has run out, and he no longer owes for his student loans. Is that right?

ANSWER:

Trying to avoid paying a legitimate debt is unbiblical. *"The wicked borrows and does not pay back, but the righteous is gracious and gives"* (Psalm 37:21). God says if you owe money you are to pay it; that's a vow we make as Christians. We are obligated to pay our debts.

Further, as far as I know, there is no statute of limitations on student loans. Not only is there no statute of limitations, but also you can't go bankrupt to avoid repaying a student loan. Therefore, he's going to have to pay the money back, and the interest can compound greatly.

Recently I had a caller on the program who started with a $25,000 student loan, failed to meet the minimum payments of the loan for about fifteen years, and now owes almost $90,000 on the $25,000 debt.

So my advice is to pay it. Work out a payment plan and meet the payment schedule. You cannot avoid it; nor should you.

QUESTION:

What are my options in paying off a student loan that I have had for almost five years?

I looked at the amortization schedule they sent me, and I was aghast that I had only paid a small amount of principal on this loan. If I continue to pay on it at this rate, it is going to take me the better part of thirty years to pay off my veterinary school debt of about $140,000.

ANSWER:

There is a way to pay it off sooner, but it requires both discipline and sacrifice. Yours is a simple interest loan, meaning that the interest is calculated on the unpaid balance each month. I recommend that you make your regular payment, the minimum amount that is required, and then make an additional payment each month.

Further, commit that, from this point forward, 50 percent of all additional monies that come in—whether from fees you earn at the clinic, gifts of money, an inheritance, or whatever the source—will be used to pay off your student loans. By doing this, you'll pay them off much sooner and save yourself a lot of interest. Do not string out this debt for thirty years.

QUESTION:

> Perhaps the most valuable result of all education is the ability to make yourself do the thing you have to do when it ought to be done whether you like it or not.
>
> THOMAS HUXLEY, BIOLOGIST

Should I keep my children in a Christian school, even though I am unable to pay my other bills?

I just went through a very bitter divorce and my husband has now remarried. My three children are eight, ten, and twelve years old. They've gone through so much that I don't want to unsettle their lives any further by taking them out of the Christian school they attend. However, if I just make the minimum payments to the school, it's going to consume nearly half my income. I'm really torn between helping my children and being able to pay my bills.

ANSWER:

There are fourteen million single mothers in America, most of whom are working two or more jobs just to keep their households together. I understand your concerns about your children's lives being disrupted; however, you must leave this in God's hands. Pray about it and let your friends know your needs. Share your needs honestly with your Bible study group, Sunday school class, and circle of friends.

The apostle Paul says, *"At this present time your abundance being a supply for their need so that their abundance also may become a supply for your need"* (2 Corinthians 8:14). I believe that the money will be provided by God's people, if that is God's will for your children.

However, if the money hasn't been provided prior to the next school year, put your children in the best schools that you can find—within your budget. Make a commitment to stay in close contact with them and with their teachers and do the best job that you can. Private school is not for everybody, Christian or otherwise, and not all public schools are bad.

There is another alternative. You might want to consider some kind of work plan with the Christian school they now attend. I've known several single mothers over the years who have done a variety of things, including cleaning classrooms after hours, in order to keep their children in the school. But, for every one of those I can recall, ten or more others have had their needs met by God's people.

So pray about this and don't give up. God is still in control.

QUESTION:

How do I go about finding more information about college grants, particularly those offered by corporations?

I read the book about finding grants and loans that you recommended on your program. It was interesting to find out that a grant doesn't have to be repaid, much the same as a scholarship doesn't have to be repaid.

ANSWER:

The best way to get information is to go to the Office of Student Affairs and ask to talk to the person in charge of grants and scholarships.

Generally, grants are offered by corporations and typically are available to students who will study in a specific field, such as electronics, physics, chemistry, or medicine.

These grants are more beneficial, in my opinion, because often the companies offer a work program for the students during the summer, which not only prepares them for college but also prepares them for a career.

QUESTION:

Do you think it would be better for us to pay off our undergraduate school loans before going to graduate school?

My husband and I have about $14,000 in undergraduate school loans still unpaid. We will accumulate about another $60,000 of debt if we go to graduate school.

ANSWER:

With the exception of a few chosen careers, it will be very difficult, even with both of you working, to repay $75,000 in school loans. What happens if you have children and want to stay home with them? Then you would lose your income and make it even more difficult to pay on the loans.

My personal recommendation would be not to accumulate that much debt. One of you, preferably your husband, should go back to school part-time. Stretch out the education over a longer period of time so that, rather than accumulating so much debt, you accumulate only a minimum amount.

Some graduate schools make provisions for working adults to go part-time, until they have accumulated all but one year of credit hours—then go to school full-time for one year. As a result, that total indebtedness will probably be closer to $10,000 than to $60,000 and will make it much easier to pay back those loans.

Just be very careful about accumulating so much debt. It's very difficult to pay it off. In your case, it would be the equivalent of buying a small home and never being able to live in it—a very tough thing to do.

QUESTION:

How can I help my children avoid making the mistake I did?

My father encouraged me to study to be a pharmacist in college. I went through five years of undergraduate school, plus the necessary schooling to get a pharmacist's credentials. Then I found out that I hate it. I don't want this to happen to our children.

ANSWER:

It is vital for everyone to discover what natural abilities and talents they have. One way to do that is to take a vocational aptitude test, and there are some good ones that have been developed in the last few years. Our ministry, Crown Financial Ministries, has what I believe is the best overall aptitude test in the country, *Career Direct* (see item 5.0 in the Appendix).

Whatever you do, don't tell your children that they must study what you've chosen for them or what you, your spouse, or your parents studied in college. Allow them to be the people God has created them to be. It's really a shame that your father didn't allow you to do that, but it's never too late.

I also encourage you to get a copy of the *Career Direct* evaluation and discover what God has equipped you to do best. Then go do that. The money is not the most important factor in choosing a career; peace is. If you do what God has equipped you to do, you'll have the greatest peace and the greatest success.

> **The great thing in this world is not so much where we are, but in what direction we are moving.**
>
> OLIVER WENDELL HOLMES

QUESTION:

Do you think we should continue paying for our son's college education when he keeps changing majors and still doesn't know what he wants to do?

He's a junior—at least we think he's a junior, but it's hard to tell because he's changed majors at least four times that we know of, and perhaps more. I feel like we are wasting our money.

ANSWER:

I suggest that you get him pointed in the right direction and not waste a lot more money. On average, today it takes five years for an undergraduate student to complete college. That means one entire year is lost in changing directions because they don't know who they are or what they want to do. By the time a child is sixteen years old, his or her personality, interests, and aptitude have been established.

Children should be tested early, to find out what skills and abilities they have, and then pointed in that direction. That includes finding the right college major. A simple assessment can do that for the majority of people, and you will find information in the *Career Direct* test (see item 5.0 in the Appendix).

QUESTION:

Should we require that my daughter not go to college until she can identify her proper career field?

She wants to go to college, but she doesn't know specifically what she wants to study. I've often heard you discuss the issue of kids in college changing their majors and how expensive that is.

ANSWER:

My recommendation is to have your daughter tested with the *Career Direct* assessment (see item 5.0 in the Appendix) to determine what her interests and skills are. This might not tell her the exact job she should pursue, but it will point her in the right direction.

> It is a wretched taste to be gratified with mediocrity when the excellent lies before us.
>
> ISAAC D'ISRAELI

Then, if she goes to college and still hasn't chosen a career field, she should take more general subjects for the first year or two. In most colleges you don't have to choose your major until the third year. By that time she should know what she wants to do. If she doesn't know by the third year, then I would ask her to sit out a year.

As I have often said, a student who goes to a community college for the first two years will save tens of thousands of dollars in education costs. And no employer that I know of asks where you went the first two years. They generally ask, "Where is your degree from?" And the last two years will determine the college that will issue her degree.

QUESTION:

Do you believe there are any vocations that are not suitable for a Christian?

ANSWER:

I believe there are. The obvious ones are those that involve anything illegal, immoral, or unethical. That covers vocations all the way from drug dealing to abortions. If you're referring to working in a gambling casino or liquor store, that decision must be based on your conviction as a Christian. The same can be said of a hotel manager who works for a company that allows pornographic movies in the guests' rooms.

These represent a compromise to God's Word and a stumbling block to others. I encourage you to seek the counsel and prayer of mature Christians in your area.

"Listen to counsel and accept discipline, that you may be wise the rest of your days" (Proverbs 19:20).

QUESTION:

Is gambling wrong?

I have worked at a casino for several years. Recently, I became a born-again believer and now I have a conflict about gambling.

ANSWER:

As far as I can tell, gambling is not prohibited scripturally. God judges motives, and the motive for modern gambling is to get rich quick.

Several instances of gambling can be found in the Bible, though not necessarily wagering on money. One reference in the New Testament describes the apostles drawing lots to replace one of the other apostles: Judas. Was that gambling? They weren't wagering money, but they were wagering on something far more important and believing that God had led them to do it. You can review this in Acts 1:26. The argument might be made that that's not really gambling. In my opinion, it was. The stakes were not monetary, but it was gambling.

The opposite side of gambling can be found in Proverbs: *"The plans of the diligent lead surely to advantage, but everyone who is hasty comes surely to poverty"* (Proverbs 21:5). Clearly, we see evidence of this in America today. Most people who gamble cannot afford to lose the money. To them it's an addiction that costs them their families and everything else. It's not that the gambling is wrong; it is the attitude about gambling that we see today.

Gambling always caters to people's weaknesses, and it is very addictive for many people. As I said, usually those who can least afford to lose the money do the vast majority of gambling. How many wealthy people do you think gamble on the lottery? Not very many.

Lotteries and other gambling are aimed at the poorest in our society. It's another way of taxing them. Gambling and lotteries prey upon the poor. In my opinion, for a Christian to be involved with gambling is a very bad witness, and it lends credibility to those who promote it. As a Christian, I would have a difficult time participating in the gambling community, either as an owner or as an employee, simply because I believe it would lend credibility to an area that, in fact, has no credibility biblically.

6

FAMILY MONEY ISSUES

MANY FAMILIES STRUGGLE WITH A VARIETY of financial issues that range from whether to pay allowances to their children to whether they should charge their grown children to live at home.

Just as there is no single personality that fits all children, there also is no single financial answer that fits all situations. One child may hoard and save money to the point of stinginess; another may spend every dime on frivolities. Sounds like a lot of adults, huh? That's because kids turn into adults—for better or for worse.

God's Word tells us that if we train our children in the ways of the Lord they will not soon depart from it. And the results of God's way are peace, happiness, and successful marriages.

The Word promises that if we don't train them they'll end up in debt, depressed, and divorced.

It's really our choice. Let's help our families succeed.

QUESTION:
Should I help my adult son who still lives at home?

Although he is working, he isn't helping with any of the expenses. It seems to me like he's always spending his money and then asking me for help. As a widow, I still have enough money to be able to help him, but I question if I should.

ANSWER:

I advise you to be very cautious. It's possible to cripple your son by helping him too much. If you are going to help him, you need to require some accountability from him. If he doesn't want to be accountable to you, refer him to a volunteer counselor from your church. You'll find how to contact our volunteer counselors in item 2.2 in the Appendix. Then be sure that both of you do what the counselor says.

> **If you want to recapture your youth, just cut off his allowance.**
>
> AL BERNSTEIN

If your son is wasting his money and getting further in debt and you keep bailing him out, you need to exercise restraint. If your son is incapable of handling his own finances, get someone to work with him very closely. Talk to the counselor and do what he or she directs. In other words, if the counselor suggests that you help him, do so; but if the counselor says to back off and not help, you must be willing to do that.

Many parents say that they're willing to step back, until a difficult situation arises, and then they cave in to the emotional pressure. Remember, God's Word says that He disciplines those He loves. Sometimes tough love is the best way to manage this kind of situation.

"Those whom I love, I reprove and discipline; be zealous therefore, and repent" (Revelation 3:19).

QUESTION:

Should I help my mother handle her money?

She isn't handling it very well and is constantly getting into debt and then asking me to help her. I don't mind helping my mother. I love her, but I wonder if I'm doing the right thing.

ANSWER:

It is very difficult for children to give financial advice to their parents. My suggestion would be to work through a third party. Go to your pastor and ask if he knows someone in the church who can help your mother manage her finances. If he does, encourage your mother to meet with the counselor.

If there is no counselor in your church, contact us and we'll put you in touch with one of our volunteer counselors (see item 2.2 in the Appendix).

Scripture does command that we honor our parents, but that doesn't mean to feed their weaknesses. If your mother is not handling her money properly (especially if she's being frivolous with it) and you continue to help by giving her more, you aren't helping to solve the problem; you're making it worse. A third party—a good counselor—might be the answer to your situation.

QUESTION:

Can you help us get out of debt?

We're a young couple, married for nearly six years. We came into this marriage with debt, and the debt continues to accumulate. Our budget is already very tight, so I'm not sure at this point how we can pay off our bills on a month-by-month basis. I have no idea how to deal with this.

Answer:

First and foremost, you and your husband need to get on a budget. You'll find budget information in item 2.2 in the Appendix. Also, you need to accept the responsibility that you have to manage your money in a biblical fashion, which means you cannot spend more than you make.

You must make whatever sacrifices are necessary to bring the spending level down, and there's only one way to do that: discipline. That means you have to evaluate each category in your budget and compare the guideline with your spending (see the Percentage Guide for Family Income table in the Appendix item 17.0). Be sure you're not spending too much on any category. For instance, if you are spending too much on your home and you're more than 10 percent above the suggested percentage, it's very likely you won't be able to balance your budget.

Don't make the mistake of allocating more to Housing and nothing to Clothing or Entertainment, because in reality people do buy clothing and they do take vacations. So, for your budget to work you must allocate a percentage to each category and limit your spending to those percentages. Otherwise, no budget will work.

Remember that God understands what your needs are and He will provide. All He requires is that you submit your rights to Him. If you find yourself worried and distressed over this, turn it over to God. "[Cast] *all your anxiety upon Him, because He cares for you*" (1 Peter 5:7).

Question:

Do you think I should go to work to help pay my son's medical expenses?

We've gotten ourselves into debt through a lot of medical expenses because of my son's incurable illness. The way it looks now, unless I go to work we won't make it. However, my conflict is that my children need me at home.

ANSWER:

No, I don't think you should have to go to work. The body of Christ should be willing to help you. You have a legitimate need over which you have no control, and God puts surpluses in the hands of other Christians so they will be able to help you. I believe that God wants you to let people around you know about your problem and then turn this over to Him. He will provide through other people.

God's Word says, *"That their abundance also may become a supply for your need"* (2 Corinthians 8:14). Unfortunately, that's not being done very much in our society—mostly because we don't depend on each other very often. We rely so much on insurance, the government, and other sources of help that we simply don't rely on each other.

If you're going to do anything to help the situation, in my opinion, the most you should do is get a part-time job and dedicate that income specifically to paying the medical expenses and nothing else. The reason I say part-time work is because the more you begin to work and generate more income, the more you'll get trapped into working full-time, and then you'll be a full-time employee, rather than a full-time mother.

Trust the Lord (and His people), and you'll see that He is faithful. *"The LORD is good; His lovingkindness is everlasting, and His faithfulness to all generations"* (Psalm 100:5).

QUESTION:

How can I keep my daughter from having the same financial problems we've had?

She's getting married in the spring, and I'd like to be able to help her understand the role of a wife in managing finances. Unfortunately, I never had much training myself, and throughout our married life we seem to have had nothing but financial problems. We've stuck it out, and now we're close to getting out of debt, but I don't want my daughter to have to go through what I have.

Answer:

Your daughter and her fiancé need to talk about their finances *before* they get married. About half of all first-time marriages will fail within the first six years, and over two-thirds of those will fail because of poor financial management (or at least that's the focus of their problems). So you need to help them understand good stewardship.

> **Children are natural mimics who act like their parents despite every effort to teach them good manners.**
>
> Anonymous

I suggest that they read *Money in Marriage* (listed in item 3.1 in the Appendix), discuss their finances honestly, and fill out a budget that shows how they are going to spend their money the first year. It also will force them to face reality.

Ask your pastor to find an older couple in your church who know how to handle money well and who will check on your daughter and her husband for the first year—in other words, hold them accountable month by month to ensure that they're living within their income and sticking to their budget.

If you'll do that, their marriage will have a much greater

chance of prospering. If all pastors would follow this pattern, the majority of the potential divorces among these young people could be avoided.

QUESTION:

How can we teach our children about money in a productive way?

We have two boys, ages fourteen and twelve, and a girl who is nine. They're so caught up in materialism that they look at us as money trees. I don't like that, and I think it's going to harm them in the future.

ANSWER:

It's true that many American kids are very materialistic. They have been raised in a society that directs billions in advertising dollars toward them, and most of them do think money grows on trees—with an unlimited harvest.

Your fourteen-year-old is old enough to begin managing his own money. I suggest that you have a plan: Whether he earns his own money or you provide an allowance, hold him accountable to a budget. For instance, have the first tenth of his money allocated to giving, another portion to savings (say, 25 percent), and the remainder can be his to spend—if he shows you how he's going to use it. That's called a budget.

You can help your children become financially wise adults, but it's important to start right now. You'll find some materials on teaching your children in item 11.1 in the Appendix. Whether you get those materials or others, start teaching your children and do it consistently. And be sure you apply the same rules to yourself, because it's very difficult to teach others what you aren't doing yourself.

"The mouth of the righteous utters wisdom, and his tongue speaks justice . . . Wait for the LORD, *and keep His way, and He will exalt you to inherit the land"* (Psalm 37:30, 34).

QUESTION:

What would you say is the most important thing we need to teach our daughters about money?

I have two daughters, ages sixteen and fifteen, and we know that when they get married they're going to be faced with a lot of financial choices. Since we don't know their future husbands, all we can do is teach our daughters how to manage money.

ANSWER:

The most important thing to teach them about money is that everything we have belongs to God and that we are merely managers (stewards) of the money God gives us. *"It is required of stewards that one be found trustworthy"* (1 Corinthians 4:2).

The majority of family money handlers in America are women. They write the checks and pay the bills, and if there's a budget they're usually the ones who are responsible for it.

I suggest you teach them the basics. For instance, teach them how to balance their checkbooks. (In America, you can go through grammar school, high school, college, and get a Ph.D. and still not know how to balance a checkbook.) Then teach them what a budget is and how to live on one. (See items 11.1 and 11.3 in the Appendix.) Teach them how to live within their incomes so that they're not spending more than they make. They will be wiser than 90 percent of all the young women of their generation who are getting married.

QUESTION:

Do you think we should pay my father-in-law's medical and funeral expenses?

My mother-in-law really doesn't have any money, and my husband believes that we are responsible for his father's medical and funeral expenses. I'm not so sure that we are. They never handled their money properly. We have always handled our money well, and now we're being asked to pick up the expenses for their frivolous habits.

ANSWER:

God's Word says, *"Honor your father and your mother, that your days may be prolonged in the land which the LORD your God gives you"* (Exodus 20:12).

We're told to honor our parents, and the word *honor* in this instance includes finances.

Are you legally responsible for your father-in-law's medical bills or funeral bills? Absolutely not. Are you morally and biblically responsible? You'll have to pray about that and make your own decision. In my opinion you are, and I believe God's Word supports that position.

Nevertheless, you are responsible to help your mother-in-law, even if you feel they were frivolous with their finances. Possibly they were, but that doesn't abate your responsibility to help her. You need to pray about this and turn it over to God. Don't let bitterness or resentment keep you from doing what's right. Remember, money is an outside indicator of what's going on inside.

"If anyone does not provide for his own, and especially for those of his household, he has denied the faith, and is worse than an unbeliever" (1 Timothy 5:8).

QUESTION:

How can I tell my husband about the debt I brought into our marriage, which I've been keeping a secret?

> We somehow fail to realize that once we marry and become part of a family, whatever we do has life-shaping and, many times, irreparable implications.
>
> GARY SMALLEY/
> JOHN TRENT

I've always had bad credit, and after listening to your radio program I realized I have dishonored my husband. When we married, over a year ago, I decided not to tell him about my debt, which resulted from my misuse of credit cards. I have been juggling my finances, trying to keep this quiet, but I don't want to do this anymore.

ANSWER:

The best way to tell him is to be totally honest. Show him exactly what you owe and ask for his forgiveness for not being honest with him. He married you, he is your husband, you are both one, and your responsibilities are his responsibilities.

Obviously this can be a tough lesson, but it also can be a positive experience in your marriage. He may get a bit irritated when you confess, but let me assure you that most husbands appreciate honesty.

"He who walks in integrity walks securely, but he who perverts his ways will be found out" (Proverbs 10:9).

After you get your finances squared away, you might consider getting some training so you can help other young couples manage their money. After all, you can honestly say that you've "been there and done that."

QUESTION:

How do you feel about the husband staying home with the children and the wife working?

We believe that one of us should stay home with our two children, instead of putting them in day care and kindergarten, and I make a lot more money than my husband does. I think it makes sense for me to go to work and for him to stay home with the children. He says he's willing to stay home but wonders about the biblical responsibility of the husband to provide for his family.

ANSWER:

Let me say up front that there are very few couples who can handle the situation you propose. When the wife works and the husband is the stay-at-home mom, so to speak, most men feel that they aren't providing for their families. The pattern laid out in Scripture is for the husband to provide for the family and the wife to be the caretaker of the home and family.

I know that in our generation we don't think that way, because we try to be so politically correct by claiming that men and women are equal. In my opinion, women are far better at raising children than most men are; they are more caring and perceptive and make better role models for their daughters.

Does that mean that a man can't raise a family in a godly fashion? Absolutely not. There are exceptions to every rule. The difficulty is that the Scripture doesn't leave us many alternatives when we're looking for the pattern of how a family works. That pattern is for the father to work and the mother to keep the home and raise the children. Obviously, both must work together to accomplish this plan.

"An excellent wife . . . looks well to the ways of her household . . . Her children rise up and bless her; her husband also" (Proverbs 31:10, 27–28).

QUESTION:

What do you think about separate checking accounts for husbands and wives?

My husband and I were separated for over two years. We have now reconciled and are determined to make our marriage work. However, at this point we are still keeping separate checking accounts. We both work and contribute part of our income to a fund to pay the bills, but we are not responsible to each other for the remainder. I'm not sure this is right.

ANSWER:

In my opinion, it isn't right. The Bible teaches that husbands and wives are to be *one* (see Genesis 2:24). Couples should pool their finances and their bills and have a common budget and common goals.

A short-term goal would be a consolidated budget; long-term would be things like college education for your children, getting debt free, and ultimately retirement. You can't achieve these goals as long as you function like two individuals living together. That's not a marriage. You must merge your finances and make a commitment to doing this God's way or it won't work. You can't make a partial commitment.

QUESTION:

Am I liable to pay a credit card bill if I didn't sign the credit card?

My husband died several months ago, and now I find he had some bills that I knew nothing about, two of which are fairly sizable credit card bills. I didn't sign for the credit cards myself, but the credit card companies are contacting me to pay these bills.

ANSWER:

Are you legally liable for these bills? Probably not. If you didn't sign the credit card application, they can't hold you legally accountable. Are you morally and biblically responsible for them? I believe Scripture supports that position. A husband and wife are to operate as one unit; and, whether or not you knew he was accumulating these bills, you are still one unit (at least you were when the debts were created).

My suggestion would be to pray about it, don't sign any legal documents with these companies, and do the best you can to pay the bills.

"I will say to the LORD, 'My refuge and my fortress, my God, in whom I trust!' For it is He who delivers you from the snare of the trapper . . . His faithfulness is a shield and bulwark" (Psalm 91:2–4).

QUESTION:

How should we handle our children's spending?

We're trying to teach our children to be financially responsible. After listening to your radio program, we got one of your savings banks, and we help them save their money. Part of it goes to tithe, part to long-term savings, and part to spending. My question is, What do we allow them to spend their money on? One of my sons is more of a saver; he wants to save up his money and never spend it. The other one is a spender who will blow his money on anything he wants, including video games and things I don't approve of.

Answer:

I believe you should hold your children to some standards. The idea of starting with the savings bank is good. When they're older, teach them to save their money in a savings account at a bank. Also teach them how to do other things, like balance their checkbooks and use credit cards responsibly.

In the meantime, however, you should hold your children accountable for what they spend. Decide on a fair and realistic standard. If you don't think video games are a good thing to spend their money on, just say no and don't allow them to rent or buy video games. You're the parent. They're the children. You set the standards.

You may say that this sounds a little bit like a dictatorship. It is. God didn't establish a democracy within the family; He established a benevolent dictatorship. Remember, we are raising future adults, and the things you're teaching them today must last them for the rest of their lives.

"Hear, my son, your father's instruction, and do not forsake your mother's teaching" (Proverbs 1:8).

Question:

Since I'm a far better money manager than my husband, should I take over the family finances?

My husband and I have had some real arguments about finances, particularly because he doesn't pay the bills on time.

And he tends to buy things impulsively, so we end up getting ourselves into debt. Then I have to work at paying these debts off. I'm very frustrated about it. I offered to be in charge of the finances, but he resents it.

Answer:

In large part this depends on what your goals are. Are you working on your marriage, or are you working on being right? If you're working on your marriage, then you need to approach it from a different perspective. This should be a project that you can do together.

You and your husband need to make out a budget. If you can't do it together, find a good counselor (you'll find a reference for counselors in item 2.2 in the Appendix).

If you adopt the idea of "I'm right and he's wrong and I should be in charge because he's (either stupid or frivolous)," you're going to destroy your marriage. You can be right and end up totally wrong, let me assure you.

If you're the better money manager in the family (and quite often that is the case), you probably should be paying the bills and balancing the books. But you must work on a budget *together*. If you don't, this problem will drive a wedge in your marriage, and that's not what you're trying to accomplish.

"A gentle answer turns away wrath, but a harsh word stirs up anger" (Proverbs 15:1).

Question:

Is it all right to give our children money for the chores they do around the house?

I've been listening to your radio programs for a long time, especially those about children and allowances. I understand that you think children shouldn't have allowances. I can't say that I agree or disagree with that right now, but should we pay them for the chores they do?

Answer:

I'm not against giving children allowances. It's just that I believe we should be raising children in a manner that prepares them to be adults, and very few employers give allowances. Employers pay for work that's done well; and that's all I'm trying to say.

If you're going to give your kids an allowance, tie it to something positive: an attitude, a performance, something you can measure. It's perfectly all right to pay your children for the non-routine chores they do around the home. In fact, I encourage it.

For young children, make the chores simple and match them to the ability of each child. One size does not fit all when it comes to children and finances. Later, as they grow and begin to make more money, you should help them learn how to live on a budget, how to manage that money, and even how to invest their money.

"Train up a child in the way he should go, even when he is old he will not depart from it" (Proverbs 22:6).

Question:

Do you think we should approach some friends who are indulging their children if we feel it's harmful to the children?

These are dear friends with children about the same ages as ours. Their boys are fifteen and seventeen. They recently bought their seventeen-year-old a brand-new automobile, which he ended up wrecking; and then they replaced it with another new one. We feel like they are hurting their children because they continuously bail them out of every situation they get into, and they seem to indulge them.

Answer:

Walk softly; you can very easily lose friends over this situation. My suggestion is to provide them with some teaching materials on finances for teenagers and let God do the convicting.

I think you're right—that your friends are teaching their children the wrong values, which may hurt them long-term—but until they're willing to hear that you'd better be cautious. Look in the Appendix, find some materials that fit the situation, and make a gift to them for their anniversary or Christmas. You can share that these are some of the things you've learned that have helped your family. Perhaps this is the best way to approach the situation.

"You were called to freedom, brethren; only do not turn your freedom into an opportunity for the flesh, but through love serve one another" (Galatians 5:13).

Question:

Do you have the answer to my dilemma?

We now have two children and I would really like to stay home with them. However, we owe a lot of money on credit cards and other bills that we've accumulated over the years. I'm on maternity leave right now, and I hate to go back to work. But as I look at our budget, I don't see any way for us to make it if I stay home.

Answer:

No, I don't have an answer, but I do have a suggestion. I can understand your desire to stay at home with your children, but you must plan carefully. I suggest that you get on a budget immediately and trim your spending as much as possible. If necessary, sell your house and one of your cars to cut expenses. Go back to work with a specific plan to concentrate on paying off your debts. Then, when the bills are paid, you can be a permanent stay-at-home mom.

I caution you not to just quit your job. You'll more than likely have to go back to work at some point, because the debt and the pressures it creates will get worse. Even worse, you might have to go back to a lower-paying job.

It would be far better to continue to work for a while and concentrate on getting out of debt than it would be to quit work and make the situation worse. *"The plans of the diligent lead surely to advantage, but everyone who is hasty comes surely to poverty"* (Proverbs 21:5).

You might get a copy of *Women Leaving the Workplace* (see item 3.2 in the Appendix). It will answer most of your questions.

QUESTION:

How do we teach my son to manage a very large sum wisely?

Unknown to him, he has inherited almost $100,000 from his grandparents. It's been in an account under his name for the last six years, but when he turns eighteen in a few months the money will be his, and he will have total control over it. How can we guide him?

ANSWER:

This is something you should've been doing during the last six years. It will be very difficult in the time you have left to teach an eighteen-year-old how to handle $100,000. I don't know your son, but if you aren't very careful, and if he's like most eighteen-year-olds, he may end up buying himself a nice sports car and blowing the rest of the money.

What you have to do at this point is, sit down with your son and be totally honest with him. Tell him what you think would be the best for him to do in terms of saving the money for college or business or whatever. If you haven't taught him any biblical principles for handling money before now, you may have waited too long to make a significant impact on your son. These principles are best taught when children are younger. But, remember, it's never too late. *"If you consent and obey, you will eat the best of the land"* (Isaiah 1:19).

You may find some resources in the Appendix that will help you.

QUESTION:

What can I do to prevent my teenagers from having access to easy credit?

I'm concerned about the amount of credit cards now available to teenagers, and my teenagers are rapidly approaching the age when they will have access to this credit.

ANSWER:

There's not a lot you can do about preventing the access to easy credit. As soon as children are eighteen years old, and considered adults in our society, they will have access. The best thing you can do in the meantime is to diligently prepare them. Teach them how to handle money properly.

One thing you can do is lead your children through a study on the biblical principles of handling money (see item 11.1 in the Appendix). Then you need to train them in how to handle their own money, including balancing their checkbooks and living on a budget. And, most significant in this specific instance, teach them how to handle credit cards responsibly.

The best way to do that is to get them credit cards while they are still in your home and help them learn how to manage them. My suggestion would be to go to your local bank and see if they have a family debit card available. A debit card is limited because it can be used only to the extent of the funds in the debit account.

All parents need to remember that they are not raising children; they're raising future adults. So teach your children how to manage credit cards while they're still in your home. Credit is going to be a fact of life for them, so the sooner you teach them about it the better. The best time to do that is while you have them under your control.

Let me suggest some simple rules to establish for your teenagers. First, they must have budgets *before* they can have credit cards. They need to know where their money is coming from and where the money is going to be spent. Second, don't let them use credit or debit cards for anything that isn't in their budgets.

Third, they must pay off every charge every month. Fourth, the first time they can't pay off their credit card charges in any month, destroy their cards, and don't let them use credit cards again until you're sure they are able to handle them properly.

"The lovingkindness of the LORD is from everlasting to everlasting on those who fear Him, and His righteousness to children's children" (Psalm 103:17).

QUESTION:

How much should we allow our children to know about how much money we make?

We're a family that's pretty well off financially. Even though my husband makes a lot of money, we don't spend a lot. I just wonder if the children should know how much we make and if they should know about our budget. Would this overwhelm them, since we are rich, or do you think it would help them adjust to the future?

ANSWER:

I think it's best for parents to be honest with their children. You should pray about whether you're doing the right thing by telling them now. If you're living disciplined lives and managing your money, you need to share that with your children. They should understand that they may never make as much money as you're making; therefore, they may not have the same lifestyle.

Also, and most important, even though you're making what looks like a large amount of money, let them know that it is not really yours; it belongs to God and you're managing it according to His rules. I encourage you to reinforce this many times while they're under your authority. Your giving habits should be revealed as well. This will help them see where your priorities are.

"How much better it is to get wisdom than gold!" (Proverbs 16:16).

QUESTION:

Should we continue to help our married son?

He is very slothful with money, and he manages his own family's finances so poorly that sometimes they don't even have money for groceries. My husband and I have helped them a lot, but I don't think it is right that we should continue, because I want him to learn some self-discipline. My husband doesn't agree with me. Also, my son and his family go to our church and now I find that he has asked our church for help, and that really has embarrassed my husband. Can you give us some guidance?

ANSWER:

Well, unfortunately, this is not an unusual situation. It's difficult to give you an exact answer to this, except to say that you don't want to support your son's slothfulness, because you love him and want what's best for him. Don't bail him out simply because it makes you or your husband feel less guilty. You were responsible for his training, but now that he's an adult you aren't responsible for his decisions; he is. Instead of giving him more money, you need to help him learn how to manage his own money.

> **Every Christian family ought to be, as it were, a little church consecrated to Christ, and wholly influenced and governed by His rules.**
>
> JONATHAN EDWARDS

There's probably nothing you can do about his asking the church for help, and you very likely will alienate your son if you ask the church not to help. You and your husband need to go to your son and tell him you love him but you realize that more money is not going to help him anymore. He must make a decision to become responsible for his own actions.

Let him know that if he's willing to get the necessary help—and that means a good counselor to help him manage his money and hold him accountable—you're willing to help him financially, but you're not willing to just give him more money with no accountability.

"A poor, yet wise lad is better than an old and foolish king who no longer knows how to receive instruction" (Ecclesiastes 4:13).

Question:

At what age do you think children should begin paying for their own clothes and contributing to the family expenses—food, rent, and other living expenses?

My husband and I both agree with what you said on your radio program about not giving your children everything.

Answer:

That depends largely on the personality of each child and what's necessary to teach them God's principles. Some children come with built-in budgets; others come with built-in spending habits. So you have to weigh this decision based on your own children's personalities, because what works for one child may not work for another.

I personally didn't charge my children to live at home while they were in high school, but if they weren't in school I felt that it was their responsibility to provide most of their own living expenses, because essentially they were adults. I didn't need the money, so that wasn't a part of the decision.

However, you need to make financial decisions based on what you think is best for them and will help them most in the long term. You want your children to feel they're contributing to their own needs. I believe it gives them a greater sense of self-worth and responsibility. And remember the point I have made so many times: You're not raising children, you're raising future adults.

"Whoever loves discipline loves knowledge, but he who hates reproof is stupid" (Proverbs 12:1).

Question:

Should we co-sign for our son to buy an automobile?

Our seventeen-year-old son has come to us and asked if we would co-sign for him to buy an automobile. We have the ability to buy him an automobile outright, but he's not always responsible.

ANSWER:

As with many questions, there is no simple black-and-white answer. The principle of co-signing from God's Word is, *"A man lacking in sense pledges, and becomes guarantor"* (Proverbs 17:18).

As a general principle, Scripture tells us not to co-sign; however, as parents we are responsible for the debts of our minor children. When your son is over eighteen, you are not legally responsible for his debts, but if he still lives in your home, to some degree you are morally responsible for him, and he's still responsible to you.

Since your son is nearly an adult, it's not a good idea for you to co-sign a loan, because likely you will alienate him if he can't pay the money back (and you'll be stuck with the bill). With the best of intentions, you may end up losing him for a period of time.

Also, as a cosigner you are liable. The only reason the bank asks for a cosigner is because it believes that whoever is borrowing the money can't pay it back and they want someone else who will be good for the money.

Should you give your son a car? I think that depends on two things: the needs of your son and the kind of car. If you're saying that he needs a car to get back and forth to work and he wants a small used car, that's a decision you have to make on your own. In our society, an automobile is as necessary as a horse was one hundred years ago.

However, it's a large expense and you can go overboard by providing a lot more car than he really needs. Some young people learn to manage a car well, but for others it can be a great distraction and a money burner. So you need to pray about this and do what you believe the Lord wants you to do.

There are no hard-and-fast rules. I don't believe you'll spoil your son by giving him a car. However, if he's going through life expecting you to do everything for him, all you're doing is reinforcing a bad habit. *"Discipline your son while there is hope"* (Proverbs 19:18).

QUESTION:

How can I convey to my parents that constantly giving money to us and our children is not the right thing to do?

My parents are wealthy, but we really don't want their money and we don't need it. In fact, in some ways I think it is a hindrance to our being good managers of our own resources, because every time we set up a budget to try to discipline ourselves they just dump money on us, and they do the same thing with our children. I love my parents and don't want to hurt their feelings.

ANSWER:

The solution is not going to be easy, but the best thing to do is to be totally honest with them. Let them know that you're trying to manage your money, and show your children that you can live on what you make. This will help them live on what they will make. Tell your parents that you'd like to make it on your own and you want your children to do the same.

Ask them to put the money into a trust, where you and your children don't have access to it until you're ready to manage it. Be very careful with them. First, you don't want to hurt their feelings but, more important, you don't want them to spoil your children to the point that they'll be irresponsible adults.

Very possibly your parents are not trying to usurp your authority at home, so you need to be sensitive to that. Let them know that you care about them and that you appreciate what they're trying to do but that you have a responsibility to be good managers of your own money.

You need to insist that they do not give directly to your children, no matter what. Many times, when you're trying to teach your children the right value system and large amounts of money are available, even if the money is in trust and your children know about it, it can undermine your efforts to teach them to be good stewards.

"It is required of stewards that one be found trustworthy . . . The one who examines me is the Lord" (1 Corinthians 4:2, 4).

QUESTION:

Should we buy a home for our married children?

We've been watching them for several years, and they both seem to be good money managers; they are living on a budget. Neither of them makes a lot of money, and we're quite able to buy a home for both of them. What do you think?

ANSWER:

In my opinion, if you're able to help your children you won't spoil them by buying them either a decent car or a decent home—or both—as long as you keep it within reason and as long as you're not using your money to control their lives.

If one is a daughter, you need to be sure that you don't usurp her husband's authority or undercut his self-esteem. After assessing the situation, if you don't think that represents a problem, then I encourage you to do it. There is nothing unscriptural about buying your children a car or a home. But I repeat: First you should carefully evaluate your children's personalities, their abilities, and their attitudes—to make sure that you don't spoil them and that you don't undercut their spouses.

I encourage families who have the resources to do so to either help their children buy homes or to buy them outright. But do that only if you know they are diligent with their own money. I have yet

> **I'm still not sure what is meant by good fortune and success. I know fame and power are for the birds. But then life suddenly comes into focus for me. And, ah, there stand my kids.**
>
> LEE IACOCCA

to see a young couple spoiled by not having to make car payments or house payments. The important thing is to pray about this decision and do as the Lord leads.

I caution you about supplementing their monthly budget long-term, unless there are some very unique circumstances, because you can encourage them to become dependent on you, rather than on God and each other. You might also be encouraging them to live beyond their means, and you don't want that.

Remember this: God can provide for your children, just as He has provided for you. *"God will supply all your needs according to His riches in glory in Christ Jesus"* (Philippians 4:19).

QUESTION:

Should we help our grown children even though we know they aren't handling their money properly?

I've heard you say on your radio program many times that it isn't wise to step in and help children who are not careful with their money, but we have an unusual situation. Our grandchildren are literally going without clothes and sometimes without food, as well as other necessities. We're financially able to help, but we're not sure that we should or, if we should, how to do it.

Answer:

I applaud you, because your caution shows very good judgment. If God is trying to teach your children discipline and you always step in and bail them out, they probably will repeat the same mistakes. If you're going to help, make your help contingent on their getting some professional assistance in handling their finances.

Regardless of anything, I would not let my grandchildren go hungry or go without clothes. They aren't responsible for what their parents have done. If your children or grandchildren are truly needy, in other words if they don't make enough money to get by and they are literally going without food and clothing, there's nothing wrong with helping them. However, if they're not handling their money properly, rather than helping them directly, go through your local church (or theirs). Give the money to the church and designate it for them (this would not be tax deductible).

I recall something that R. G. LeTourneau said in his book *Mover of Men and Mountains.* He had a similar situation with an employee so, rather than give the family money, he would actually go buy the food and give it to them. That might be awkward for you to do with your children, so that's why it's a good idea to work through a church.

Your children need to learn to be accountable for their money, so you need to locate a financial counselor for them. If one is not available in the church, call our office. That information is in item 7.0 in the Appendix.

"A wise man will hear and increase in learning, and a man of understanding will acquire wise counsel" (Proverbs 1:5).

Question:

How soon do you think I should teach my children the principle of giving and tithing?

Answer:

There is no age too young to start teaching your children God's principles of giving. However, you should avoid what I call the quarter-in-the-plate syndrome. That means when the collection plate comes around you give them quarters and they drop them in. That means absolutely nothing to them. There is no sacrifice on their behalf, and it doesn't teach giving.

Children should be encouraged to tithe from their own resources, including their allowances. Rather than giving directly to the local church, help them find needy families or missionary families to help. When your children see what can be done with offerings, it will mean much more to them than it does to drop quarters from you in the plate. *"Instruct them to do good, to be rich in good works, to be generous and ready to share"* (1 Timothy 6:18).

At the very early ages you probably need to insist that your children give a portion of their money to the Lord's work, but as they get older—twelve, thirteen, fourteen—you should begin to allow them to make their own decisions about giving. How and where they give is a window into their spiritual lives.

There are many verses in the Bible about giving. Read them to your children regularly and let them see that giving is a part of God's plan for all of us. It is a privilege. *"Little children, let us not love with word or with tongue, but in deed and truth"* (1 John 3:18).

Question:

Do you think I should bring my children into my business?

I own a sizable company and my desire is to bring them into the business. I am concerned, however, that I'm not objective and I don't treat them fairly—I'm actually harder on them than I am on anyone else. Also, some of my employees, particularly my executive employees, have expressed concern over bringing my children in; I assume they fear it will cut them out of their positions. How do you think I ought to handle this?

ANSWER:

Let me say first and foremost that it is biblically acceptable for family members to be involved in your business. We read in the Bible about how David passed along the leadership of Israel to his son Solomon. Why? Because God chose him.

You need to be fair, and your children should be willing to start in positions they can handle—not according to their genes but according to their abilities. They shouldn't automatically expect to take over the operation. God determines talents, and your children's talents need to be matched to particular jobs.

> **The only place you find success before work is in the dictionary.**
>
> MAY V. SMITH

It is quite possible, also, that a younger child will prove to be a better administrator to run the company than one of your older children. That's a problem you're going to have to deal with early on. Help them understand that God determines gifts and talents; you don't. *"To show partiality in judgment is not good"* (Proverbs 24:23).

I recommend that your children work outside of your business for some period of time before bringing them in so that they have some creditability in the workplace. Also, if you do employ your children be sure that you're objective with them and don't try to shelter incompetent children. You need to evaluate their performances as you would anybody else's. You can love them but still promote somebody over them if necessary. If

God has provided a leader among your children that's fine, but if He hasn't you don't want to sacrifice your business simply to appease your children.

There may come a time when your children will voice disagreements over company policies, and you should allow them the room to express their own opinions.

If you find that you're unable to handle your children working in your business, be honest with them. It may be that the timing is wrong for them and for you, or it could be that God has equipped them to do something else. And remember, it's truly God's decision, not yours.

QUESTION:

How can I support two families?

Since my divorce six years ago I've been supporting my two children. I recently remarried, and my new wife has two children. Her ex-husband does not give her child support, so I'm having great financial difficulties trying to support my two children and my new family. What do you suggest?

ANSWER:

I'm glad that you understand your obligation to your children. And now that you've taken on a new family, regardless of how you acquired them, they are your responsibility also. My suggestion is to immediately get on a budget that allows for supporting both of these families.

If you find that you don't make enough money to support both families, a viable alternative is to take a second job. I know that's very difficult to hear, because it will take time away from the family. However, this is a financial commitment that you've taken on, and as a Christian you must meet it.

God's Word does not provide a plan for postmarriage finances. The truth is, you now have two families to support and must do whatever it takes to do so. I encourage your wife to pursue her former husband and require him to support his family. If she has to force him to do so legally, so be it (in my opinion).

"If anyone does not provide for his own . . . he has denied the faith, and is worse than an unbeliever" (1 Timothy 5:8).

You'll find some helpful budgeting resources listed in items 2.2 and 3.1 in the Appendix. I wish I could give you more detail and more help, but there simply isn't any that I know of. We all make choices and then must live with the consequences.

QUESTION:

How can I learn to manage my finances?

My husband, who died recently, handled all the finances in our family. I don't even know how much money he made. He wrote the checks, paid the bills, and did the investing. Since he did everything, I feel like I'm totally lost and about to panic.

ANSWER:

You need to seek help right now. Go to your pastor and tell him exactly what your problem is. Ask if he has another widow in the church who can work with you and share her experiences.

Somewhere in your husband's records is all the information you'll need to reconstruct your finances. If he had an accountant, make an appointment to meet with that person. If he didn't, ask your friends to recommend someone and take all the information you've found to him or her. Someone with financial expertise can help you sort it all out.

You must now learn how to handle your money, which includes managing the real estate you have, paying the bills, and handling the taxes. You can learn to do it, but I do recommend that you get someone to help you—at least for a while.

I've been through this many times with widows. I know it's very confusing at first, but within six months you'll know most of what you need to know, and in a year or so you'll be handling your finances properly, if you work at it.

Just take the first step. God will do the rest. *"The LORD's loving-kindnesses indeed never cease, for His compassions never fail. They are new every morning"* (Lamentations 3:22–23).

QUESTION:

How do I decide if something is a need, want, or desire?

We don't have a debt problem. We have the money to buy pretty much whatever we want, so money is not a problem. We make over $300,000 a year, so we have a surplus of money. But I find our spending is continuing to increase along with our income, and that concerns me.

ANSWER:

You have a problem that lots of people would like to have, or at least they think they would. And you're right: It is difficult to deal with. I think of what the prophet Agur said in Proverbs: *"Two things I asked of You, do not refuse me before I die: Keep deception and lies far from me, give me neither poverty nor riches; feed me with the food that is my portion, that I not be full and deny You and say, 'Who is the LORD?' or that I not be in want and steal, and profane the name of my God"* (Proverbs 30:7–9).

For better or worse, you fit in the category of having riches. It's a great position to be in if you have a heart for giving, but a bad position to be in if you have a heart for spending. It's very difficult to discern what is a need, want, or desire. Let me explain.

When you're about to buy something and the price is not the determining factor, you need to ask yourself, "Is not having this causing a lack in my life?"

Let me give you an example: If you were a carpenter you would need a hammer. Hammers and nails are not very expensive, and for a carpenter they're necessary for making a living. But if you're an earthmover, you might need a bulldozer. A bulldozer often costs hundreds of thousands of dollars. The amount it costs isn't the real issue; it's what you're going to do with it.

So, before you buy, ask yourself, "Will this thing I'm considering have utility in my life?" I find that most people buy things that have little or no utility in their lives and they end up in storage or parked in their backyards, gathering rotten leaves. That includes motor homes, boats, airplanes, and all kinds of toys that we buy.

Pray about this and decide if your life is suffering as a result of not having whatever you're about to buy.

Remember, God has ordained some of your surplus to help others. *"He who is gracious to a poor man lends to the LORD, and He will repay him for his good deed"* (Proverbs 19:17).

QUESTION:

When you say that you don't approve of accepting government welfare, does that include unemployment compensation?

My husband is unemployed and hasn't been able to find another job. He does have unemployment compensation available to him but won't take it because, he says, "Larry says welfare is wrong."

Answer:

My objection to government welfare is not a biblical objection; it's a personal one. I believe the government is too intrusive in our lives and that by accepting government handouts we make them more so.

In my opinion, unemployment compensation does not fall under the same category. You contributed a percentage of your salary, as long as you were working, into a common pool to take care of people who are unemployed.

You have a right to that money, so there's nothing wrong with accepting unemployment compensation. In fact, I encourage you to do so.

7

GIVING

WOULDN'T IT BE GREAT TO SEE GOD'S people open their hearts and give the way they should? We have enough money in North America to fund all the Christian work in the world if the people would just give.

Giving should be an outward, material expression of a deep spiritual commitment, an indication of a willing and obedient heart. We should give out of grateful hearts in an attitude of joy. Sacrificial giving is a way to honor God, but it should be the result of a good attitude.

There are wrong motives for giving: fear (that God will punish you if you don't give) and giving to impress others (giving should be done modestly and humbly—we are not to draw attention to ourselves when we give).

Being doers of the Word and not hearers only is solidified through our giving to God. Regardless of the work to which we're called, few Christians really cannot afford to give, and when giving is done in love it exemplifies the greatest sacrifice ever made for mankind—the death of Jesus on the cross.

QUESTION:

What should I do about tithing?

I owe too much money to be able to tithe, but I would really like to be able to give to God. Should I stop paying my creditors to give to God?

Answer:

My suggestion is to trust God and give what He tells you to give in His Word. If people waited until they were out of debt to tithe, most American Christians would never tithe.

If you have a commitment to your creditors, you have an obligation to do what you've promised. God is not an accountant, but He says that we should always pay our vows.

"It is better that you should not vow than that you should vow and not pay" (Ecclesiastes 5:5).

So, if you can't pay your creditors and also give to God, you should pay your creditors and honor that commitment. In most instances you can do both, but it means making sacrifices. Believe that God will provide what you need if you make the commitment to do it. The word *believe* means to make it a reality in your life.

There is a caveat that I must add: If you are married to an unsaved person who does not see the necessity or does not have the will to give, in my opinion you need to let the Lord guide you. That doesn't mean not to give, but it also means don't drive a wedge between you and your spouse or a potential wedge between your spouse and the Lord. It would be better to start off giving a small amount and let God convict your spouse than it would be to start off with a large amount, not be able to pay your creditors, put your family in great need, and alienate your spouse.

Remember, giving is an outside expression of an inside conviction. God blesses the heart attitude more than the dollars given. It has been my scriptural and personal observation that the giving habits of individuals usually are direct reflections of their value systems.

Those who sincerely care about the needs of others give, according to their means, to help alleviate those needs. They are the "doers" as described in James: *"Prove yourselves doers of the word, and not merely hearers who delude themselves"* (James 1:22). Those who say they care but fail to back up their words with their money are the "hearers" who delude themselves.

To be sure, we have frauds, phonies, and the lazy in our society who make it easy not to give, on the premise that there are frauds, phonies, and lazy people sopping up charity and tax dollars. But with a little effort you can locate the truly needy who do the best they can and still come up short.

They are the single moms who work three jobs to keep their families fed and housed. They are the families of Chinese Christians who are in prison simply because they believe in Jesus Christ. Or they may be the thousands of kids on the streets of Delhi or the garbage dumps of Jaurez, where they eat other people's discards.

One day we'll all stand before our Lord and give an accounting of our lives: *"They were judged, every one of them according to their deeds"* (Revelation 20:13). What we do for the Lord is important. There is an adage that says, "Actions speak louder than words." That is absolutely true when it comes to giving.

John tells us to love not only with words but in truth and with deeds (giving). We are admonished that *"whoever has the world's goods, and sees his brother in need and closes his heart against him, how does the love of God abide in him? . . . Let us not love with word or with tongue, but in deed and truth"* (1 John 3:17–18).

QUESTION:

How much is a tithe, and should I tithe on my net or gross?

I have a friend who teaches the Bible and she says that the tithe is not applicable to New Testament Christians—that it is a Jewish law, not a New Testament principle. Is that true?

ANSWER:

The word *tithe* or *zela* means "one-tenth"; therefore, when you see the word *tithe* used in reference to giving, God is saying that He wants His people to give a minimum of one-tenth. The tithe was not a law in the Old Testament; there was no punishment for not tithing.

> **Nothing is more pleasing to God than an open hand and a closed mouth.**
>
> FRANCIS QUARLES

Think of it this way: Suppose you know there's a law that says you cannot drive through a red light, but you drive through one anyway. A police officer stops you and asks, "Did you know that you drove through that red light?"

You answer, "Yes."

He says, "Okay, just wanted to let you know about it," and he drives off.

If there's no punishment, that really isn't a law. And there was no punishment for not tithing. However, there is a consequence. *"You are cursed with a curse, for you are robbing Me!"* (Malachi 3:9).

In my opinion, the Word teaches that we are to give from our gross personal income. God says, *"Honor the LORD from your wealth, and from the first of all your produce"* (Proverbs 3:9).

I believe that *"from the first"* means that we are to give from our gross income. But remember to do what God convicts you to do, not what anyone else says.

Don't get hung up with rules. *"It is acceptable according to what a man has, not according to what he does not have"* (2 Corinthians 8:12). Give freely what He tells you to give, and He will bless your life.

QUESTION:

Should I claim what I give to God as a deduction on my income tax?

How does that deal with the principle that God said about me giving in secret?

ANSWER:

I believe the principle of giving in secret is like the principle of praying in secret. If we are praying to be noticed, then we should "go into the closet to pray." But God also said that we are to pray together; in fact, where two or more are gathered, God said He is there. In giving, as well as in praying, God is dealing with heart attitudes.

I suggest that you claim the tithe on your income tax and take that refund. Then, if you have a problem with that, give it back to God, because He can do a lot more with your tithe and the refund than the government can.

No one at the Internal Revenue Service is going to reveal your giving or tithing habits. All that person is interested in is that you provide the right figures. I would not consider that a violation of the principle of giving in secret.

QUESTION:

Could I take money from my tithe to help my elderly mother, who is in great need?

We really don't have a lot of surplus money.

Answer:

Yes, I believe you can. However, you should do so only if there are absolutely no other funds from which you can help her. Rarely is that true. What it might mean is that you will have to change your habits or your desires.

"Honor your father and mother . . . that it may be well with you, and that you may live long on the earth" (Ephesians 6:2–3). We are told to honor our fathers and our mothers, so if you have no other funds available from which you can help your family, I believe that God would have no difficulty with you helping them from your tithes or offerings. It's something you need to pray about to get direction from Him.

Question:

Will I be denying God if I don't give to the Lord's work?

I'm married to a really good man who is not a Christian. I'd like to be able to give to the Lord's work, but he doesn't want me to. In fact, our only arguments are about giving. And, if I decide to give, should it come from my income only and not from his?

Answer:

God's Word says, *"Wives, be subject to your husbands, as is fitting in the Lord"* (Colossians 3:18). If your husband is not a believer and doesn't want to give, in my opinion, you should not give against his will.

I encourage every Christian woman to do this: Challenge your husband with Malachi 3:10: *"Bring the whole tithe into the storehouse, so that there may be food in My house, and test Me now in this . . . if I will not*

> **What I gave, I have; what I spent, I had; what I kept, I lost.**
>
> ANONYMOUS

open for you the windows of heaven, and pour out for you a blessing until it overflows." Then ask him if you can give a small amount of money, with the agreement that you'll give for one year, and if you're worse off financially at the end of that year's time you'll cease giving. But indicate that if you're better off financially, you would like to be able to give some more.

This is one area (tithing) in God's Word where he says to test Him and trust Him. He promises to prove Himself true. On a personal note, I have seen God do it many times. If you honor your husband and agree with him on what you're doing, God will bless you. He does not want the tithe to cause separation between any husband and wife.

Another word of caution about your incomes. Don't categorize them as "my income" and "his income." When you begin to split incomes, you begin to split families. Instead, make the commitment that it is all "our income." It is all from the Lord and not from you or your husband, so you should treat it that way.

QUESTION:

I've been investing in the stock market and have quite a few unrealized gains in my stocks. Should I tithe from those gains even if the stock has not been sold yet?

ANSWER:

Yes, in fact, if you have appreciated stocks or other assets, I encourage you to give those before you sell them. You have two advantages in giving appreciated assets to your church or any other ministry: you can write off the gift as if it were a cash contribution; and the church or other nonprofit organization doesn't have to pay tax on it. It's a great way to give.

You could give when the maximum appreciation has been gained from your stock, but if you hold on too long you'll likely lose some of that gain. My encouragement is if God has convicted you to give, go ahead and give. That would be true of all appreciated assets, not just stock. You can give a percentage of the land or other assets you own to the Lord's work, and then you know that when it's sold God owns that portion and He is going to get His part no matter what. It never hurts to be a "tax-wise" giver. Use the current laws to maximize your giving.

QUESTION:

Should we accept gifts of money that we can't tithe from?

My parents, who are not believers, give several gifts of money every year to our children and stipulate that they, or we, are not allowed to tithe from it. I don't know how to handle this. I feel like I'm not obeying God if we accept these gifts.

ANSWER:

We are instructed in God's Word to put Him first in all things—even ahead of our own families. Training your children in the ways of the Lord is much more important than any amount of money that your parents could give them.

Try to communicate to your parents that you have to refuse the monetary gifts, with love, if these strings are attached. Help them understand that your commitment to your children and to the Lord is more important than anything else in your lives.

If the gifts go directly to your children, help them decide where to give, assuming that their grandparents will allow it, because the kids need to be involved in giving.

Let me add this: You shouldn't purposely alienate your parents, but it may well be that you'll be forced to give up their gifts in order to serve God. Hopefully, your commitment will influence them, but even if it doesn't you still must do what God leads you to do.

QUESTION:

Is it acceptable for me to give time rather than money?

We are really tight on money, and I have decided to volunteer time to my church rather than to give tithes. My wife disagrees with this, and she says that she thinks we are to give money and that time is not a good substitute. What do you think?

ANSWER:

I believe that God wants you to give both time and money, so I think that your wife is correct: Time is not a substitute for money. We are instructed by God to give for one reason: as a testimony. I know it's difficult to give time. Many people are more stingy with their time than they are with their money; but, we are to give both, and one is not a substitute for the other.

Your attitude about money is important, and if you learn to budget your money and give, even though things are tight, I believe it will make

> **The generous man enriches himself by giving; the miser hoards himself poor.**
>
> DUTCH PROVERB

you a better money manager and, therefore, a better steward. Bottom line, in my interpretation of God's Word, time is not a substitute for money when it comes to giving.

QUESTION:

Could I use my tithe, which I normally give to my church, to help a non-Christian friend who is having a lot of financial problems?

I would like to be able to help her and her family.

ANSWER:

I believe that the purpose of the tithe, given in the name of the Lord, is to help people—period. Ultimately, we are to help people take another step toward salvation. Giving is a way to do this. In my opinion, it's better to give the tithe through a local church or some other ministry. And I would always ask first: Are there other funds available? vacation funds? some other way that you could give out of your resources rather than out of God's resources?

If you have no other funds from which to give, I believe that your friend would qualify for the tithe, as any other person would for your help. However, you need to require some accountability of your friend. Help her get on a budget. We're not supposed to put strings on our help, but if your friend is not a good money manager, giving her more money is not the solution to her problem. You're just treating that symptom.

QUESTION:

Should my entire tithe go to my local church?

We're members of an excellent church that is part of a denomination that I strongly disagree with. I think that we should not give our money to our church, since a large portion goes to the denomination; my husband disagrees. What do you think?

ANSWER:

The purpose of the tithe is to help other people. It pays your pastor, it supports mission work through your local church, and it helps the widows and orphans of the Christian and non-Christian community. My counsel is that if you cannot entrust your funds unreservedly to your local church, and therefore to your denomination, then you're probably in the wrong place. Unless you have been called there as a missionary of the Lord, you need to leave this denomination. The Lord may be telling you to move on by creating this lack of peace about where your tithes should go.

QUESTION:

Should we tithe on the significant profit we made when we sold our home?

I would like to, but my husband doesn't agree with me.

ANSWER:

We are instructed in Proverbs 3:9: *"Honor the LORD from your wealth."* If you believe that the profit you made from your home is part of God's blessing in your life, and I would think so, then in my opinion you obviously should tithe. But remember, husbands and wives should pray about this together. Let the Lord do the convicting; don't nag.

QUESTION:

Can you help me make my husband understand the purpose of the tithe?

He is a deacon in our church and has been for over ten years, but he doesn't tithe and has no desire to. This causes a lot of friction in our marriage. I don't understand why he doesn't tithe, and I don't have any idea what to do.

ANSWER:

If someone has been a Christian for an extended period of time and has no desire to tithe, in my opinion you're seeing an outside indicator of what's going on inside that person's life spiritually. The finances are merely a symptom.

The evidence of salvation in anyone's life is a changed life. Part of that change is going to evolve around the area of giving. That doesn't mean that once somebody becomes a Christian he or she automatically wants to give a tithe or wants to give everything away. But I'm inclined to believe that a person who has no desire to give to God's kingdom over an extended period may not have had a personal experience with the Lord.

When I was doing a lot of counseling, I decided that those who weren't tithing probably did not know Jesus as Savior. Therefore, at some point I would share Christ with them during the counseling. In the majority of the cases, these people turned out not to be Christians.

Help your husband understand the truth that giving is an outside indicator of an inside spiritual condition. If he really accepts the admonition from the Lord to come under God's authority, it will be reflected through his finances. Thirty-seven percent of all Christians in America, people who confess to being born-again Christians, give nothing into God's kingdom.

Only about 3 percent of God's people in America today actually tithe. I believe that's an indicator of what they truly believe.

> Let him that desires to see others happy, make haste to give while his gift can be enjoyed, and remember that every moment of delay takes away something from the value of his benefaction.
>
> SAMUEL JOHNSON

QUESTION:

What do you think about us using our tithe to help my brother and sister-in-law adopt a child?

They really don't have any money to adopt, and I would like to be able to help them.

ANSWER:

I suggest that you go to your pastor, present this need, and ask him to pray with you and help you make the decision. Having said that, I believe that the tithe is to be given so that others will come to a saving knowledge of Jesus Christ.

If you have the funds to be able to help this couple out of your own resources, you should do so. But if you don't, I believe that your idea is a perfectly legitimate use of the tithe, and I believe that if you seek the counsel of your pastor he will feel the same way. Perhaps you can even do it through the church.

Remember, we are instructed that if we give even a glass of cold water to a child we have served the kingdom of God.

QUESTION:

Since we are currently between churches and looking for the one God would have us join, should we give our tithe to the churches we are visiting?

ANSWER:

The Scripture says that we are to support those who teach us. *"The Lord directed those who proclaim the gospel to get their living from the gospel"* (1 Corinthians 9:14). If you're going to a church, even though you aren't a member, and you attend for any substantial period of time, I encourage you to give to that church.

However, you need to be careful where your funds are going and be sure they are being used wisely. That's something you can't discern if you just visit a church one time. One suggestion would be to open a special savings account for the tithes that you're not giving currently. Put your tithes in this account until you're a little bit more settled on a church home.

But be careful. There will be a temptation to dip into those funds for other things, so you need to commit the money for your tithes. There are some community foundations that will allow you to put the money into their foundation and direct where it will go later. These are called self-directed funds. You'll find a reference to some in item 12.1 in the Appendix.

QUESTION:

What should I do about giving?

I'm a Christian but my wife isn't. I really want to give, but she vehemently disagrees with me and we always end up in an argument.

Answer:

According to God's Word, husbands are to be the leaders of their homes, but you shouldn't let your giving cause a rift in your marriage. Make every attempt to share with your wife the biblical truths about tithing and giving. Then challenge her to tithe as a family and see how God will bless you.

But as the authority of your family, even if your wife doesn't agree, you must do what God is telling you to do. This may, in fact, temporarily alienate your wife, but most wives are looking for strong, godly leadership—not a dictator but a leader. And if these principles are real in your life, she will see that tithing is a commitment in your life, not a legalism. Let me encourage you not to force the decision on your wife just to assert your authority. Do your very best to convince her that this is a heartfelt conviction within you.

Pray about this, give it a lot of time and prayer. I believe that God is going to prove Himself through your finances, but ultimately, if you are to be the leader of your home, you have to do what God is convicting you to do. And remember what Jesus told us in Matthew 10:37: *"He who loves father or mother more than Me is not worthy of Me; and he who loves son or daughter more than Me is not worthy of Me."* This is a tough biblical truth, but I believe that God will bless you through it. I have yet to see a marriage dissolve over the husband obeying a conviction from the Lord to give, though I realize it's always possible.

Question:

Is it proper for my wife and me to use part of our tithe to keep our children in a Christian school?

Answer:

This is not an easy question to answer. All I can tell you is what I see in God's Word, which says that the tithe belongs to the Lord. It is our material testimony that God owns everything in our lives. When you take a portion of your tithe and give it in your own self-interest to keep your children in a Christian school, then I believe that it becomes a gift made to you or your family, not to the Lord. That's my personal opinion.

Education costs are a normal responsibility for all of us. I believe that if you will commit your tithe to the Lord and not use it for your children's school, He will either provide for them a way to attend Christian school, or He will convict you and your wife that that school is not where He intends for your children to be.

Question:

What do you think about giving a portion of my tithe to the United Way?

I believe that if these organizations are doing the work that God really wants to have done, they are worthy of getting a portion of my tithe; however, my wife strongly disagrees.

Answer:

The tithe you give is a portion of your income that has been committed to God and is given as a testimony in God's name. There are many organizations that do great work, but the ministries that serve in God's name, not secular organizations, should be the recipients of our tithes. That doesn't mean that you can't support them, but don't use your tithe to do so.

This is our testimony that God owns everything in our lives, including our finances, and the tithe should not be used to support secular organizations that don't serve in the Lord's name. That does not mean that they are not worthy. It's fine to support them, but do it with your money, not with God's.

QUESTION:

What's the difference between a pledge and a faith promise?

My church has asked us to pledge against a building project. My husband says he thinks that is unscriptural. I'm not sure. Can you help us?

ANSWER:

It may be that the definitions your church is using are not literal. A *pledge* is a legally enforceable commitment to pay over a period of time. If the church is actually asking for a pledge, they will give you a commitment card and ask you to sign it. That is a legally binding contract between you and the church. In fact, there are churches that take those pledges and discount them or resell them to a lender, so you end up paying your pledge to the lender and the church has already received their money.

A *faith promise*, on the other hand, is a commitment to give if the funds are available. In other words, you are not presuming upon the Lord. If God provides, you will give; if God doesn't provide, the church understands that you have no legal obligation to give.

Remember what God's Word says in Hebrews 11:1: *"Faith is the assurance of things hoped for, the conviction of things not seen."* Therefore, a faith promise is a future money commitment, although you may not see a way to fulfill it right now. In my personal opinion, I believe that a faith promise is scriptural, a pledge is not.

A faith promise allows a church to plan, based on the anticipated income. That doesn't in any way give them the right to borrow the money against that faith promise; it simply allows them to plan.

I believe that a pledge is unscriptural because it is an absolute commitment with no certain way to pay. In other words, it is surety, which is a violation of biblical principles.

QUESTION:

Do you think that some people try to bribe God?

I've been listening to a preacher on television talk about giving, and he says that it is like priming the pump—that God can't give to us unless we have given to God first. Just like you can't get water out of a well until you pour some water down the well first. Sounds a little bit to me like I can pressure God into giving something, but if He really owns everything, how can I pressure God or bribe Him into doing something for me?

> **He is no fool who gives what he cannot keep to gain what he cannot lose.**
>
> JIM ELLIOT

ANSWER:

This is called the name-it-and-claim-it philosophy. The most common Scripture used in this philosophy is Luke 6:38: *"Give, and it will be given to you; good measure, pressed down, shaken together, running over, they will pour into your lap. For by your standard of measure it will be measured to you in return."* I've heard many preachers, television and otherwise, use this scripture to make the point that whenever you give to God, God is then obligated to multiply it at least tenfold and then give it back.

I don't believe that's what Jesus meant at all. I do believe in the principle of sowing and reaping—that you can't get more crops if you don't plant some seeds. Committing a seed to the ground in faith that a plant will come up and dropping a seed in the ground and demanding that the ground give it back are totally different in my opinion. I believe that you are correct: You cannot bribe God.

The apostle Paul once said, *"Who has known the mind of the Lord, or who became His counselor? Or who has first given to Him that it might be paid back to him again?"* (Romans 11:34–35). In other words, we cannot force God to do anything. God gives to us based on our attitudes, not the money we give. And the minute that you demand, God stops giving. But, by way of balance, every faith promise requires some action on our behalf; therefore, it is necessary to act.

But those who give and demand it back from God very quickly find out that it is God who owns and runs this universe, not us. We serve God, God does not serve us. The scriptural principle behind Luke 6:38 is giving and receiving, but it is not giving to receive. You have to go back and read Luke 6:27–37 to find out what is necessary to start this process, and it is a total surrender to God.

QUESTION:

Do you think we should tithe on a gift from my parents?

My husband says that because it isn't income we shouldn't tithe on it. However, I think we ought to tithe on everything that comes in.

ANSWER:

I believe that you're right. God's Word does not tell us to tithe only on earned income. It tells us that we should give from the firstfruits of everything that comes into our possession. But bear in mind that, as I have said before, God is not an accountant, and He's not sitting up there with a ledger book trying to determine whether you have given the right amount of money into His kingdom.

The purpose of the tithe is to act as an outside indicator of an inside spiritual condition. If your husband is not committed to giving and is doing it grudgingly or under compulsion, there really is no reward for doing that. My encouragement to you would be to read Malachi 3:8–10 to your husband and help him understand the purpose of the tithe. Then allow God to convict him about what he should do.

QUESTION:

Should we stop tithing until we pay off our debts?

My husband says that he thinks we should stop tithing because we owe so much money in credit cards and other debt. I don't think that we should do this; however, he says that it is a better testimony to pay our creditors than it is to give to God while we owe so many people. What do you think?

ANSWER:

To some degree I think that both of you are correct. It is not a good testimony to owe people money and not be paying them. However, in my opinion, it also is not a good testimony to claim that we belong to God and that Christ is first in our lives and then not be willing to give from our material assets as evidence of that.

If you can make the minimum payments on your debt, even if it requires working through one of the credit consolidators, it would be better to pay the minimum amount and give God the tithe than it would be to pay more than the minimum amount and not give the tithe.

QUESTION:

What should my attitude be about the church taking up an offering at every service?

I find myself getting resentful when I see the offering plate going around. It's like the church is begging us to give to them, and I wonder how offensive this is to our visitors and perhaps to the non-Christians who are in our congregation.

ANSWER:

Scripture doesn't dictate how an offering should be collected. I've been in churches that put an offering box at the back of the church and never ask for money. I've been in churches that passed around a plate. And I've been in other churches where the pastor would cajole his people into giving more.

Other than from a personal perspective, I don't know that one is more right than the other. The apostle Paul tells us about giving in church: *"Now concerning the collection for the saints, as I directed the churches of Galatia, so do you also. On the first day of every week, let each one of you put aside and save, as he may prosper, that no collections be made when I come"* (1 Corinthians 16:1–2).

The first day of the week for us is Sunday, as it was in the apostle Paul's time, so what he was saying to them was, put aside some money so I don't have to gather this offering when I come.

If I were a pastor, I would try not to offend people, but I would do what I believed was right. I don't think passing around an offering plate is wrong; nor do I think it's begging. It's interesting to me that we will give to a variety of causes whose representatives call us on the telephone or come to our doors—everything from supporting our local fire department and police department to collecting money for muscular dystrophy—but somehow we think it's wrong for God's people to ask to keep the church going. I don't feel that way.

I would suggest that your motive may be wrong. Test your motive and see if it's the giving you object to or the passing of the plate.

QUESTION:

Do you have any guidelines for giving?

I have difficulty with so many groups always asking for money. I'm sure many of them are doing good work, but I don't know where I should give.

ANSWER:

First and foremost, you need to pray and be sure that wherever you're giving, it's where you believe God wants you to give. But when you are testing an organization, first get some information from them to find out how much of their money they spend in fund-raising versus programs. If more than about 25 percent goes to fund-raising, in my opinion, the organization is out of balance. Too much of your money is going to raise more money.

Second, do you know that the organization teaches a message that is true to God's Word, and are people responding by either accepting Christ or becoming better disciples of Christ? Are the lives of the leaders of this organization consistent with Christian principles? And is the organization multiplying itself through the teaching of God's Word?

I realize it's difficult to ascertain this information, particularly when you're talking about just giving $10 to an organization that comes door-to-door. Personally, what I would do is get the Form 990, which tells where their money goes every year. I would try to get some literature from the organization and find out what they stand for, and I also would pray about it. If you're considering giving any sizable amount of money, I probably would go visit the organization personally. You want to be the best steward of what God has given to you.

QUESTION:

Should I stop giving to organizations who promise to give me something in return for my money?

I am regularly solicited by organizations that are asking for money. In return they promise to give me books or materials. Should these organizations be giving away products that dilute my giving, and should I eliminate organizations because they do that?

ANSWER:

It's unfortunate that some Christian ministries have gone to extremes, and fortunately they are not the norm, but unfortunately they are often the most visible. I recall doing a television program for a Christian organization that was soliciting money. During the program I was on, this ministry said that if the viewers would mail them $1,000, they had the right to expect God to give them $10,000 back—a 10-for-1 return. If a viewer gave them $100,000, they had the right to ask for $1,000,000. This group suggested that if someone gave enough money they had the right to ask God to heal someone of a physical problem.

In my opinion, this kind of teaching is pure heresy. It should have no part in our lives and cannot be justified on the basis of the Word of God. Those who do this are peddlers of the Word of God for self-benefit.

However, I believe there's nothing wrong with a Christian organization offering to send a premium, such as a Bible or a book or a cassette tape, provided it's a part of their ministry—in other words, the teaching is complementary to the ministry and they reveal to the donor that the value of the product must be reduced from the donor's charitable contribution. If the promised item is an extension of the ministry, I don't find that offensive.

QUESTION:

Wouldn't it be better if I contributed directly to needy people rather than going through a church or some other organization?

I've really been turned off by so many ministries soliciting money, supposedly to help the poor, but I suspect that much of my money is going into buildings and travel and other overhead.

ANSWER:

Sometimes it's proper and better to give to an individual, particularly if you're trying to reach somebody in your own community or perhaps even in your own neighborhood. In fact, I've often suggested to people to find a single mother in their church to help. If they do and she's the average single mother, they'll be helping a needy person.

But what about the people who aren't in your community or your local church? What about people who live in other countries who are needy? Without distribution organizations, we would never be able to meet their needs. Number one, you probably couldn't go to the country; number two, you couldn't get through the political system to bring anything into

> **If everyone gives one thread, the poor man will have a shirt.**
>
> RUSSIAN PROVERB

the country; and number three, you wouldn't know who is needy and who is not. So there's a legitimate purpose for these organizations.

Giving is the true evidence of caring. *"Whoever has the world's goods, and sees his brother in need and closes his heart against him, how does the love of God abide in him?"* (1 John 3:17).

I do recommend that if you are giving to someone, do not give cash. You might help buy food, pay rent, pay a utility bill, or something else, but unless you're well trained in how to counsel people and determine if the money is being used properly, you might just be adding to somebody else's weakness. That's particularly true when you give to beggars on the street. You may think that you are feeding them, but in fact you may just be feeding a very bad habit. Well-organized charities do a much better job of sorting out the needy from the greedy than most individuals can.

QUESTION:

How can I give money but be sure that it's spent for the right things?

I know of a family in my area who is in need, but I am concerned that if I just give this family money they may misspend it. I've seen evidence of that in their lives before. Would I be better off just lending them the money so I have some control over it?

ANSWER:

If you really want to help this family, you need to give with some strings attached—meaning that you require some degree of accountability from them. I would go to the family and tell them that you want to help but you'd like for them to go see a financial counselor first and then you'll give according to what the counselor recommends.

> **A bit of fragrance always clings to the hand that gives you roses.**
>
> CHINESE PROVERB

If, however, you want to give anonymously, I'd go to their church and talk to the pastor, tell him what you'd like to do, and then have the pastor recommend that they see a financial counselor. If they're not willing to do that, perhaps it's better that you back off and not help.

Do what the Lord tells you, and act out of conviction; don't respond only to emotions. Under the supervision of a good financial counselor, you'll help the family get out of debt—and stay out. Remember the old adage that it's better to teach a man to fish and feed him for the rest of his life than to give the man a fish and feed him only for the day.

QUESTION:

Could you help me decide what to do with some appreciated assets?

I've heard you suggest giving appreciated assets to your church or other Christian ministries because it is a much better way to give, and you avoid taxes on it. I tried to do that, but my church doesn't want to be bothered with receiving things like real estate or stocks or bonds. My pastor has asked that we sell them ourselves and just give the money to the church. What do you suggest?

ANSWER:

Giving appreciated property is far better stewardship under our tax system. If you sell an appreciated property, you're going to be taxed on the profit. However, if you give the asset prior to the sale (stocks, bonds, land), you can avoid the income tax and still get the same tax deduction, and the church will not have to pay any tax.

For example, let's say that you gave to your church a stock that you bought for $100 and it is now worth $200. If you sell that stock, you're going to be taxed on the $100 gain; if you give the stock to the church, you won't pay any tax. You can write off the $200 gift on your taxes, and the church will get the $200 without being taxed itself, so everybody benefits. I believe that this is a very good method to be able to give more to the ministry.

Explain to your pastor that this is a good tax advantage and will cause no difficulty to the church. Any broker within the church would be more than happy, I'm sure, to sell the stocks and remove that responsibility from the church.

QUESTION:

How would my church set up a program to help single mothers and needy people inside and outside the church?

I'm a member of a very good church, and we truly are committed to helping people and serving God.

ANSWER:

I always try to remember what the apostle Paul wrote about this: *"Because of the proof given by this ministry they will glorify God for your obedience to your confession of the gospel of Christ, and for the liberality of your contribution to them and to all"* (2 Corinthians 9:13).

Remember that benevolence is not an option for a local church, and it's important to point this out to your pastor and the staff. It's a responsibility according to God's Word. It's not our government's responsibility to care for people; it is the responsibility of Christians and the local church.

> **He who gives when he is asked has waited too long.**
>
> ANONYMOUS

I suggest that you help your church begin a ministry of benevolence with established, written standards for whom you're going to help, how you're going to help them, under what conditions, and how much. People should be screened by a benevolence committee before you give to them, but you need to set up the benevolence committee first. You'll find information on that listed in item 12.2 in the Appendix.

Benevolence is an essential part of God's plan for every local church, and it has to be done in a way that ensures that the church is really helping people. Those who are undisciplined should learn to become disciplined; those who have a surplus should help those who don't have a surplus.

"At this present time your abundance being a supply for their need, that their abundance also may become a supply for your need, that there may be equality" (2 Corinthians 8:14).

8
Housing

HOUSING IS THE LARGEST SINGLE EXPENSE category for most people. It also represents the biggest problem area for most families. Expectations in the current generation demand a home that most people only dreamed about a generation ago. Available long-term loans have made expensive housing the norm, rather than the exception.

However, what people can buy and what they can afford are generally at odds today. Lenders often look at two incomes when qualifying home buyers, which is unfortunate because children frequently come along after the home is purchased, and one of those two incomes is interrupted.

In general, a family of three making $50,000 a year or less can afford to spend no more than 35 percent of their net (after-tax, after-tithe) income

> A man builds a fine house; and now he has a master, a task for life; he is to furnish, watch, show it, and keep it in repair the rest of his days.
>
> RALPH WALDO EMERSON

on a home. And that amount includes payments, taxes, insurance, utilities, maintenance, and the like.

In reality, many buyers consume 60 percent or more of their income on their homes. There is virtually no way they can balance their budgets with such a large percentage committed to one category. The question is often asked, "What do we do now?"

QUESTION:

Is it better to buy or to rent?

We have been married six years, we're still renting, and I'm concerned that we're just throwing our money away. My husband says that he can make more money by investing the funds that we would otherwise put into a home. However, totally outside of the area of investing, I would like to have a home for our family. P.S. We have two children.

ANSWER:

We're really dealing with a couple of issues here. In the area of buying versus renting a home, the budget is really the key. The question you have to ask is, "Can we afford to buy, considering what our net cost would be?" In other words, when you rent you know what your net outlay is: the amount of money you pay per month, since you don't get to write any of it off.

When you buy, there are some expenses that you can deduct from your income tax (if you itemize). This includes the interest you pay on the loan and the real estate taxes. So you're really concerned about the *net* amount you're paying to buy a home.

Basically, if you can afford to buy for what it costs to rent per month, in my opinion, you're better off buying, because you can't accumulate equity in rent. All things being equal, therefore, it is better for most families to buy rather than to rent. However, if your rent is substantially cheaper than what it would cost to make house payments, and your budget is limited to what you are now paying in rent, obviously it would be better for you to rent.

The other issue is whether it's better to invest, as opposed to buying a home. It has been my observation that, for the majority of people who decide to invest the difference, most don't do very well. A few people are committed investors who stick to the plan, but the majority of people who have money available in an investment plan, other than a qualified retirement plan like a 401(k) or an IRA, often end up spending the money.

Again, remember the bottom line: It's better to buy, but only if it fits your budget. You'll find additional information on this topic in the Budget section (see item 2.2 in the Appendix).

QUESTION:

We're going to the mission field. Is it better to sell our home or rent it? And if we sell it, what do we do with the proceeds while we're on the mission field?

ANSWER:

There's one critical question I would ask anyone who is thinking about going to the mission field and wants to rent his or her home: Do you have a close friend or family member who lives near your home and would be willing to *totally* take care of it? By totally, that means finding renters, evicting renters, repairing the home, and fixing any damage to the property during the time that you're gone. If you don't have someone like that, no matter what the economics, do not rent your home; sell it and get out from under the burden.

If you do decide to rent your home, I encourage you to rent it at below-market value to the extent that your finances will allow.

That way you're able to choose your renters more carefully than would be the case at the going market rate.

Another question I would ask: Will you return to this area when you leave the mission field? If the answer is yes, it may be more beneficial for you to rent out your home. That would be the same for a military family who is being transferred out of the area but plans to come back in the near future to retire there.

In regard to the question about where to keep your money in the short term, if you decide to sell, my recommendation would be to keep it in an investment that is very safe, such as a CD (certificate of deposit), a Treasury bill, or a money market account, which gives you maximum security. Granted, potentially you probably can make more money by investing your house proceeds in more speculative ventures; however, if you can't replace the money and you lose it, it's going to be very difficult to buy another home. In this case, the risk is greater than the potential return.

"Do not boast about tomorrow, for you do not know what a day may bring forth" (Proverbs 27:1).

QUESTION:

Is it better to put more of our money down on the home we're going to buy or just a little bit down?

ANSWER:

If you can pay 100 percent on your home, I believe it's better to do that. You don't make money by borrowing somebody else's money. If you don't believe that, just look around at the biggest buildings in your city. They're usually banks.

However, in reality, when you're buying a home, if you can't put 100 percent down and own the house debt free, you're probably better off not using all your cash assets. In other words, put down enough to afford the payments.

One issue that you need to consider is Private Mortgage Insurance (PMI). If you have 20 percent equity in your home you can avoid the PMI, which typically adds 1 percent to your mortgage cost per year. So if you're financing a $100,000 home, you'll pay about $1,000 per year in PMI, but with 20 percent equity or greater you can avoid paying it.

Otherwise, just consider that you're buying the home in lieu of rent—in other words, you're buying the home as a substitute to renting, in which case it's better to put a small amount of money down. The other question I would ask is, Do you plan to stay in this home long term? If you do want to own the home, then it would be better to put more money down. In fact, try to accelerate the payments on your home on a monthly basis.

QUESTION:

Should we use our IRA money for a deposit on a home?

We plan to buy a home, but we don't have the down payment. However, I understand that we are allowed to borrow the money out of our IRA or 401(k) to make a down payment. Is this a wise thing to do?

ANSWER:

In general, owning a home is a good investment for most families, but remember that when you borrow the money out of your IRA or out of your 401(k) that money must be repaid in a timely fashion—typically within seven years, with interest. If you don't repay the loan on time, the penalties are significant. You'll pay a 10 percent premature withdrawal penalty, plus the federal, plus the state, income tax. That's a pretty steep price to pay to get into a home.

You might look for options, other than your own retirement account, such as assuming a loan on a home that would not require a large down payment. Or perhaps you could borrow the money from a family member who would not charge interest so that you wouldn't be penalized if, for whatever reason, you were unable to meet the payment schedule.

There's nothing wrong with borrowing the money from your retirement account to get into a home as long as you budget in the repayment costs. But remember that the penalties are high if you don't pay that money back in a timely fashion.

QUESTION:

How much can we afford to pay on our home mortgage?

Our lender has qualified us at about 40 percent of our gross income. When I calculate the payments, it seems awfully high for a family of five to afford on a $40,000 salary.

ANSWER:

In my opinion, 40 percent is the maximum that should ever be qualified, but it's 40 percent of your Net Spendable Income (that's income minus taxes and tithe). And remember that 40 percent, in our budget system, must include your mortgage payments, taxes, utilities, maintenance, telephone bills—every expense associated with your home.

Also bear in mind that the number one financial problem facing most young couples is that they spend too much on their housing. In reality, based on your income, your housing allowance at $40,000 in income should be around 35 percent of your Net Spendable Income (after taxes and tithes). Many young couples are spending 60 to 65 percent of their total income on their home, and that's why their budgets won't balance.

In the area of housing, it's better to do with less—initially. Buy a smaller home until you can handle a larger home more comfortably—that is, when income increases. Actually, if you buy a home that is within your budget and you can control your other expenses, you should be able to pay off the mortgage in about seven years. Obviously, for the majority of young couples today, that is virtually impossible. They can't pay their homes off in 100 years, because they have overcommitted.

QUESTION:

Should we use a home equity loan to consolidate our debt?

We've gotten ourselves into severe debt problems. We owe about $17,000 in credit cards; we still owe about $10,000 in school loans; and now we owe doctor bills that probably amount to more than $12,000. We don't have that much equity in our home, but we do have about $30,000. Should we borrow the money out of our home to consolidate as many of these debts as possible so that we can make our payments on a timely basis?

ANSWER:

There's at least one positive factor when you use your home to consolidate a loan: The interest is deductible. In reality, debt is debt. But having said that, there are some prerequisites that you must meet before I would recommend that you use your home equity to consolidate debts.

> Small rooms or dwellings discipline the mind, large ones weaken it.
>
> LEONARDO DA VINCI

You need to make sure that you're treating the problem and not the symptom. The symptom is the debt that you owe: credit cards, school loans, and doctor bills. The problem is, you're living beyond your means.

So I would first recommend that you get on a budget and live on it for at least six months, making the current payment schedule that you now have. If you can't make the current payment schedule because you're too far in debt, in all probability a consolidation loan will not solve the problem; it will merely treat the symptom. You need to pray about this together and agree together on the sacrifices necessary to pay down this debt.

One of the things I recommend, particularly when dealing with credit cards, is that you make an agreement like the one below and tape it on your refrigerator.

> Lord, from this day forward we will pay off any new credit card purchases each month, without interest. The first month we fail to meet this promise we will destroy all our credit cards.
>
> **Husband** _____
>
> **Wife** _____
>
> **Date** _____

Basically, you're promising that the next time you use your credit cards and don't pay off the current charges that month, you'll destroy them. Without this commitment, all the consolidation loans will do is ease the pressure you're under right now. And within a year, or two at the most, you'll be right back in the same trouble you're in now, only you'll owe a consolidation loan in addition to the other debts.

Let me assure you that I've seen many couples who consolidated their debts, using their home equity or something else, and they went right back into the same difficulty—only worse. Often, the next time it ended up in something more severe—like bankruptcy or divorce.

From this day forward, you must make a commitment to incur no more debt, no matter what the circumstances. I believe that you also need to make yourselves accountable to somebody else. I would suggest you go to your pastor and see if he can suggest a good budget counselor in your church who will work with you. If you're willing to do this, perhaps the consolidation loan is a reasonable thing to do.

QUESTION:

We want to build a home debt free, but is it a good thing to do?

I've been listening to your radio program for many years now. We've been married for two years, and I have told my wife that I am committed to the Larry Burkett principle of being totally debt free, including our home. We're not going to build a home until we can pay cash for it. My wife doesn't agree with this and wants your opinion.

ANSWER:

The answer to this question is best answered by you and your wife. It is possible to build a home debt free, but certain things are required: great communication and cooperation between husband and wife. Another is being willing to sacrifice virtually everything else for five to seven years. And remember that both of you must be committed to this project totally; you must pray about it together and have no reservations, because it's going to be a very difficult thing to do. You'll need to save enough money to buy the land for cash, and you'll have to be willing to do much of the work on the house yourself in order to keep the expenses down.

Obviously you have to have surplus money to be able to do this. I would say it is unrealistic for a couple with children to accomplish this. So if you have no children, and if you're willing to take no vacations, do away with your Entertainment/Recreation budget, and make a commitment to buy no new cars during this process, you might be able to do it. For the majority of couples, I would say this is not the way to go. It's not for everybody.

I jokingly say something that's not really a joke: Unless you have been married for ten years you probably shouldn't even try to build a home, much less try to build a home debt free. Perhaps the compromise that you could make is to finance your first home, accumulate enough cash that you can buy the land for cash, and then try to use the equity plus whatever surplus you have above that to build your next home debt free.

Even then, without both of you being absolutely committed to this, it will not work. I have known several young couples who set out to build a home debt free. The majority of them did not succeed. About 1 in 20 actually stuck it out. And, unfortunately, in some cases their marriages did not make it either. So, as I said, it's not for everybody.

Two staff members of Crown Financial Ministries have built debt-free homes. They discovered it could be done because they and their spouses were willing to be totally committed to the concept. Though it was difficult, they had the resolve to put in a lot of sweat equity, and they sacrificed in the short term in order to enjoy the future benefits of debt-free homes.

QUESTION:

Should we buy our home using a conventional or a government loan?

We're looking at buying our first home and are checking into mortgage rates. It seems to us that buying a home through the FHA or VA is a less expensive way. Can you tell me if there are any downsides to this?

ANSWER:

In most instances government loans will be cheaper, at least initially. They require less down payment: typically about 5 percent (or zero) down, depending on the type of loan you get. But, in reality, many conventional loans today are very competitive and offer the same interest rates—and many times the same money down. In fact, there are conventional loans available that will lend you more than 100 percent of the total loan amount. I don't recommend these loans.

Basically though, the bottom line is that it doesn't matter what kind of loan you get, if you know that you can work it into your budget and that you can afford the payments on the home.

QUESTION:

Is a biweekly mortgage refinancing a good deal?

My bank has offered us a deal: For $500 they will renegotiate our loan so that we can make mortgage payments twice a month. Is this a good idea? They say that this will save us thousands of dollars on our mortgage.

ANSWER:

The idea of prepaying your mortgage in order to retire your home loan earlier is a good plan. A biweekly mortgage basically allows you to make one extra month's payment per year. Simply put, there are 26 weeks in a year, so you pay 13 payments rather than 12 and it helps you pay your home off earlier. However, I don't normally recommend biweekly mortgages that require an up-front cost like $500, because essentially you can do the same thing yourself by simply making an extra partial payment per month.

For instance, you make your regular monthly payment and then write a second check, marked "payable to principal only," in the amount of one and one-half of your regular payment. You will, in fact, make one extra payment per year. You will accomplish essentially the same thing without incurring the front-end cost.

Remember though, you should write two checks, one to the regular payment and a second that is marked "principal only." And then, at least annually, you need to verify that the extra payments have been correctly credited to your principal account. Refer to item 13.0 in the Appendix, where we have suggested some computer programs that will help you do that. They are also available on our Web-site: www.crown.org.

QUESTION:

What is the best way to pay off our mortgage early?

We would like to retire our thirty-year mortgage early.

ANSWER:

The best method to prepay your mortgage is to make additional prepayments monthly. For instance, you make your regular payment; then you write a second check, made payable to "principal only." And, you do need to verify, at least annually, that all of the payments have been credited properly. Otherwise your bank may take your prepayment and allocate it as part of the next regular monthly payment, in which case interest would be taken out of it, and you don't want that.

The chart in "Mortgage Prepayment" (see item 16.0 in the Appendix) shows a $100,000 loan, financed at 7 percent for thirty years, and shows how paying an extra $50 per month can retire that note early and how much interest it will save you.

Mortgage loans are simple-interest loans, meaning that the interest is calculated on the unpaid balance at the beginning of the month; therefore, you do have prepayment privileges. And the more principal you pay down, the less interest you pay in the next payment as well. The advantage of prepaying, using this method, is that there are no up-front fees.

QUESTION:

Is it better to pay off our home mortgage or invest the difference?

My husband thinks it's crazy for us to pay off our home mortgage since we will lose our tax write-off. In fact, he says he can make more money in the stock market with the money we would use to pay off our loan; therefore, it makes no sense to pay off the loan early.

ANSWER:

Well, he's probably both right and wrong, but first let's discuss the issue of making interest payments. You don't make money when you pay interest unless you're in a 101 percent tax bracket, which no one is. For example, if you pay $1,000 in tax-deductible interest and you're in the highest tax bracket in America today, you're paying about 38 percent federal and probably around 6 percent state income taxes for a total amount of 44 percent. And most people are not in that high a bracket.

In a 44 percent tax bracket, when you pay $1,000 worth of deductible interest, you get $440 back from the government. However, the way I figure it, since you paid the $1,000 and got $440 back, you lost $560. Therefore, you didn't make money by paying interest; you lost money.

Certainly, the argument could be made that you might invest the money and earn more with that money than paying off the loan. That's a different argument altogether. Your husband may be right about investing the money and making more money on it; but, remember, there are no guarantees.

I would suggest that you pray about this and determine if God wants you to be debt free. If you believe God has called you to be debt free, then pay off your home, because that's God's will for you. Also let me say that, by observation, I've found most people don't invest the money they would've used to pay off their home. The majority of people take that money and spend it. So, as a result, they aren't further along in paying off their home; they just have more toys that wear out quickly.

One idea is to pay off the mortgage loan and then see if you have peace about it. I have never heard anyone say that they hated being debt free. Husbands and wives should pray about this together and let God guide. It is my considered opinion that God wants His people to be debt free and invest at least some of the interest they're paying into kingdom work. Theoretically, it may make more financial sense to invest the money and keep the debt on the house, but usually that's the husband's thinking, not the wife's.

Question:

With interest rates down, we want to refinance our home, but would it be better to use a thirty- or a fifteen-year note?

Answer:

Refinancing generally makes good sense if you can recover the refinancing cost in two years of payment reductions. In other words, let's assume that you're going to refinance a $100,000 loan at 8 percent down to 6.5 percent (saving 1.5 percent), and it will cost you $2,500 to do that. For every percent of interest your loan is reduced, you save $1,000 in payments per year, so a reduction of 1.5 percent will save $1,500 per year. In two years you will have saved $3,000, less whatever the tax savings on the interest would be; but, essentially, you will have recovered your refinancing cost in two years. In my opinion, that's a good idea.

Whether you use a thirty- or a fifteen-year loan is totally dependent on whether the shorter loan will yield a large enough interest break. The first consideration is not to refinance a home with any loan that is more expensive than what your budget can handle. In other words, if choosing a fifteen-year loan will make the payments so high that it's difficult for you to make them, you'd be better off with a thirty-year loan. You can make any thirty-year loan into a fifteen-year loan simply by prepaying principal each month.

For instance, you could convert a $100,000 loan at 6.5 percent for thirty years into a fifteen-year loan by simply making an additional principal payment per month, which is totally under your control. However, if there were a time when you couldn't afford the additional payment, you aren't obligated to do so. Therefore, in my opinion, you're probably better off with a thirty-year loan. The only exception to this would be if the fifteen-year loan carries a substantially lower interest rate, which would make it beneficial for you in lower costs.

I would suggest that you shop rates. Look to your present mortgage company first. It may be that they will give you a preferential refinancing rate to keep your loan with them; therefore, your cost would be lower. But, make the decision between a thirty- or a fifteen-year loan based on your budget.

QUESTION:

Can someone else assume our home loan?

We're trying to sell our home, and we have a 6.5 percent loan rate. Somebody who was looking at our home asked if it would be possible to assume our loan. How can we tell whether our loan is assumable?

Answer:

Whether your loan is assumable will depend on your contract with the mortgage lender. Unless you have an extremely old loan, probably one that was issued in the 1970s or earlier, it likely is not assumable. If the loan carries a balloon clause, as most do, so that when you sell the entire payment comes due, the buyer is forced to take out a new loan.

However, I do know many people who have assumed mortgage loans, even though the contract said the loan was not assumable. Essentially, the way this works is that the many mortgage companies don't really care as long as somebody continues to make the payments. However, when someone assumes your loan under these conditions, your name is still on the note, and if he or she doesn't pay it is still your obligation.

Nonassumable loans often are adopted by commercial home resellers. For example, a businessman I know buys homes from couples in distress—usually as a result of a divorce and they need to sell the home quickly, or they have moved and need to sell the home. He then takes over the nonassumable loan, continues to make the payments, and resells the home to someone else, who then continues to make the payments. Usually he adds a fee for managing the loan.

The good news is that the banks usually go along with these loans, even though they are not assumable, but the bad news is that they have the right by law to call the loan. For people who have been through bankruptcy, often this is the only way they can buy a home: by going through a reseller and assuming the mortgage of a previous owner.

QUESTION:

I'm a minister and we live in a parsonage. Should we try to buy a home?

ANSWER:

Personally, I believe that pastors should try to buy their homes—for two reasons. First, when a pastor leaves the pastorate, by retirement or by transfer, he may go into an area where homes are highly inflated. The second reason is because pastors get what's called the *double dip* in taxes, meaning that the housing allowance is not taxable and yet the interest and taxes are deductible on his income tax. That is a significant advantage over most other home-buyers in America.

If the church owns a parsonage and the pastor opts to buy his own home, the church can either rent the parsonage and allocate the rent to help the pastor buy his own home, or the church can sell the parsonage and allow the pastor to buy his own home.

In my opinion, parsonages made a lot of sense until the mid-twentieth century, with pastors moving around and not a lot of available homes in many areas. But today they fundamentally are not a good idea. There are plenty of homes available, and many pastors do move around and often get caught in housing markets that are highly inflated, with no funds to buy their own homes.

Let me reiterate: For most pastors it is better to buy a home than to live in a parsonage. Let the church rent the parsonage, sell it to the pastor, or sell it outright. Because of the double dip, pastors can actually make money because of the nontaxable housing allowance and the fact that the interest is deductible. That's a rare opportunity not available to most homebuyers.

QUESTION:

Should we borrow the equity out of our home to invest?

My husband would like to borrow the equity out of our home to invest in the stock market. I personally don't have a good feeling about this, but I don't have an argument against it either, because he says he can make more money than what the loan would cost us in interest.

ANSWER:

First and foremost, I would ask your husband, "Have you prayed about this?" "Have you talked it over with your wife?" and "Are you in agreement?" Unfortunately, many men look at their homes as investments, but most wives look at their homes as family dwellings. The purpose of a home is to provide comfort for your family and not necessarily to maximize the return on your money.

There is a risk any time you invest, especially in the market, because you can lose some or all of your investment. The question your husband has to ask himself is, "Would I mind coming home in the evening, facing my wife, and explaining that I had lost some or all the money I borrowed from our home with no way to pay it back?" If he wouldn't like to do that, my recommendation to him is, don't do it.

There is always a risk. Remember, the higher the rate of return you're seeking, the higher the degree of risk you must assume. I've known many people who've taken equity from their homes to invest—either in the market or their businesses—and I would say that more have failed than have succeeded. Theoretically, it seems like a good idea, but quite often it doesn't work out.

QUESTION:

What do you think about a mobile home as an investment since we can't afford to buy a home in our area?

ANSWER:

In many areas, mobile homes represent a good alternative to high-cost housing, particularly for young couples and also for older couples facing retirement. However, there are some assets and liabilities associated with mobile homes. New mobile homes normally depreciate very rapidly. Therefore, in general, used mobile homes are a better buy, because someone else has taken some of the depreciation on them—much the same as in buying used cars.

However, before I would buy any mobile home, I would verify its quality, because the most important thing with any mobile home is how well it is manufactured. And if I were going to consider buying a mobile home, I would check it out through *Consumer Reports* magazine, either on their Web site or in the magazine itself, and verify the quality of the mobile home as compared to others.

Also remember that when you buy a mobile home, particularly if you're in a high-energy market—which would be northern or western states that are very cold or some southern states that are very hot—you'll normally be facing higher heating and/or air-conditioning bills, because typically a mobile home is not as well insulated as a constructed home.

Another price factor to consider when you buy a mobile home is the space rent or a lot on which to locate it.

For many couples mobile homes represent a good alternative to high-cost housing. But the thing to remember is that they depreciate rapidly and require higher maintenance costs.

QUESTION:

Are condominiums a good value?

We're a newly married young couple looking for a place to live, and housing in our area is very expensive. We looked at condos and found that they are much less expensive—by about one-third—but we're not sure about the resale value.

ANSWER:

Usually, the purchase of any property, including a condominium, depends on the area of the country and what's going on in your economy. There are areas, such as South Florida and some of the recreational areas, where condos sell just as readily as homes; but, in other areas condos do not sell as readily as homes, even at lower costs.

Also remember that there are some additional costs associated with condos, such as the association fees you must pay every month. Because you're in a complex that is physically linked to other units, you must pay common fees for the upkeep of the grounds, the roofs, and the buildings. Sometimes these fees are substantial, so you need to verify what they are before you buy.

Another factor to remember is that since the sale of condos is somewhat more difficult, you don't want to buy one if you're going to have to move often (for instance, if you're a military person or perhaps a pastor who moves a lot).

If you only plan to rent a condo, typically they do cost less than a stand-alone home. However, if you're buying a condominium in an area where you plan to live for a reasonable period of time and you can get a good deal, in my opinion, condos can be an excellent bargain for many people.

What I believe makes a condo particularly attractive is that you don't have much personal maintenance and upkeep, because much of that is done by the homeowners' association. Anytime you don't have yard work or maintenance, I'm for that!

QUESTION:

Would it be better to borrow against our home for our children's education or would it be better to go for school loans?

We have two children, seventeen and sixteen, who are going to be going off to college—one of them in the next year and one the year after that—and we've been looking at school loans. School loans have a great advantage, we think, but we want to know if it would be cheaper for us to borrow against our home.

ANSWER:

Well, let's look at this issue intelligently. The first big advantage to school loans is that generally they have deferred interest, meaning you don't have to make payments until after the child graduates or quits college.

However, be aware that school loan interest is not deductible, as home loan interest is. So, when you're comparing net cost, be sure that you deduct the tax savings from your home loan interest rate. For instance, if you had a 7.5 percent rate on your home and you were in a 33 percent tax bracket, your net interest would be only 5 percent, which probably would be lower than the school loan.

The thing I would say about this is, a loan is a loan, so you need to pray about which suits you best. Couples need to discuss this and be sure that they are doing what God wants them to do. One of the difficulties I have with either home loans or school loans for education is that people tend not to watch the costs as well as they would if they were paying for the school out of their own pockets. That's true with almost everything we do, whether it's automobiles, housing, or education.

It has been reported that about one-half of all school loans are used for nonschool items: things like stereos, TVs, automobiles, and vacations. So, you need to be aware of that. Personally, if I had the option of borrowing against my home or going with a school loan, I would probably borrow against my home—mostly because I don't believe in government-backed loans. In my opinion, they are a negative option, and there is the tendency to use them too readily and spend too much.

QUESTION:

Should we let the home go back to the bank?

Our housing percentage is much too high for our budget and it's ruining our monthly finances, but we have tried to sell our home and can't find a buyer.

ANSWER:

Remember that when you signed your home mortgage you signed a contract that guaranteed the lender you would make the payments. As long as it is humanly possible to do that, I would encourage you to make the payments. If you have to let the home go back, you're far better off selling it yourself. Arrange with the lender to allow you to sell the home. If it sells for more than the outstanding loan, you get to keep the difference. If it sells for less than the outstanding balance, you'll owe the difference. That's not good, but even so, often it's less than what you would lose if the bank sold the home.

Generally, if a bank sells a home they won't press for the highest price. If the sale price is less than the loan value, they'll sue you for the difference—called the deficiency. That's why I warn couples against creating a back-loaded mortgage.

For instance, let's assume that your payment is $750 a month, the majority of which is interest, and because of economic circumstances you make an agreement with the bank to pay only $500 a month. The bank takes $250 of the interest payment and tacks it on the end (back) of your loan. Essentially, you have created an upside-down loan, which means that eventually you'll owe more on the home than what it's worth. That doesn't avoid the problem. It delays it and makes it worse.

You're better off to face the reality that you bought a home that's too expensive, sell it as quickly as you can, and absorb the loss, if necessary. *"Thus says the LORD, 'Set your house in order'"* (2 Kings 20:1).

9

HUSBAND AND
WIFE COMMUNICATION

MONEY AND ITS ASSOCIATED PROBLEMS do not necessarily cause poor communication in a marriage, but they certainly reveal it. Most of our daily lives revolve around money—including making it, spending it, saving it, giving it, and the like.

It has been said that 80 percent of our lives is spent in the accumulation and distribution of money, so it's little wonder that the lack of communication will be reflected in money as well.

Many couples (and singles) talk *at* each other about money, but few really talk about money in a way that allows both to voice their true feelings. Most couples are opposites (they really *do* attract) and, as such, each brings a different set of wants and needs to the table. The couples who learn to use money as a tool for communication learn a lot about each other and about balance.

Money is a great area in which to learn how to communicate, because it is objective and measurable. Use it wisely, and your relationships will grow stronger. Ignore it, and perhaps you'll find yourself starting over again with somebody new, who may be remarkably like the previous spouse.

God's plan is that your marriage should prosper and grow, and money can help.

QUESTION:

Should we rent or buy?

My fiancée and I are getting married soon and we're getting a lot of conflicting advice. My parents tell me that it's foolish to waste money on rent and get no return. Unfortunately, most of the homes that we've looked at are beyond our financial capability. My fiancée's father is willing to lend us a down payment and make the monthly payments for the first year if we want to buy a nice home. It sounds very appealing to me, but I wonder if it is the right thing to do.

ANSWER:

There are two factors to consider about buying or renting. The first is what your budget allows. The second is whether it's the right decision for *you*.

If you have the money to make a down payment and you can afford the monthly payments, it may be a good financial decision to buy. However, I usually advise young couples not to buy in the first year of their marriage. There's enough stress on your life, just getting to know each other, without adding any additional stress.

If you let someone loan you the down payment and assume a monthly payment larger than what you can afford, you're taking on a contingent liability. Scripturally, what you're doing is taking on surety: an obligation to pay without a certain way to pay it.

Even though I appreciate the concern of your parents, remember that you and your fiancée are adults, and you need to make these decisions yourselves. The number one cause of financial problems with many young couples is that they buy a home that's too expensive for them. And although your father-in-law said that he would make the monthly payments for the first year, let me assure you: That year will pass very quickly and then you'll be stuck with making the payments. What happens after the first year if you can't afford those payments?

Bear in mind this simple proverb: *"Prepare your work outside, and make it ready for yourself in the field; afterwards, then, build your house"* (Proverbs 24:27). I think that's very good wisdom. In other words, get your life squared away, settle into a comfortable routine, live on a balanced budget, and then think about buying a home. And be sure it's a home that's within your means.

In your situation, I recommend that you relax for a year, get to know each other, and then think about buying a home.

QUESTION:

Can you tell me what my options are since my husband left us high and dry?

My husband of sixteen years left recently and went to live with another woman. That was a shock, but it's been an even greater shock that he's giving us only a minimal amount of money to live on. I haven't worked outside my home in over ten years, but now I feel like I need to go back to work to make ends meet. I hate to, because the change for my children—ages ten, twelve, and fourteen   has been traumatic enough, and if I leave home to work it will be even more traumatic for them.

ANSWER:

It's sad that divorce is such a common thing in our society, and abandonment is even more common. To deal with the issue of your husband leaving, you need to pray about it, present it to God, and let Him take control. Try not to let this experience make you bitter.

You need to make out a realistic budget, based on your minimum needs. There's information in item 2.2 in the Appendix about budgeting. You might get someone in your church to help you with it. When you go to court (and in my opinion you should), you can present your budget to the judge as your reasonable needs. With the court system as it is today, you're never sure what a judge is going to do, so it may be that yours will grant you an adequate amount of money—or not. It's always possible that the judge won't.

If you have to go to work, my recommendation is to look for a job that will allow you to work during the time your children are at school. Depending on your skills and your personality, there are things you can do to work out of your home. Home sales for products is a very common area today.

To help you understand what you are best equipped to do, I suggest you take the *Career Direct*® assessment (see item 5.0 in the Appendix).

There is no easy answer to your situation. God has to convict your husband to do what is right for your family. Don't give up though; God is still in control. Put your trust in Him. *"Oh, the depth of the riches both of the wisdom and knowledge of God! How unsearchable are His judgments and unfathomable His ways!"* (Romans 11:33).

I recommend that you let your family, church, and friends know what your needs are. Don't let pride rob you of God's blessings. Pride is Satan's best weapon.

QUESTION:

Can you tell me if the Bible teaches that women should not work outside the home?

I've listened to your radio program for a long time. I'm a Christian wife and mother, and I do work outside the home. I enjoy my home, but I also enjoy my job a lot. However, some of my Christian friends have been hinting (pretty strongly) that I am sinning because I don't stay home with my children.

Answer:

I'm going to give you some biblical principles, and then I'll give you an opinion, based on a lot of counseling. I don't believe that God's Word teaches that a wife can't work outside the home, but I do believe that Scripture establishes some priorities.

> **Liberty means responsibility. That is why most men dread it.**
>
> George Bernard Shaw

First, if you're working because the family needs the money, it's the wrong motivation. Unless your husband is disabled, you're probably like everyone else—working just to buy more things. And until a couple learns how to get along on one income, let me assure you that two incomes won't be enough either, and you'll be trapped into working for the rest of your life.

Second, if you're working to satisfy your ego, that's also the wrong motive. Don't listen to the media or you'll find yourself with loyalties divided between your job and your home.

An excellent wife is described in Proverbs 31:16, 24. These verses describe her doing business ventures as well as household duties. Although she isn't working for somebody else, she's definitely working outside the home. And she's described as a working wife and mother who is able to keep her priorities in balance. I believe it is the *balance* that determines whether you should or should not work outside the home.

In most instances, I believe that it's God's plan for women to stay home and raise the children. Mothers are the homemakers, and in America we have this totally out of balance. Paul states in Titus 2:5 that women should be workers at home and subject to their own husbands.

Since women are described elsewhere in Scripture as holding

down some outside jobs, I don't believe that Paul is giving any new counsel. He's simply stating a biblical principle: that women should not neglect their family responsibilities by getting absorbed in things outside the home.

Let me outline what I think are the priorities for a working wife.

Number one, she should have her husband's approval: *"Wives, be subject to your own husbands"* (Ephesians 5:22). That doesn't mean that she nags him until he finally agrees for her to work outside the home.

Number two, her children must be well cared for: *"She looks well to the ways of her household"* (Proverbs 31:27). It's obvious that some children are ready for outside training at age five or six; others don't seem to be ready at thirty-six. So you have to weigh your own family and their needs. I believe that the family needs a parent at home.

Number three, a mother and wife should maintain her home well: *"She rises also while it is still night, and gives food to her household"* (Proverbs 31:15). If you are frazzled at work, you will be at home too.

And number four, she should be able to balance that dual authority between the home and the job and not be double minded. I believe there is a strong biblical case that Christian women should be homemakers, not workers outside the home. But that does not imply that Scripture teaches she can never work outside the home. That's a decision that each wife and mother must make together with her husband and the Lord.

QUESTION:

Do you think Christians can have problems that are not sin related?

I've heard you talk many times on your radio program with people who have severe financial problems. I've been taught, as a

Christian, that problems in people's lives are an evidence of sin. I'm concerned about this philosophy, because I hear about committed Christians who are having problems.

ANSWER:

There's a common attitude among certain groups of Christians that we should never have problems, and if we do it's because we lack faith and we're being punished by God. In my opinion, that is a very defeatist philosophy.

God's Word says, *"Consider it all joy, my brethren, when you encounter various trials, knowing that the testing of your faith produces endurance. And let endurance have its perfect result, that you may be perfect and complete, lacking in nothing"* (James 1:2–4).

I believe that a paraphrase of that verse would say that if you really want your faith to grow it must be tested. Therefore, we can know with certainty that not all problems are caused by sin or are the evidence of sin. In fact, many difficulties are allowed by God for our growth.

However, even though financial problems *can* be an indicator of sin, there are going to be a lot of other indicators; money is just the outside measurable objective of what is going on in someone's life. Christ has promised peace if we will yield our rights *when* we have problems (not *if* we have them).

Jesus obviously had plenty of problems during his time on Earth, and He certainly didn't sin. He told us that if we follow in His steps problems will occur. *"These things I have spoken to you, that in Me you may have peace. In the world you have tribulation, but take courage; I have overcome the world"* (John 16:33).

Our difficulties are not all sin related. If you look into your life and you know that you have violated one or more biblical principles and you're having problems, then you probably have created them for yourself. But, in general, that's not going to be true for everyone. Through our difficulties we can be witnesses to other people who are having similar problems. They look at us and know that our God is real because we are able to handle whatever happens.

The last thing that anyone who is having a serious problem, financial or otherwise, needs to hear is, "Are you sure that you have confessed your sins?" Let me assure you that people who are experiencing difficulties, particularly major kinds of problems, have confessed not only their sins but sins they never even thought of committing. So, they don't need Christians to condemn them; they need Christians to comfort them.

QUESTION:

Even though I want to be a good wife, and I know that the Bible says that my husband is the authority in the home, shouldn't I have some input in this marriage as well?

My husband acts more like a dictator than a leader in our home. He's chosen to manage all our finances, even though I believe that I'm a better bookkeeper than he is. I have absolutely no say over anything about finances: He buys our food, pays the bills, even selects my clothes.

ANSWER:

Yes, you should have input in the marriage. God directs a husband to give his family balanced, godly leadership—not establish a dictatorship. A husband who wants to be a godly leader should take Jesus as his example. Jesus was a gentle leader. He never crushed somebody else's spirit to assert His authority.

The apostle Paul said, *"The husband is the head of the wife, as Christ also is the head of the church"* (Ephesians 5:23). But he also said, *"Husbands, love your wives, just as Christ also loved the church"*

> **Marital freedom: the liberty that allows a husband to do exactly that which his wife pleases.**
>
> ANONYMOUS

(Ephesians 5:25). And, *"Be imitators of God, as beloved children; and walk in love, just as Christ also loved you, and gave Himself up for us"* (Ephesians 5:1–2).

A marriage between two people is much like the relationship between a right hand and a left hand: They are well matched but opposites. The key to a good partnership is to determine each other's assets and liabilities and then work together in love (no dictator needed).

It helps to remember that to have authority doesn't mean to be a ruler. Authority implies responsibility. Being a good authority figure means being a strong enough person not to be threatened by somebody else's strengths, particularly a spouse's. There is nothing better a husband can do for his children than to unconditionally love their mother.

The Bible tells husbands to love their wives and treat them as partners—literally coheirs: *"You husbands . . . live with your wives in an understanding way, as with a weaker vessel, since she is a woman; and grant her honor as a fellow heir of the grace of life"* (1 Peter 3:7).

Acting as a dictator is a sure sign of being insecure. Try not to take it personally. Your husband is an insecure person and you need to get to the source of it. Ask him to go for counseling, and if he won't go you need to pray about it—but don't badger him. *"The way of a fool is right in his own eyes, but a wise man is he who listens to counsel"* (Proverbs 12:15).

Even though the apostle Paul said that wives were to be subject to their husbands, that doesn't make you a nonperson in your home. You are to be your husband's helpmate, and one responsibility that any wife has is to help her husband make godly decisions.

My counsel is to share honestly with your husband how you feel. If you can't say it verbally, write it down for him, and then offer some alternatives. He may not even be aware of how important it is to you to be making some of the decisions or at least to be involved in the decision process. You might consider saying (or writing) something like this: "I believe that God has created me to be your helpmate. I love you and I would like to help by handling the budget for our household items, at least the ones that affect the home." Try to find some common ground on which you both can agree.

If, after sharing your feelings, your husband doesn't respond, go to your pastor, describe the problem, and see if he can help. Both you and your husband would need to attend this counseling, because he has to understand how you really feel.

QUESTION:

Is it taking authority away from the husband if the wife is the primary wage earner while the husband attends school?

My fiancé is in school, and we're getting married next year. I'm wondering if it would be proper for me to support us while he is in school?

ANSWER:

The two of you need to discuss this issue very honestly. Also, ask yourself if you are willing to work, without any bitterness or resentment, while he goes to school. Do you want to do it? Will it bother you that your husband isn't working? What will happen if you decide to go back to school, or what if you get pregnant? Can he accept that? Would he be willing to drop out of school if necessary? These are all questions you both need to answer honestly.

Personally, I can see nothing wrong with the wife working while her husband is in school, as long as you don't have any children. The apostle Paul says, *"If anyone does not provide for his own, and especially for those of his household, he has denied the faith, and is worse than an unbeliever"* (1 Timothy 5:8). That doesn't mean you can't work while he's in school, but it does mean that over the long-term the husband is to be the provider.

I have real concerns for any couple when the wife immediately goes to work to support them. She can easily become resentful. I've seen it many, many times, particularly if she doesn't want to be the sole provider. I've also noted that sometimes it makes the husband feel very inadequate.

I've known of situations in which the wife worked and the marriages were fine—they didn't have a problem—but I've also seen marriages dissolve because of the role conflicts that were caused. That's just as true when the husband was in seminary and the wife was working full-time.

So be very careful. Pray about it before you make your decision.

QUESTION:

How can I face the future without fear?

I find that as I get older I seem to worry more about our future; how I could earn a living if I lost my job, now that I am over fifty, and what will happen if we can't afford to retire. It seems like I am paralyzed by fear of the future. I know this is wrong, but I don't know how to change it.

ANSWER:

Worry has been described as "taking on a responsibility that belongs to God," and that includes being preoccupied with your future. You have to know where to place your trust.

God's Word says, *"Do not worry then, saying, 'What will we eat?'
or 'What will we drink?' or 'What will we wear for clothing?'* . . .
*Your heavenly Father knows that you need all these things. But seek
first His kingdom and His righteousness; and all these things will be
added to you"* (Matthew 6:31–33).

I encourage you to work first on your spiritual outlook—learning to trust God. If it means starting to give more than you have
been giving, then stretch. Get out of your comfort zone. If it
means that you're hoarding money because it makes you feel
secure, stop doing that. Give that money away and trust God.

It's better to trust God than to have a big retirement account. God is
going to provide for you. Obviously there are things that can happen
over which you have absolutely no control, but God knows that. Most
of our worries are based on future expectations of problems, not our
current circumstances. It's the "what-ifs" that give us the most trouble.

Most people can handle whatever is happening currently, no
matter what it is—cancer or heart disease or loss of a job—but
they go into a depression worrying about what might happen in
the future. You must not expect the worst.

How can you stop worrying? Number one, confess that it's not
your responsibility, turn it over to Jesus, and trust Him. Trust is
the only cure for worry. *"Casting all your anxiety upon Him,
because He cares for you"* (1 Peter 5:7). Do what you can to prepare
for the future and let God do the rest.

QUESTION:

Do you think that God can use a woman to head the household if her husband is weak-willed?

I've heard you talk many times about the wife supporting her
husband and allowing him to be head of the home. However, I
know that I am a better leader in our home than my husband is.
He lets the kids come and go as they want, leave the cars without

gas, leave their rooms a mess, and so forth. He's their buddy and I end up always being the ogre in our family. He never questions a price or challenges any salesperson either. I call around checking on home insurance costs and trying to get the best buy I can; my husband won't do that because our agent is a friend from church.

Answer:

As I've said so often: God never puts two similar people together, because if He did one of them is unnecessary. One of you is going to be a leader and the other is going to be a follower. Sometimes that's the husband, sometimes it's the wife.

The husband's authority is established in God's Word: *"Encourage the young women to love their husbands, to love their children . . . being subject to their own husbands, that the word of God may not be dishonored"* (Titus 2:4–5).

No, I do not believe that you should usurp his authority in the home. Even though he may not have your willpower, he still has God's authority, and God is going to bless your husband. You should work with him, support him, help him to make these decisions, and point out, when necessary, that maybe he didn't get the best buy or make the best decision. But do this in a nonaccusatory manner. That's the role of the supporter. "Not fair," you say? I agree, but it still doesn't change God's Word.

It would be no different from a good general who had a colonel under his authority who was the better military adviser. Napoleon Bonaparte was probably the best example of this. He was a brilliant strategist, but he was not an implementor. After Napoleon's brilliant motivating speeches were over and the battle plans were drawn up, it was the colonel who drew the plans and directed the troops, because Napoleon knew his own strengths and weaknesses.

The same principle is true in your situation. You may be a better manager and organizer and have a more forceful personality, but your role as a wife is to be a helpmate for your husband. Don't undermine his authority; build it up. And every chance you get, rather than telling people how much better you are at managing the household than he is, tell them how much you depend on him and what a godly man he is.

The fact that he wants to be a buddy to his children may not make him the best disciplinarian, but if that's his personality, build on it. Let me assure you that there are many women who would trade their "bully" husband for a "buddy" husband.

QUESTION:

Do you think two people from vastly different financial backgrounds can make a go of marriage?

I'm from a family of modest income and we managed our money very closely. My fiancée is from a very affluent home and her father's annual income is the equivalent of ten years of my father's income. It has caused some problems already, because the restaurants I want to go to she considers to be beneath her. Also, I know what kind of a honeymoon we can afford, and her expectations are at least ten times greater than mine. Her father is willing to pay for it, but I still wonder if this will cause a problem after we're married. Do you believe that these differences are so great that we shouldn't get married?

ANSWER:

Different financial backgrounds can have an enormous impact on a marriage, but different backgrounds don't always dictate a failed marriage. Interestingly enough, the spouse from the wealthy background isn't always the spender—any more than the spouse from a poor background is always a saver. Often the opposite is true.

If your fiancée's family, even though wealthy, managed their money wisely, then she may become a prudent money handler. However, you do need to discuss this very honestly *before* you get married.

I recommend you read *Money in Marriage* (see item 3.1 in the Appendix), because it will help you understand each other: your goals, your aspirations, and how you think about money. Although you come from a lower-income family, it's great that your father and mother helped you learn how to manage money properly.

Very often, though, people from poorer families may feel that they did without while growing up, so now that they're out on their own they're going to live it up; so you need to watch for that as well.

A successful marriage depends on your backgrounds, your training, your personalities, and, most of all, your commitment to the Lord. The most important thing is that you understand each other, know what your goals are, discuss them thoroughly, and see if you can work out these things before you're married. Let me assure you, if you can't work it out before you're married, it won't get any easier once you are married. If you can't agree, you probably do need to postpone your marriage.

Many couples think that because they are Christians they will always be able to work out their problems later. Sadly, Christians get divorced as often as non-Christians do and over the same issues—generally money problems. *"The prudent sees the evil and hides himself, but the naive go on, and are punished for it"* (Proverbs 22:3). So you don't want to go into a marriage without facing a possible problem.

QUESTION:

What can I do about a fiancée who won't discuss financial matters?

I'm twenty-eight and engaged to a twenty-four-year-old Christian woman from a very fine family, but she is totally unwilling to discuss anything financial. I believe that God has called me to the mission field, and I know that I'm not going to make a lot of money. I need to know exactly how my fiancée feels about this, but her parents never talked about money in her home and she won't either. Her father handled all the money and her mother never even knew how much he made or where it was spent. I am in a quandary. I love her, but I don't know what to do.

Answer:

In my opinion you should delay your marriage until you and your fiancée can discuss your finances. You should be very honest with her about your plans for the mission field, and find out how she feels about it. Initially, many young couples say, "Well, God will just provide for us." That's true, but the Bible also says, *"The mind of man plans his way, but the LORD directs his steps"* (Proverbs 16:9).

We're to be a part of God's plan, not just observers of it. If you marry with these uncertainties about your wife's feelings, you may find out too late that she resents your career path and the tight money that's going to accompany it. It is going to be a difficult life at best, and unless you are both absolutely committed it very possibly won't work out.

Don't think that this will get easier once you're married. On the contrary, it will become more difficult. I recommend that the two of you go through our workbook, *Money in Marriage* (see Appendix item 3.1). If you find that she isn't willing to do this, go to her pastor and explain your problem to him. Perhaps he can talk to the two of you together.

If you can't work this out, cancel the marriage plans. Otherwise, you're courting disaster.

Question:

Is keeping the records and paying the bills always the husband's responsibility, or can it be the wife's?

I keep our home financial records because I have more time to do it than my husband, and I believe that I'm more detailed. But I heard a Christian teacher recently say that all these kinds of things should be the husband's responsibility.

ANSWER:

If a wife has the ability to manage the home finances, there's absolutely nothing unscriptural about her doing so, as long as she and her husband work together. They should both develop and maintain the budget—in other words, they both have a part in it. Then the wife can keep the records, but she and her husband should make the decisions together.

It's important, though, that the husband be in control if there are financial problems. That's especially true with delinquent bills. The husband should take charge and work out the arrangements with the creditors. As the biblical authority in the home, the husband should bear the emotional pressure of creditor harassment. Remember what Ephesians 5:25 says: *"Husbands, love your wives, just as Christ also loved the church and gave Himself up for her."*

In the final analysis, if you're the better bookkeeper and paying the bills doesn't create a rift in the marriage, I say go for it. That's why God gave you the gifts you have.

> **Action springs not from thought but from a readiness for responsibility.**
>
> DIETRICH BONHOEFFER

QUESTION:

Do you think husbands and wives should work together in business?

Our children are grown now and I'd like to work in the business again, but my husband says that I shouldn't be involved in the business. He thinks we will have too many fights about it.

Answer:

God established a husband and wife to work as a team. Working together in a business is an option—not a requirement. If you're already having problems and argue a lot and those arguments carry over into the business, perhaps you shouldn't work in the business. Not every couple can spend the long hours together that most businesses require. If that's your situation, get some professional marriage counseling.

God created husbands and wives to be a team, and that relationship is not limited to the home. A husband who refuses to involve his wife in business decisions has, in my opinion, lost the very best counselor that God provided. Some men think their wives don't understand business. Well, let me assure you that most husbands didn't understand the business when they began and some still don't. Learning a business is a process; it's not a revelation given only to men.

How involved a wife should be in the day-to-day operations is going to depend on a lot of things. It will depend on her skills and abilities, her desire to work in the business, and her willingness to accept authority. There is no biblical principle about a wife being excluded from her husband's business.

Since your children are grown, that shouldn't be an influence. How involved you should be in business policy is really a matter to be decided by you and your husband. (All too often husbands want to run things their way, without interference from the ones who know them too well.)

In my opinion, you and your husband should seek godly counsel before this causes a marital rift. I also recommend that you read *Business by the Book* (see item 4.4 in the Appendix). If either of you would prefer, there's a set of cassette tapes available on the same subject. Then, pray and let God help you both make the right decision.

QUESTION:

Do you think it is scriptural for my husband to be employed by me?

I started a small home business several years ago, which has been quite successful. It has grown into a full-time occupation for me, and now that our children are grown my husband would like to quit his job, which he is very dissatisfied with, and work with me. Since it's a business that sells primarily to and through women, though, they're always going to look at me as the boss. I'm afraid this will be a detriment to our marriage and hurt his ego.

ANSWER:

As well as I can tell, there's nothing unscriptural about a man working for a woman. Now whether a husband should work for a wife is a different matter. The Bible gives us a few guidelines, or at least some references to wives who held positions of authority. One of the most familiar is the wife of Lappidoth, Deborah, who was judge over Israel. Her husband obviously came under her authority (see Judges 4:4).

It's difficult for some women to lead and still honor their husbands. Some couples manage it very well, but I would say that the majority I have counseled don't.

The apostle Paul says that *"each individual among you also [is to] love his own wife even as himself; and let the wife see to it that she respect her husband"* (Ephesians 5:33). Any wife needs to be honest about whether she can do that when her husband is in her employ.

However, I would say also that for many couples the issue is not so much the relationship as it is the image. And in our society image can be all-important. If it hurts a man's image and self-esteem to work for his wife, it's better not to do it. But that's a decision that must be worked out, and you and your husband will have to explore that possibility.

If you can still honor and respect your husband while making the decisions in the business that affect him as well, then you are really closer to being one flesh than most couples will ever be. My advice is to forget about the image and do what God leads you both to do. Pray about it, and if you have a peace about it do it.

"The mountains may be removed and the hills may shake, but My lovingkindness will not be removed from you, and My covenant of peace will not be shaken" (Isaiah 54:10).

QUESTION:

Is it a good idea to leave money to my wife in a trust, so she can spend the income but not the principal during her lifetime?

I'm concerned that if I die somebody might come along and trick her out of our insurance money and other assets.

ANSWER:

There's nothing wrong with leaving assets in trust for your spouse. In many instances, if the person doesn't really want to be bothered with the management of the money, it's a good financial planning tool.

However, I must caution you about something. If you're committing these assets (including the income) to be used only for your widow, in my opinion, that is unscriptural. If your wife remarries, she is bound to her new husband and they are to be *one.* And whatever assets she has available should also be available to him.

I understand the argument against that very well: What if she marries a scoundrel? Well, you have to trust her judgment, and she has to be smart enough not to marry a scoundrel, but once married they are to be one person, with no barrier between them. If you leave this money only to her and her future husband has no access to it, even for living expenses, you have created an artificial barrier between them.

The apostle Paul said, *"Wives, be subject to your own husbands, as to the Lord"* (Ephesians 5:22). As a Christian, you don't want to be guilty of interfering in a future relationship. So you need to discuss this with your wife and have a clear understanding. Ultimately, if you do leave it in trust, make the trust flexible enough that her future husband can have access to the funds.

I know that this counsel runs contrary to most of the advice in our generation, but that advice is based primarily on what the world says, not on what God's Word says.

QUESTION:

Can you help me with a frightening situation?

My husband seems to have suffered some deep emotional trauma over the last several months and, in my opinion, is acting very irrationally. He spends money on a whim and he never did before. He'll go out and buy a brand-new boat, a car, maybe even a condominium without even asking me. This is totally out of character for him, and it really frightens me. As the co-owner of our business, I've been hiding money in the company so that I could pay all of our bills and/or employees. Otherwise, I think he would spend it all. Do you think I am wrong to do this?

ANSWER:

You have a unique situation. It is possible that your husband has suffered some kind of emotional or physical trauma that is causing the irrational behavior. However, many men go through what are called midlife crises in their forties or fifties, and that could be what's happening to your husband. If so, it will pass; usually it's just temporary.

Encourage your husband to seek some professional help—to make sure it isn't something more emotionally or physically serious. I agree with you that you cannot, at this point, turn over all the finances to him while he's in this irresponsible stage. You have a responsibility as a wife, a Christian, and a co-owner of this business to ensure that your bills are paid and the payroll is met.

There is an example in Samuel 25 when a wife had to assume the responsibility because of her husband's irresponsibility. When Nabal was acting foolishly before David, his wife, Abigail, intervened to keep David from killing him. She was blessed for her action by God, and Nabal was punished for his irresponsibility.

In Proverbs 12:4 we are told, *"An excellent wife is the crown of her husband, but she who shames him is as rottenness in his bones."* Therefore, you want to do everything you can to support your husband. I encourage you to go about your duties in a quiet and confidential manner, so as not to shame him in front of your employees or the creditors.

QUESTION:

Should we leave our daughter's inheritance in a trust?

My husband and I are both committed Christians. Over our lifetime we have accumulated a large estate, and we'd like to begin sharing that estate with our children. After hearing one of your radio programs about the wife who separated from her husband as a result of her personal affluence, we wonder if we should leave an inheritance to our daughter. If we do, should it be left in trust for her alone or should we include our son-in-law?

ANSWER:

There's nothing wrong with leaving assets to your children. An inheritance, at least in the Old Testament, was a very common Jewish tradition. Typically a daughter would inherit property only if the family had no sons, but if she was married they would give her a dowry that she would take into her marriage. Then she would pass that dowry along to her own family.

If you're going to leave an inheritance to your daughter, I would suggest that you carefully consider how much you're going to leave her. I'd be cautious about putting it in trust so that the funds are never under the control of your daughter and her husband. By doing that, you are usurping God's authority over their lives.

When a wife brings assets into a marriage and they are "protected" from her husband, with very few exceptions this creates tensions in the marriage, particularly if a husband feels his wife doesn't trust him and is independent of him. I've witnessed this in couples I've counseled. All too often those marriages dissolved. I encourage you not to do that to your children.

QUESTION:

Should husbands and wives ever keep their assets separate?

I'm a widow who recently remarried. My husband and I are both in our late sixties. We have been wondering if it would be right if we keep our assets separated? He would keep his assets for his children, and I would keep my assets separated for my children.

ANSWER:

A great thing about God's Word is that it is clear and concise, and it doesn't regard ages, assets, or opinions. According to God's

Word, once you're married, you and your new husband are one. Period.

If you both willingly agree to keep the assets in trust for your children, that's fine. However, you need to be very sure that neither of you is doing this because of intimidation—either from each other or from other members of the family. I'm concerned that if you keep your assets separate your marriage will suffer. Spend some time praying about this, seeking God's plan for your life, and seeking some good counsel.

Even though you are in your sixties, God has still given the leadership of the home to the husband, and you as his wife are to honor him, as he is to love you unreservedly. I trust that after you pray about this and seek God's wisdom you'll be in agreement about the distribution of these assets.

QUESTION:

Should an engaged couple have money saved before marriage?

My fiancé believes that we need at least $10,000 in the bank before we get married. However, by the time we have paid off our school loans and the other small debts that we have, this could take several years. I'm not sure that is the right thing to do or that I'm willing to wait. Can you give us some guidelines?

ANSWER:

If I could, I would tell every young couple getting married, "Go into your marriage with a surplus, not with a debt." Unfortunately, most young people go into marriage owing money. Having a surplus is not absolutely necessary, but it does make the transition a lot easier.

When two people enter marriage, it's a difficult adjustment, under the best of circumstances, because each is an independent human being. But if they go into the marriage with a debt, it's even more difficult, because then they have to deal with financial pressures.

I would say that, as a minimum, you should have enough money saved to pay for your honeymoon and the incidental expenses that will occur over the first couple of months of marriage.

The actual amount that any one couple is going to need is going to vary. If both of you need cars and clothes and all of the expenses associated with setting up a household, then your need for savings may be somewhat higher. In my opinion, most young couples should have a couple thousand dollars or more after the wedding and honeymoon expenses have been paid.

But beyond that, the amount of savings is not all that critical. Keep in mind the biblical principle: *"There is precious treasure and oil in the dwelling of the wise, but a foolish man swallows it up"* (Proverbs 21:20). You do need some savings in anticipation of your marriage, because there will be expenses. Without savings, you may end up in debt for the necessary expenses. Do you need $10,000? Probably not. Your fiancé is probably going to the extreme.

Obviously, many couples get married without a savings account and they still make it; however, the statistic in our society is that about half the marriages in America don't make it and about 80 percent of them point to financial problems as the cause. You're a lot better off if you go into your marriage without a preexisting difficulty called debt.

10
INSURANCE

THE AREA OF INSURANCE HAS GOTTEN increasingly confusing for most people. That's hardly surprising since there are so many different types of insurance that come in an almost infinite variety of options. If you can say it, there's an insurance company out there somewhere that will write a policy to cover it.

Almost as soon as a child can walk you're faced with the choices about life insurance, health insurance, prescription coverage—even long-term care insurance. Once you determine that your newborn needs life insurance to protect his or her insurability, you must decide on term or whole life or single premium annuity versus dividend-accumulating universal life.

Wow! Things used to be a lot simpler back when doctors

> When you stop to think about it, there is no such thing as a future decision. You face only present decisions that will affect what will happen in the future.
>
> DENIS WAITLEY

made home visits, babies were birthed by midwives, and Uncle Charlie fashioned Uncle Bob's coffin in his carpentry shop.

I hope this section will help sort out some of the most commonly asked questions about insurance for you.

QUESTION:

Can you give me some information about life insurance?

We are the parents of two children, and I don't know what type of insurance is best for us. I'm confused about buying whole life insurance versus term insurance.

ANSWER:

Buying life insurance depends on your age, health, and how much money you have in your budget to spend on it. *Term insurance* is usually the cheapest in the short term. You buy term insurance for a determinable period of time—perhaps for one year, five years, ten years, or twenty years—hence the name "term." The cost of any life insurance is going to depend on two things: your age and how long you'll need the insurance.

Term insurance is the least expensive and the most common kind of insurance available. However, the longer you keep term, the costlier it gets. One of the arguments for buying *term* insurance is that you can buy the cheapest insurance and invest the difference elsewhere—typically mutual funds, or the like, that will accumulate more money over the long run. When you look at it financially, that argument seems to be true; but, in practical fact, the majority of people don't get around to investing the difference in the money. They usually spend it.

Conversely, when you buy *cash value* insurance you pay a fixed price per month for the duration of the contract period—often the rest of your life. Obviously, because they are insuring you over a much longer period of time, the insurance companies are going to charge more for the policy up front. Then the companies take a portion of that premium overcharge and the accumulating cash value to offset the company's increasing liability as you get older.

Common sense says that a thirty-year-old is at less risk of dying than a sixty-year-old. Therefore the company overcharges the younger person and keeps part of that money in reserve, so that when the insured is sixty years old the company can offset some of its risk. That's the basic difference between *term* and *cash value*. It's not that one is more or less costly; they average out essentially the same over your lifetime. The only difference is that at a younger age you can afford more *term*, which is when most people need the maximum amount of insurance.

Bear in mind that, with few exceptions, most of the cash in your *cash value* policy belongs to the insurance company and not to you. There are some very good policies—both *term* and *cash value*—now available. Some *cash value* policies invest in mutual funds and other investments that help offset the increasing cost of the premium. Some will return a portion of the accumulated cash or dividends to the insured.

Let me make it clear that no one insurance plan fits everybody. *Term* insurance is great for younger couples and people who have a short-term need, and I heartily recommend it. Usually the maximum amount of insurance is needed during the most critical years of your life: generally when you're a young family with children. As you get older, the *term* insurance is going to get decidedly more expensive, and you can drop some of it. So my advice about buying insurance is to shop, shop, shop.

The majority of people do need some kind of permanent insurance, but as they get older the tendency is to drop the *term* and carry no insurance, which is not a good idea. I also recommend that you avoid buying life insurance, or any other financial product, from a part-time salesperson. Stick with a professional—someone who is in the business to make a living from it. The reason I say that is because I have seen many part-time people who've sold insurance, investments, and other financial products and then went on their way, and the people they insured were left with nobody to follow up later. You'll get a lot better service if you buy from a professional, even if you have to pay a little more in terms of commission.

QUESTION:

After we buy insurance on my husband, do you believe that my children and I also need life insurance?

ANSWER:

In general, if you are working and generating income that is necessary for your family's welfare, I'd say that you do need insurance. However, when in doubt, put the insurance on the primary wage earner, which in most instances is the husband.

Because your children don't generate income for the family, the only reason to insure them is to cover the potential cost of a burial. Therefore, if a tragedy happened, the burial costs would not be a great financial burden on the family. One additional argument for insuring children is so that when they are older they will be insurable. However, very few young adults are uninsurable.

In summary, if funds are limited, insure the husband (or the primary wage earner) first; second, insure the wife because she has an economic benefit to the family—especially if the family is dependent on her income. Even if she doesn't work outside the home, there will be a significant financial burden if she dies.

The primary rule: Put the money where it is needed the most.

QUESTION:

Is it a good idea to cash in our life insurance to pay for our children's college education?

ANSWER:

Perhaps, but remember this: If you cash in your life insurance, the face value (death benefit) of your policy will be reduced by the amount of the loan—that's the initial loan plus accumulated interest. If you decide to borrow from your policy, make a commitment to pay that money back.

Actually, unless you have an extremely large insurance plan, you probably don't have enough money in your insurance plan to provide for your children's college education, so you'll probably need other resources also.

QUESTION:

We're sixty years old. Do we need long-term care insurance?

We've been looking at what would happen if one of us went into a nursing home. We know that nursing home care is very expensive, so we've been looking around at some long-term care insurance, but it's all very confusing. Do we need long-term care insurance and, if so, where is the best place to buy it?

ANSWER:

Let's look at the purpose of long-term care insurance. Essentially, long-term care insurance is designed to cover the costs for those who go into nursing homes—either for a short period of time or,

> ## The best way to predict your future is to create it.
>
> ANONYMOUS

more normally, for the rest of their lives. Like all insurance contracts, the long-term care policies vary widely, so you need to read the contracts carefully or buy from a professional agent who will explain the options to you. The normal purpose of long-term care insurance is to protect your asset base.

When someone goes into a nursing home, the state draws from the assets of that person to pay the costs of care until those assets are exhausted. In most states, the spouse of the patient does have the right to withhold some assets—essentially a home, an automobile, and some amount of cash. That will vary by state. If you don't have a substantial estate, long-term care insurance is not necessary, in my opinion.

There's a mistaken notion that if nursing home patients are on Medicaid instead of long-term care insurance they don't get the same treatment in the nursing home. I have found that not to be true. We could argue about whether nursing home care is adequate or inadequate, but in general the quality of care is based on the particular nursing home—not how the bills are being paid.

QUESTION:

Do you think the ads on television that guarantee insurance even if you have cancer are legitimate?

ANSWER:

Be very careful. There is an old cliché that says, "If a deal sounds too good to be true it probably is"; and most of these deals sound too good to be true. Before you sign, read the contract. Before you pay, read it again.

Normally, existing health conditions are excluded in insurance contracts, and some exclude any unknown conditions for from one to five years. The cost of this insurance per dollar of coverage is very high, and usually there are many exclusions.

Understand that any insurance company is a profit center. They don't give away insurance, and there is no free lunch when you're dealing with a commercial entity like an insurance company. In my opinion, these plans are very deceptive and not worth the money you'd pay for them.

QUESTION:

What are my options for health insurance now that I've lost my job?

I won't have any insurance when I leave this company.

ANSWER:

There are only a few options available to most people. Under the COBRA Act, you can continue the insurance that your company offers (if they have twenty or more employees). However, you probably will pay the total cost of the insurance—the employee's portion and the company's portion, plus a small administrative fee. In general, it's about 103 percent of the total cost.

I would use that provision only if you have a preexisting condition that precludes you from getting insurance elsewhere. Usually, the coverage in a company's group plan is better than what you can buy on your own, but most people don't need that kind of coverage. More commonly, what you need is a higher-deductible disaster insurance—in other words, a major medical insurance plan with a $500 to $1,000 deductible.

There are some alternative plans available that are called *share cost* plans. In other words, you pool your money with other people and the accumulated surplus provides for the major costs of the members of the plan. You'll find information about these in item 14.1 in the Appendix. That principle is discussed in God's Word: *"At this present time your abundance being a supply for their need that their abundance also may become a supply for your need, that there may be equality"* (2 Corinthians 8:14).

Additionally, some states have state insurance health plans for those who have been turned down for health insurance—for whatever reason.

Unfortunately, the bottom line is that there are no real bargains in health insurance these days.

QUESTION:

Should I add my dependents to my company health insurance plan?

We have the option to join our company's group health insurance plan, but it's going to cost us about $200 per month and our budget is very tight. Is this a good buy?

ANSWER:

Let me assure you that whatever private insurance you could buy that would have comparable benefits is going to cost a lot more than what a group insurance plan normally will cost. Group rates usually are lower and the benefits are better. Personally, I would make the budget sacrifice to join the group plan if possible.

Many families gamble by not having insurance, but one major medical expense—one child with leukemia, one heart attack, one major accident—can wipe out their finances for a very long time.

In my opinion, if you have the option to put your spouse and children on your company group insurance plan, you should do it. You may have to sacrifice in other areas to do it, but it will be well worth it.

QUESTION:

Do I really need the group disability insurance my company offers?

ANSWER:

In my opinion, a group disability through an employer is one of the best bargains available in insurance. You do need to review the plan carefully, though, because there are many different options in any disability plan. Choose those that fit your need.

Some plans are short-term and will cover you until you're qualified for Social Security disability, some will cover you only for a few months, and some will cover you for the rest of your life. The cost of each is different, so you need to read the policies and buy only what you need.

In my opinion, disability insurance is not one of those critical areas of insurance. First, I would provide for life and health insurance, and then, if you can afford it within your budget, decide on disability. Many professionals—doctors, lawyers, pilots, dentists—often will carry disability plans so that if they can't practice their profession for whatever reason (usually health reasons), their incomes are protected. Many of those plans are very comprehensive but also very expensive.

Individually purchased disability policies are usually much more expensive than group plans; but, again, dollar for dollar many of those are also good bargains. In my opinion, if you have enough money in your budget to provide for your life and health insurance needs and a good disability is available through your employer, you should take advantage of it.

QUESTION:

Can you tell me the benefits and liabilities of long-term care insurance?

My mother is eighty years old and we are considering long-term care insurance for her.

ANSWER:

Yes, basically long-term care insurance means insurance to provide the care required in a nursing home. Usually this is in-service care (as opposed to home care). Long-term care insurance is best used by people who want to protect their assets.

Let's say, for instance, that your mother had $500,000 worth of assets. If she went into a nursing home, the state would require that her assets be exhausted before the state would assume the costs. The exception to that rule would be if she had a living spouse who was not confined to a care facility. Most states will exempt some assets. At best, in her case, she would still have $250,000 worth of assets available, excluding the house and car, that would have to be exhausted before the state Medicare would pick up the costs.

I'd estimate that an average nursing home costs somewhere around $30,000 to $40,000 per year. So, essentially, in your mother's case, the first ten years of her coverage would be her expense. The purpose of long-term care insurance is to protect those assets, because after some period of time the insurance would pick up the costs and, therefore, her assets would not be dissipated.

So, in general, people with large amounts of assets would do well to buy the long-term care; those who have a smaller asset base probably wouldn't. For instance, let's assume that a single seventy-five-year-old individual owned a home, a car, and a small savings account of about $100,000 total worth. That person's nursing home stay would consume all those assets in approximately two and one-half years. The state would then pick up the costs for as long as he or she would require.

If the premium cost of the long-term care insurance was in the range of $5,000 to $7,000 per year, it would take ten years of insurance payments to equal two and one-half years of nursing home costs. At that point, it's really a toss-up as to whether it's a good deal.

Long-term care insurance is expensive because the cost of nursing home care is expensive. However, it is generally appropriate for those with larger amounts of assets.

QUESTION:

Do you recommend supplemental insurance for Medicare?

My parents need a health care supplement. They both have Medicare but no supplemental policy.

ANSWER:

Yes, there is a substantial difference between what medical care costs and what Medicare will pay. I recommend that you purchase a Medi-Gap policy. There are a variety of companies that offer these policies (see item 14.2 in the Appendix). The nonpaid portion of medical health care can put a great strain on your parents' finances. In my estimation, Medi-Gap insurance is a necessity for the vast majority of Medicare recipients.

QUESTION:

What can you tell me about prepaid funerals and memorial societies, and would this be a benefit to my husband and me?

ANSWER:

Prepaying funeral expenses basically means that you negotiate with a funeral home or association, often at a much reduced rate, and prepay the costs. That includes the cost of transportation, the funeral home expenses, the viewing, and often even the plot. Funeral costs today can be pretty substantial, and by negotiating in advance you can often save between 25 and 40 percent of the average cost of a funeral. In my estimation that is a good investment for a couple approaching their "super" senior years.

The memorial society is a nonprofit organization that negotiates with commercial funeral homes around the country. They do it on a large scale so the costs are significantly reduced. I've been part of a memorial society for the better part of thirty years. It's a very inexpensive way to pay for a burial. You can reach the memorial society through the Web site or phone number listed in item 14.3 in the Appendix.

QUESTION:

Is variable adjustable life insurance a good idea?

My husband has been retired for about three years, and recently an insurance agent from our church recommended that my husband buy a variable adjustable life insurance policy on himself. It seems very expensive to me; it's going to cost us almost $500 per month. I don't think that we can afford it, because we are living on a fixed pension, but I don't want to be foolish, either.

ANSWER:

Because of your husband's age, I recommend that you not buy this insurance. Remember, the purpose of insurance is to provide for somebody in the event of death. If your husband has already provided for you in the event of his death, meaning through a pension, or Social Security, or some combination, then you probably don't need life insurance except for burial expenses. In my opinion, $500 a month for somebody living on a fixed pension is an excessive expense. I would avoid it. I think that your insurance agent has not done you a great service by recommending this.

QUESTION:

Should we cancel our current insurance policy, withdraw the cash value, buy some term insurance, and invest the difference?

I've heard you discuss the area of life insurance, including term and whole-life insurance, quite often on your radio program, but I've never heard you discuss this particular question. Our agent is the one who is recommending it. I feel a little bit hesitant about this and am not sure we should do that.

ANSWER:

Well, the principle of selling your insurance and investing the difference is not really much different from buying term and investing the difference. The purpose would be to make a potentially greater return, generally speaking, on the cash value of your insurance. Your insurance adviser, who probably sells investments as well, wants you to cash out the policy and invest it with him.

In my opinion (and it's one based on observation), the vast majority of people I've known who have done that have ended up with less money over the long run because, inevitably, they got into something they didn't understand—typically an investment—or they spent the money and bought short-term insurance plans, which although much cheaper in the beginning, became way too expensive as they got older, and they ended up dropping their insurance.

I'm sure this works out well for some people, and perhaps the agent has your interests at heart, but just be very careful. If you're going to do this, you need to establish a plan and stick to it.

QUESTION:

Is life insurance wise for someone about to graduate from college?

Our son is about to graduate, and he's been inundated by insurance agents on the campus trying to sell him life insurance. I don't see that he particularly needs life insurance, and since he doesn't have a job he can't afford it now, but their argument is that he won't be insurable later unless he buys the insurance now. Is that likely?

ANSWER:

What the agents are saying is that if he buys his insurance now while he's young, it will cost less and he'll be guaranteed insurability. And that is true to some degree, but let me explain.

Even though the insurance costs him less when he's younger,

he's going to pay for it for a longer period of time; therefore, essentially it's going to cost him the same. Whether he buys it younger, at a lower cost, and pays for a longer period of time, or buys it at an older age and pays more for it but for a shorter period of time, it still comes out to be about the same. The insurance company is going to make a profit.

In terms of his insurability, if he were uninsured and something happened—anything from a heart attack to cancer—he might not be insurable. However, statistically the vast majority of people below the age of fifty are insurable.

I would counsel your son to wait until he has a stable job and then take a look at insurance. He should buy insurance that is guaranteed expandable—in other words the company guarantees he can buy more at a later time—but he probably shouldn't buy much beyond a burial policy right now. Then after he's married and has a need for more insurance he can buy more.

QUESTION:

Are there any alternatives for less-expensive health insurance for people who are self-insured?

We are having a very difficult time getting health insurance for our family, and when we do qualify it's extremely expensive. Currently we are paying about $1,300 a month out of a $3,000 salary just for health insurance for myself, my wife, and our two children.

> Only man clogs his happiness with care, destroying what is, with thoughts of what may be.
>
> JOHN DRYDEN

ANSWER:

In all honesty, there are not many good alternatives available anymore. Health care and, consequently, health insurance are very expensive, depending on the coverage you desire.

My recommendation is to look at some major medical insurance policies. These are policies that have sizable minimums—$1,000 to $5,000. They're meant to cover only major expenses, like heart attacks, cancer, and the like. They're going to be less expensive because they cover less.

QUESTION:

Is there an alternative to long-term care insurance?

My wife is disabled and eventually will need nursing home care. Currently she is only forty years old, but the average person with her disease will be in a nursing home by age fifty. We've checked to see if I can purchase long-term care insurance for her, but it is very, very expensive and, in most instances, they've turned us down.

ANSWER:

There are several alternatives I would recommend. First, you need to pray about this, and you need to share this need with the body of Christ, your friends, your family, and those in your Sunday school class and Bible studies. Let them know what your needs are. Christians are supposed to help one another.

The probability that any insurance carrier would write long-term care insurance for your wife is very slight, and if they did it would be exorbitantly expensive. So you're going to be dependent on other Christians or the government to help you.

The way the system works, in most states, is that if your wife went into the nursing home she'd be required to exhaust her assets, which in many states would equate to half of your joint assets, excluding your home and an automobile and some amount of cash. I hate to think that God's people would require the state to take care of Christians, but, unfortunately, in our generation that seems to be the case.

Pray about this, and leave the results in God's hands. He can provide for her, and He will. *"He will call upon Me, and I will answer him; I will be with him in trouble; I will rescue him, and honor him"* (Psalm 91:15).

QUESTION:

How does insurance compare to other investments?

We're getting to the point of being debt free, as you have suggested. We still owe on our home, but we have a plan to pay it off in about ten years, and we're looking at some long-term investing. Our insurance agent, a friend from church, has suggested that we get into insurance and annuities as an investment. Is this a good idea?

ANSWER:

The return depends, in great part, on the insurance plan, and there are as many insurance plans available as there are agents. First, you need to separate apples and oranges, because every insurance plan has two components to it.

One component is the insurance, and that's going to cost you a fixed amount of money. Insurance companies are in business to make a profit, and they're going to do so by guaranteeing your life and charging a premium to do so.

Another component of the insurance plan is the accumulation of cash or perhaps an investment that is the equivalent of a mutual fund. You need to compare how much that part earns to other investments. In other words, if you're going to buy an insurance plan with a variable annuity component—meaning it is basically a mutual fund—compare the earnings of that fund against what you could get in an outside mutual fund if you had invested the same dollars. This may be difficult for you as a purchaser, but your agent can do it for you, and I would insist that he do so prior to buying insurance from him.

Remember, apples and apples. Insurance costs you some amount of money; the amount of money you pay above that is going to be the investment side. If you're looking at the investment return, simply subtract the cost of insurance and compare the insurance company's investment return against a good-quality mutual fund.

Question:

Should we cash out my life insurance policy to pay the bills we owe?

We're having some financial difficulties and have gotten behind on our credit card bills due to an illness. We also owe some doctors. I think that we should cash out my policy and pay these bills, but my wife doesn't think it is a good idea.

Answer:

You should be very careful about cashing out your life insurance policy to pay down bills, because it's very easy to deal with the symptom—the debt—but if you don't solve the problem, the symptom will return.

Prior to doing anything along this line, which is very much like a consolidation loan, and to be sure that you aren't going to get further in debt, you first need to get on a budget and live on it for at least six months.

As far as cashing out your life insurance, you need to exercise caution. You have several options available. One is to cancel the policy, take the cash value out, and use it, in which case then you have no insurance. Another is to simply borrow the cash value and pay it back. You'll pay the insurance company a higher interest rate than they're paying you on the policy. The difference is normally 2 or 3 percent.

The third option you have is to borrow the money out of the policy and not pay it back, in which case the outstanding loan reduces the death benefit of your insurance by the amount of the loan, plus interest. If you allow this to go on long enough, eventually it can consume the entire value of your life insurance.

There is nothing particularly wrong with your idea, but I would be very careful. Be sure that you've solved the problem first.

QUESTION:

Now that I've become a stay-at-home mom and have lost the health insurance I had when I worked, do I really need insurance?

We took your advice and paid off all of our debt, with the exception of our home. My husband has health insurance coverage through his company, but he didn't elect to cover us as dependents.

ANSWER:

Most Americans are going to need health insurance at one time or another, and that includes stay-at-home moms. You can get sick just like anyone else. My encouragement to you is to find some kind of insurance policy. Often company policies, like your husband's, will open up periodically for dependents to become a part of the plan. So if that happens I would take that option, because it's almost always going to be cheaper than buying your own insurance.

An alternative is to look into a major medical plan—one of the Christian co-op self-help health plans (see item 14.1 in the Appendix). In my opinion you should have health insurance.

QUESTION:

What are our options for health insurance?

My husband is leaving the company he has been with for nearly fifteen years to go into his own business. We are losing access to our 401(k) plan, and we are going to lose our health insurance.

ANSWER:

Under what is called the COBRA Act, your husband can continue his insurance for up to eighteen months. However, in order to do so, you'll have to pay the full cost of the insurance, plus a small premium. That means you'll pay whatever the company is paying for it plus about a 3 to 5 percent handling fee for the insurance, and that can be quite expensive.

I would say that most company policies will cost between $600 and $800 per month. The other option you have is to find private insurance, which is going to be very expensive, or perhaps look into a Christian health plan (see item 14.1 in the Appendix).

As far as your 401(k), that money is still yours. It depends on the contract with the company whether you can leave your 401(k) there. But you can always transfer it to an IRA of your own. You can call any mutual fund company or brokerage house, and they will handle that transaction for you at no expense. Just explain what you want to do.

Although you don't have the 401(k) available to invest in any longer, there are other retirement accounts, including the SEP-IRA, which is available to self-employed people. It's a very good plan. It doesn't have an employer's portion as a benefit, but it will allow you to invest for retirement up to $22,500 per year, depending on your income.

11

INVESTING

THE TOPIC OF INVESTING IS OF GREAT interest to millions of people, since much of their long-term savings is tied up in stocks, bonds, land, and other investments. From 1995 until early 2000, it seemed that investing questions dominated my daily call-in broadcast. A lot of people were making record profits in the stock markets and ordinary citizens wanted in on the action.

Then, in 2000, the questions shifted from "How can I get rich in the market?" to "How can we keep what we have?" Why? Because the markets dropped (as markets are prone to do), but the debts of the average family didn't.

Investment decisions are never easy. But if you will hear and apply God's principles, most of the wrong reasons to invest will be eliminated.

The Bible isn't mute on investing. Quite the contrary; it is quite vocal.

QUESTION:

I recently left one company for another and my new company offers a 401(k), but they won't allow me to transfer my old 401(k) into their account. What should I do with the money that is in my previous company's 401(k)?

ANSWER:

First, you should verify with your previous employer that you have the right to leave your account there and, if so, for how long. Also, ask what control you have over the money. Otherwise, you'll need to roll it out of that 401(k) into your own IRA account.

Since your new company won't allow you to put that money into their 401(k), you'll need to set up a private IRA. Though IRAs are limited in the amount you can invest in them per year, there is no limit in a rollover IRA, so you can transfer your savings into an account with any financial institution you desire. Any bank, mutual fund, or stock investment company will set up this IRA for you at no cost.

My recommendation is to choose a good mutual fund company and roll your money into one of their flexible mutual fund accounts. Then you can spread the money out among the variety of funds they offer. These range from the most conservative, which might be their bond funds, to speculative stock funds, if you desire. As I said, any financial institution you select will set up the IRA for you and will transfer the funds into that account. Most companies provide at least a quarterly accounting of your assets.

If I were choosing a company, I would use a neutral source, such as *Money* magazine or *Consumer Reports* magazine, and select one of their top five companies to do the rollover.

QUESTION:

What is the best thing to do with my wife's recently inherited $200,000?

She wants to put it into a secure savings account, like a government security, but I disagree. I think we need to invest the money. However, I have a bad investment record, and my wife is concerned that we'll lose the money. This issue has turned out to be a major conflict in our marriage, and I'm not sure exactly what to do about it. Can you give us some help?

ANSWER:

First, you need to seek godly counsel. Your wife may have just cause for the way she feels. I suspect there are other issues at play here, and you need to deal with those issues, because they are far more important than the money. Above all, don't let a disagreement about finances destroy a good marriage.

Perhaps you can seek a reasonable compromise with your wife. For example, rather than investing the entire $200,000, put $150,000 into a secure account, perhaps a one- or two-year CD (so she'll know where it is). Then you could invest the remaining $50,000. But, get your wife involved in the decisions so she'll understand the options you're choosing, why you're choosing them, and what the risks are.

You don't want to overdo the risks here either. Keep the risk reasonable and allow her to help choose the investments. My recommendation would be to use quality mutual funds, because they have professional management (and if the mutual fund doesn't do extremely well you won't be totally at fault).

The two of you should have specific plans for the money— education, retirement, or whatever—and then target your investment plan to accomplish that end. If your wife is involved in the decision making, she should be a lot more at peace. Above all else, don't let financial decisions interfere with the health of your marriage.

"He who troubles his own house will inherit wind, and the foolish will be servant to the wise-hearted" (Proverbs 11:29).

> **An investment in knowledge pays the best interest.**
>
> BENJAMIN FRANKLIN

QUESTION:

Can you tell me where to find a financial planner who can help us with our long-term goals? And what should we expect to pay?

ANSWER:

In item 15.1 in the Appendix you'll find some sources for financial planners. But bear in mind that you need to find a financial planner who fits your personality and what you're trying to accomplish, and be sure to ask the right questions up front.

The first decision you need to make is whether you're looking for a fee-only financial planner (one paid by the hour or by a set fee) or for a commission-based planner (one who earns his or her income as a result of selling products—mutual funds, stocks and bonds, insurance policies).

There's no right or wrong way to bill for financial services. I personally prefer a fee-only planner, because I feel like I have more control when I pay. Some people prefer to have it included in the investments they're buying. Over the long run, you're still going to pay the cost, no matter which way you choose, because that person has to make a living. You'll either pay it as a fee or as a percentage of your investments.

In my opinion, when you're looking for a good financial planner you need to look for a person with longevity in that field. My personal criteria is something like this: someone who has been in the financial planning business for ten years or longer, someone who has the right credentials (the CFP, indicating certification, and other credentials that reflect his or her training), and someone with references. When you get the references, make the effort to call no less than five of the planner's previous clients.

When you call, ask very pointed questions: "How did you like the service? Did that person make money or lose money for you? Is he or she readily available? Do you have good communication with this person?" Don't be bashful; ask the right questions. The bottom line is to find a person who will give you good financial advice so that you'll make more money on your money (after his or her fee) than you'd make if you just invested the money yourself in a good CD.

After all, you don't need a financial adviser to help you park the money in a CD or some other fixed income investment. So you need to weigh the planner's credentials and look at his or her results. If the results show that after the planner's fee you made less money than you could make in a CD, go do it yourself.

QUESTION:

Do you think I should accept the new plan my company has offered for its employees?

We're not a dot-com company, but we're a start-up company in the high-tech business, and the company is offering stock options for the employees in lieu of raises. Do you think this would be a good deal or a bad deal?

ANSWER:

You probably won't know that for several years. Obviously, it's going to depend on the company and how well it does. What you'll be buying into is the long-term future of the company and the long-term growth of its stock. That's what risk and return is all about. You must decide. Be advised that, in many cases, when you're issued controlled stock you may not be able to sell it for some period of time. So you must have confidence that the company is going to be around and be viable for the long term.

Tech companies in general, not just the dot-com companies, are difficult to track, simply because they haven't been around very long. There are lots of people who took stock options in lieu of income in a tech or dot-com company who find now that their options are worthless. But if you're with a good company

> An investor is a man who plays the horses on a merry-go-round.
>
> ANONYMOUS

and you trust the management, then taking a risk in the company you're working for is a great way for a lot of ordinary working people to make a lot of money. And that's true not just for the executives of the company; that goes all the way down to employees on every level.

I read someplace that if you had worked for Microsoft in the early days and had taken their stock in lieu of annual increases, your stock would be worth tens of millions of dollars today. Of course, not every company is going to be a Microsoft, but some of them will be.

I believe that a company offering stock in lieu of raises is a good idea. First, it keeps the capital working inside the company, and it encourages longevity in the senior employees, because they have a vested interest in the company. On the other hand, there are employees who have worked for a company for several years and have nothing to show for it. So it depends on your confidence factor in the company.

QUESTION:

How do I start an investment portfolio?

I'm retiring and getting a lump sum from my company.

ANSWER:

Caution: If you've never managed money before, you're in potential danger when you attempt to manage your own money. There's a tendency to look at the distribution as a surplus that can never be exhausted, and that definitely isn't true. If you don't stick to a good budget and maintain the good habits you've developed over the years, you'll find this money evaporating like ice on a hot summer day.

My first suggestion is to take that money and park it in a good safe place like a Treasury bill or a CD for at least one year, and don't touch it! You may not maximize your return, but you're going to minimize the losses by doing that. Then you need to read all you can about investing, pray about it, and seek godly counsel. Find a good financial planner who has been around for a long time who can advise you. And you need to start very slowly.

Say to yourself, "Preservation of capital is more important than gains." As Will Rogers once said, "The return *of* my money is far more important than return *on* my money." Keep that in mind, seek good counsel, pray about it, and take plenty of time.

"A tranquil heart is life to the body" (Proverbs 14:30).

QUESTION:

Should I take a lump-sum payment of all my retirement money or an annuity that would pay out on a quarterly basis?

I'm retiring from a company for which I've worked for more than thirty years, and it has offered me those two options. My wife and I need your help.

ANSWER:

Actually, it depends on your personality to some degree. But, from the financial perspective, you need to compare the two and see which would pay you the best. For example, let's assume the sum is $100,000. If you invested that money securely, you would earn about 7 percent on it—or $7,000 per year.

To compare that income against taking the annuity, the first question you have to ask is, Is it a one-life or two-life annuity? In other words, if you choose a one-life annuity the payout would be higher, but the money stops when you die. If you choose the two-life annuity, the payout is going to be lower, but your wife would be assured of the money in the event of your death. So you need to compare both options.

Let's assume that the annuity is a two-life (because if you took a lump sum it would belong to both of you) and the payout from the annuity is $6,000 per year. Then you're better off taking the lump sum, because you would make $1,000 a year more on $100,000 by managing the money yourself. So I suggest that you compare the lump sum and what you could earn on it against what the annuity would pay. In addition, I heartily recommend that you find a good financial planner to help you do this evaluation.

QUESTION:

Should our rental houses be debt free?

We've heard you discuss being debt free many times, and we believe that is a good principle, but my husband says that rental houses don't fall under the same category as a personal home and that we can expand our investments by borrowing on our rental homes to buy more rental homes.

ANSWER:

In general, your husband is correct. As investments, rental homes don't have to be debt free, as long as you have a good cash-flow plan, you understand the rental home business, and you're sure that the income from the rental homes can pay all the expenses. Those expenses include the mortgage payments (based on eleven months of income so you have one month per year to set aside for long-term maintenance). Also, that way, if the rental is vacant a month or so it won't put a strain on your personal finances.

Rental houses have some distinct tax advantages, because you're able to depreciate them. Also, rental income is excluded from self-employment tax, which is a benefit that's hard to beat. Also, because you can buy rental homes in different areas, even in different price ranges, they help to balance your portfolio.

The disadvantage, obviously, of rental housing is the hassle: repairs, upkeep, and managing renters. As long as you can handle that and you understand realistically the ins and outs of residential real estate, rental houses are a good investment.

I do believe in having your home debt free, but there's some logic in having mortgages on rental houses, and using that capital to expand your rental base. Sometime prior to retirement, though, your goal should be to have the rental houses debt free—for two reasons: it generates more income per month, and a bad economy won't wipe you out.

"The wisdom of the prudent is to understand his way" (Proverbs 14:8).

QUESTION:

Should we buy a home in the town where my husband will be attending college for two years?

We decided that he needs to go back to grad school to improve his education, so we sold our home. If we shouldn't buy a home in the town where the college is located, what should we do with the money from the sale of our house until he gets out of grad school?

ANSWER:

Generally speaking, three years in one location is the minimal amount of time for buying a home. The reason for that is when you move into a new area you need time to decide where you want to buy. Then you have to qualify and purchase a home. Then, when you're ready to leave, it takes time to sell the home. There's always the chance that it might not be the best time in the economy, so you might not be able to sell it immediately; then you're stuck with a house in a location where you don't want to live. So, if you're not going to be there more than three years, I would say don't buy a house.

However, if you can find a really good buy in the college town—less than what you'd pay in rent—then it might be worth the risk, particularly if it is a property that you know is easily sellable to another student.

If you don't buy a house, though, don't take big risks with this money. The money is there for you to buy another home and, therefore, should be secured. I personally would put my money in a money market account with one of the large brokerage firms, maximize the interest I could earn on it, and not take risks with it.

QUESTION:

Do you think I've been a bad steward?

I am a seventy-four-year-old widow and I have had no experience in managing money. For most of the time since my husband died, about ten years ago, I have left my money in CDs, lived off interest, and renewed them whenever they came due. I saw everybody else making lots of money in the stock market, and when a friend told me how much she had made I went to see her financial planner. That was about two years ago. He's lost about half of my money—almost $100,000—and I'm distraught. Can you help me?

Answer:

It's unfortunate that, instead of following their own plan, people sometimes follow other people's plans, which might not be right for them. The friend who advised you may have millions and not need her money, allowing her to ride out these downturns and recover. But for a seventy-four-year-old widow, the investment plan suggested by that financial planner was probably flawed.

I recommend that you appeal to the National Association of Securities Dealers (NASD) and determine whether the financial planner or the firm that employs the planner is liable for your losses. Probably not, since these risks fall within the realm of "reasonable losses." But, since you're a novice investor and were not warned of the risk, you might have a case.

At the very best, this was an ill-advised planner, at least in your case. You needed security, not high returns. However, no matter what happens, God is still in control. He knows what your needs are and He will provide for you.

"He who pursues righteousness and loyalty finds life, righteousness and honor" (Proverbs 21:21).

Question:

Are prepaid tuition plans good investments?

I've read in the newspaper about a prepaid tuition plan at state universities. We'd like to put some money aside for our children's college education. They are ages five and seven.

Answer:

That depends on what your goals are. In some states the money can be transferred to another state, if necessary, which gives you better flexibility. I would recommend that kind of plan.

The advantage of the prepaid tuition plan is that it sets the cost of tuition for your children, effective the year you subscribe to it. It is a contract, and with the cost of education going up the way it is, if you're fairly certain that your children are going to go to school in your state, it's probably a good idea.

The average return, if you're looking at this as an investment, is probably somewhere in the 7 to 8 percent range per year—tax free. In most states the prepaid college plans are not taxable.

> **I'm more concerned with the return *of* my money than I am the return *on* my money.**
>
> WILL ROGERS

However, if you are a Christian and you're planning to send your children to a Christian school, the state tuition plan may not be transferable to a private school, particularly a private religious school.

QUESTION:

Can you tell me under what conditions you would use a Roth IRA versus the regular IRA?

We're planning to start a retirement account, and we're trying to decide whether it's better for us as a young couple to get a regular IRA or a Roth IRA.

ANSWER:

Be aware that you can't get into either a Roth or a regular IRA if you have an employer-provided, qualified retirement account. IRAs are for people who don't have qualified retirement accounts. Also, under current law, your income has to be $150,000 per year or less. However, there are other types of retirement accounts that are available to self-employed individuals with incomes in excess of $150,000 per year.

Basically the same qualification rules apply for the regular and the Roth IRA. The difference in the two is that in a regular IRA account you're allowed to put in tax-deferred money, meaning you don't have to pay income tax on that money. But, as the account accumulates and, ultimately, when you take it out for retirement, you're going to be taxed at ordinary income rates on withdrawals, regardless of how the money was earned. In other words, even if you invested in the stock market and you had capital gains income, you would still be taxed at ordinary income rates.

The Roth IRA is different because you contribute after-tax money to the account. In other words, money you have already paid income taxes on. The account accumulates over the years (hopefully), and when you withdraw the funds for retirement purposes it is not taxable income.

In my opinion, the Roth IRA is well suited for younger people, and if I were looking for a retirement plan and qualified for an IRA, I personally would use the Roth IRA. Under many conditions I might choose the Roth IRA even as an older person. It would depend on my tax situation and whether I thought my tax structure would be higher or lower after retirement.

If I thought my tax liability was going to be higher at retirement, the Roth IRA would certainly be the way to go. If I thought my liability was going to be substantially less after retirement, the regular IRA might suit me better. As the old saying goes: Pay them (IRS) now or pay them later.

QUESTION:

Should we borrow the money out of our retirement account to pay off our credit cards and then repay our retirement account?

We have money in my company's 401(k) retirement account, but we have large amounts of credit card debt— almost $17,000—and just making the payments on this money is very difficult. I want to borrow from my 401(k), but my wife disagrees.

Answer:

You need to be very careful about doing this. Be certain that you're not just treating the *symptom*. The symptom is the credit card debt; the *problem* is something entirely different—perhaps greed, covetousness, or ignorance. Be sure you're dealing with the problem first.

First, I recommend that you get on a budget for a minimum of six to nine months. Prove to yourself that you can live within your income, including making at least minimum payments on this debt, before you even think about consolidating. That's especially true if you're using a retirement account as a means of consolidating.

If you don't pay the money back to your retirement account, it's going to cost you 40 percent (plus or minus) of the money you borrow, because you'll pay federal and state income taxes on the money, as well as a 10 percent withdrawal penalty. It might be much cheaper to consolidate by borrowing the money against your home, or some other asset, as opposed to your retirement account, especially if you don't repay that account.

Normally, I don't recommend borrowing money from a retirement account, because it's too easy not to pay back the money. An exception might be some kind of family crisis. Suppose that your wife would have to go back to work and leave the children with a sitter. In my opinion, no amount of money is worth that. It would be better to pay the penalties and withdraw the money from the retirement account, rather than be forced to make a decision that is contrary to your biblical views.

QUESTION:

Is an annuity a good retirement plan for my family?

ANSWER:

This is a difficult question to answer without knowing more details. Generally, an annuity is a contract issued by an insurance company for the purpose of retirement income.

Most annuities fall into one of two categories. A *fixed annuity* means that the issuer guarantees a set amount of money in savings and payout; a *variable annuity*, on the other hand, is much like a mutual fund. The earnings and payout depend on the markets. Whether you choose a fixed or variable annuity depends, in large part, on your age. Older people would typically lean toward a fixed annuity, because they want to know what the payout is going to be; younger people prefer variable annuities.

> 'Tis said that persons living on annuities are longer lived than others.
>
> LORD BYRON

Also, most annuities have a penalty surrender phase, meaning that if you want to cancel the annuity or take your money out, there are substantial penalties for several years; usually the penalty phase ranges from seven to ten years.

Further, when you buy an annuity, at some point you're going to have to make a decision about whether the payout is for one or two lives. In a one-life annuity, when the annuitant dies, the money stops. Two-life means exactly what it says: The contract will pay to a second person. The rate paid by the annuity varies significantly depending on which option you choose. Remember, a variable annuity is basically a mutual fund managed by the insurance company, and the payout depends on how well the investments do.

There is a great variety of annuities available—almost as many options as you can name. My recommendation is to get good counsel *before* you buy an annuity.

QUESTION:

What are our options for selling a time-share condominium that we purchased but can no longer afford?

ANSWER:

Unfortunately, in the majority of instances, time-shares are impulse purchases. Generally, they're made by people who go to an area for a vacation; they're feeling very good and they think they'd like to return every year; and so they buy into a time-share condo. Usually, most people find that they don't like to go back to the same area every year. However, unless they have swap privileges, which means they can trade their time-shares with other people in different areas, they tire of the area quickly or realize they made impulse purchases. Or worse, they realize they really can't afford them.

I have found that time-shares are very difficult to resell, primarily because if the company that sold the time-shares is still in business, anyone trying to sell is in competition with them.

But if you want to try to sell your time-share, the best way to do it is to advertise during the tourist season in the area it is located. Perhaps there will be someone else who would like to buy your unit, but be prepared not to get what you paid.

If you have a time-share, read the contract carefully to be sure that you have the right to resell your unit. Also, there may be a waiting or holding period before resale.

In my opinion, time-shares are not good investments for the majority of people.

QUESTION:

Should I be contributing to my 401(k) if our budget is extremely tight?

We seem to be borrowing on our credit cards every month just to get by. This is creating a lot of conflict in my marriage, particularly because it may result in my wife going back to work. At the same time, we're putting $300 a month in our 401(k).

ANSWER:

In general, long-term saving is a very good idea, and I heartily recommend it for the majority of people—but not at the cost of your marriage. There are other things far more important. You need to look carefully at your budget and find a budget counselor. You'll find references for budget counselors in item 15.1 in the Appendix. You need to get help immediately on this.

Be aware that many marriages, Christian and non-Christian alike, dissolve over financial arguments. In my opinion, if it takes borrowing the money out of your 401(k)—even with all the penalties—to resolve this crisis, it's worth it to lower the pressure on your marriage. But don't do it until you've met with a counselor and gotten on a budget. Then you can be sure that you're dealing with the problem, not just treating the symptoms.

Stopping your retirement savings for a while will not hurt your long-term plans; dissolving your marriage will.

"Better is a little with the fear of the LORD than great treasure and turmoil with it" (Proverbs 15:16).

QUESTION:

Do you consider owning a bass boat an investment?

My husband has a bass boat that takes about 15 to 20 percent of our total budget to maintain. He believes it's necessary for his long-term mental health and that it's a good investment.

ANSWER:

Well, I would rather not get caught in the middle of a family argument, but I do believe that rarely, if ever, is a bass boat an investment. It's a purchase—usually it's a hobby—and it consumes a lot of money.

Bass boats, in general—like many other luxuries: motor homes, vacation homes, and the like—fit in the Entertainment/Recreation budget. If you'll look at our budget Percentage Guide table in the Appendix (see item 17.0), 15 percent of total spending won't fit in the recreation budget. But I would say to pray about this, let your feelings be known to your husband in a loving way, but don't plague him. Turn this over to God. He will handle it.

If your husband refuses to make any adjustments in his recreational spending (and you know this spending is outside the budget), then you need to prayerfully give the budget to him and let him pay the bills. Tell him you're more than willing to help, but you are no longer willing to absorb the pressure of a budget that won't balance. But, remember to do this in a gentle and a loving way. Don't (literally) throw the book at him.

QUESTION:

Should we help our children, ages eight and twelve, invest their money?

Their grandparents give the children about $1,000 per year, so they presently have $8,000 and $12,000 in their accounts. They're bright kids, but they have no idea how much money is in their accounts.

ANSWER:

I think you should tell them how much money their grandparents have given them. First, have them thank their grandparents, and then help the children understand the concept of investing for the future. What a great opportunity this is for them!

You'll need to observe your children carefully to determine how much control they should have. Each child is different, and what works for one may not work for the other. I recommend giving them one of the youth profiles listed in item 15.2 in the Appendix. It will give some good insights into their personalities.

There are some excellent investments available to your children. I recommend good-quality mutual funds, because mutual funds offer professional investment management. You can find mutual funds that are oriented to kids if you will check both the *Money* magazine and the *Consumer Reports* magazine annual edition on mutual funds. In addition, I refer you to item 15.3 in the Appendix, where other investment advice is available.

There are mutual funds that are oriented specifically to kids. These require a low down payment (although that would not be a problem in your children's case) and low periodic payments. Sometimes you can set up nonmonthly payments—in other words, they can put the money in as they receive it.

It would be best to take a diverse approach to investing their money. Don't risk everything in any one place. Start with about a fifty-fifty balance between investing in mutual funds and pure cash investments, like money market accounts or CDs. I would use one of the good computer tracking programs for investments, and you'll find some listed in item 2.2 in the Appendix.

In general, you and your children should read as much as you can about investing before you get started, and then let them help you choose the investments they like. It can be a great learning experience for your children, both positive and negative, but that's what investing is all about.

QUESTION:

Can you tell us where the best place is to make money on our money?

We've saved some money for our household contingencies, about $10,000 to date. We would like to be making money on that money, but I want it to be absolutely safe. My husband says we should have it in the stock market where it can grow, but I would rather have it in something secure. We have agreed to follow your counsel.

ANSWER:

I also suggest that this money be put in a very safe place. It is not money that's meant to be invested. If you want to take half of it and use it for long-term savings and keep the other half for short-term expenses, that's fine. If it were my own money, I'd put it in a money market account or something equivalent; I wouldn't be taking stock market risks with it.

Those funds need to be accessible when breakdowns or emergencies occur.

A good place to keep this kind of savings is in a money market fund offered by one of the large brokerage firms. Generally speaking, a money market account is going to make the maximum amount of interest with a minimum risk, and your first priority is minimum risk. You're looking for a return *of* your money, not the return *on* your money in this particular situation.

QUESTION:

How safe is a money market account?

My son has recently told me that I should be keeping my spare money in a money market account rather than a savings account at my local bank, but I don't understand money markets.

ANSWER:

A money market account is basically an interest-bearing account in which many people pool their funds, and it is managed by a professional investment company—like a brokerage firm. Money market accounts yield some of the highest interest rates available for on-demand accounts—where the money you have on deposit is available to you, usually on a daily basis.

In general, a money market account is an at-risk investment, meaning that it is not guaranteed by the FDIC or by any government agency. But if you select one of the large brokerage firms, the probability of you getting your money back, in my opinion, is 100 percent. Many of them have billions of dollars in these accounts, which are used by the brokerage houses for internal operations and for investing, and they are very secure.

The brokerage houses keep a large supply of cash on hand to

repay these accounts—far more than your bank does to pay your savings account—and generally you earn a higher interest rate.

The majority of the brokerage firms that offer these kinds of accounts also offer government-backed mutual funds, meaning that your money is backed by the U.S. government, but these funds usually don't pay the same rate of return. Also, be aware that some accounts that are called government securities are not actually secured by the government. They are repurchase agreements, meaning that the government securities are owned by the institution and they back your money as collateral, but the government is not actually guaranteeing the money. In my opinion, money market accounts satisfy the requirement of prudent security and they offer total liquidity.

QUESTION:

What are Certificates of Deposit?

I've recently received my deceased husband's insurance proceeds, and my accountant recommended that I put the money into a Certificate of Deposit. I am not familiar with these. Can you help me?

ANSWER:

A Certificate of Deposit (CD) is an interest-bearing note that is issued by a bank. The Federal Deposit Insurance Corporation (FDIC) backs these notes—up to $100,000—by the full faith and credit of the U.S. government. The time period in which these CDs mature can be anywhere from 60 days to as long as 10 years. Usually, the longer the maturity date, the higher the interest they will pay. And if you need your money before a CD matures, you can recover it, but you will pay a substantial interest forfeiture.

QUESTION:

Could you help me understand what a mutual fund is and what is involved?

My husband would like for us to put our retirement money in mutual funds, but I am not familiar with mutual funds, except by name.

ANSWER:

A mutual fund is an investment in which many people pool their money together to buy different kinds of securities—like stocks or bonds. In essence, it is a large group of people pooling their money into a common account. Then a professional manager uses that money to invest in stocks or bonds, depending on the type of fund.

In my opinion, mutual funds are good investments for low-budget investors, because they provide a lot of diversification (they invest in many different companies) and they provide professional management. However, bear in mind that the same principle of risk and return always applies: If you want a higher return on your money than you can get by leaving it in a CD or a savings account, then you must be willing to assume a higher risk. Mutual funds go up and down with the markets they represent, and you can lose money as well as make money.

So you need to select your particular fund based on your personality and your ability to handle risk. Look at the track records of the mutual funds very carefully. Mutual funds

> **If a little does not go, much cash will not come.**
>
> CHINESE PROVERB

are profit-making entities; therefore, there are certain risks that every investor must assume.

The companies and salespeople who sell mutual funds make their money through a fee system. There are two kinds of fees in mutual funds: the front-load and the no-load mutual fund. The front-load mutual fund basically means that the service charges for handling the funds and the commission to the salesperson are taken out when you buy your shares, so you have less money working for you up front.

The no-load funds don't take those commissions and fees out up front; therefore the costs are amortized over a number of years. In theory, the no-load mutual funds should have higher earnings, because more money is working for you initially. But if you keep a mutual fund for a substantial period of time—typically six years or longer—statistically, there is virtually no difference in performance between a no-load and a front-load mutual fund (at least that's what the experts on both sides tell me).

Many mutual fund companies will give you the flexibility of shifting your investment among different kinds of funds—what they call their family of funds. So you can invest in low-risk funds, high-risk funds, and mid-risk funds, and you can shift your money back and forth—normally, without a fee.

If you're going to buy into mutual funds, I recommend that you first do some reading. You'll find information about some good materials in item 15.3 in the Appendix. Then, start slowly, don't invest all your money at one time. And, finally, only invest in companies that are secure, have been around for a long time, and have verifiable track records. At least then you'll know the risks you're taking.

QUESTION:

How risky is it to invest in art or antique rugs and furniture?

My husband and I have recently come into some inheritance money, and I've been thinking about using this money to invest in items that we can use in our home while they are appreciating. What do you think about this idea? How would I get started?

ANSWER:

Be very cautious about investing in what are called *collectibles*. The potential profits or losses on collectibles typically depend on two things: first, how much you know about them when you buy them; and, second, how much somebody else knows about them when you buy them. In general, collectibles are complicated investments, requiring years of expertise, and only specialists make money from them. These are people who know their area well, whether it is collectible coins, gems, furniture, or other specialty areas.

The items you mention can be excellent investments. However, for the majority of people I've known, usually they turn out to be purchases—meaning they bought them and were never able to resell them. In most cases those that were resold resulted in significant losses.

We read in Ecclesiastes 5:14: *"When those riches were lost through a bad investment and he had fathered a son, then there was nothing to support him."*

The best way to acquire the knowledge you need is to buy books or subscribe to magazines that specialize in a particular collectible area that interests you. When you feel that you've gained enough insight and knowledge to take a risk, then commit a small amount of money, invest on a limited scale, and decide up front whether you're investing or purchasing. If you're purchasing, you need to realize that you probably aren't ever going to sell.

For instance, I've heard many men say they bought investment-grade diamonds for their wives' wedding rings, because they would appreciate in value. In reality, it's irrelevant whether the rings appreciate in value, because the wives will never sell them. Outside of using a hatchet, those rings are going to stay on their fingers. They are purchases, not investments, and besides that, very few people have the expertise to know a good diamond from a bad diamond; most are totally dependent on the appraisal, which can vary widely.

Collectibles in general can be a good area of investing for some people, but they are not good for the average investor.

QUESTION:

What do you think about commodities?

I'm a physician, and I am thinking about doing some investing. The area that interests me the most is commodities. It seems to me that if you know what you're doing you can invest a small amount of money in commodities on margin and make a large return. I understand there are risks, but I think that I'm intelligent enough to assess the risks. My wife doesn't agree with me. She asked me to contact you, and we have agreed that we'll abide by whatever advice you give.

ANSWER:

I don't want that kind of responsibility. It's not my money. I'm not going to lose it, and I'm not going to make a profit from it. It's your money; nobody cares more about your money than you do. All I can do is give you counsel, based on what I know about the commodities business.

The commodities market does serve a legitimate function: It provides farmers and other growers with the opportunity to pre-sell the crops so they know how much profit they will make before the season begins. However, when most people deal in commodities, they have no interest in the delivery of any product. It becomes pure speculation—literally, a gamble. Most are guessing whether the markets will go up or down.

A typical speculator in the commodities market buys a contract for a future delivery of a commodity but never actually intends to receive that commodity. If the price he or she has agreed to pay is less than the market price when the contract matures, the buyer sells the contract and reaps a profit. If the market price drops substantially, the person who sells the contract takes a loss.

If you buy on margin, you can exaggerate the potential profits and exaggerate the potential losses. For example, let's assume that you bought a contract worth $1,000 and bought it on 50 percent margin—meaning you only had to put $500 down to hold the contract. At maturity, the contract was worth $1,200. Super! You made a substantial profit. You had $500 at risk, and you made a $200 profit—or 40 percent.

But, if when the contract came due the market was down to $800, you took a 40 percent loss on the deal. Therefore, buying on margin, and in this case 50 percent, has greatly exaggerated the potential profit *and* the potential loss.

Remember that for the majority of amateur commodity speculators (those who don't trade commodities for a livelihood) there's little risk involved—generally speaking, the vast majority of them are going to lose.

A professional broker reduces the risk through knowledge and market timing. For the vast majority of amateur traders, the commodities market is a very high-risk, volatile business. It is akin to gambling. In fact, in many cases the odds are worse in the commodities market than they are on a roulette wheel.

"If any man's work is burned up, he will suffer loss . . . Let no man deceive himself. If any man among you thinks that he is wise in this age, he must become foolish, so that he may become wise" (1 Corinthians 3:15, 18).

QUESTION:

What is your opinion about stock market investing?

I've been investing in the stock market for four or five years, and initially I made a lot of money—on paper at least. However, in recent years I've lost a substantial amount of money. I'm probably even with the market right now. My wife thinks the stock market is gambling and that Christians shouldn't be involved.

ANSWER:

We are warned in Proverbs about having the wrong attitude toward worldly riches. I believe that the majority of stock market investors need to heed Proverbs 23:4–5: "*Do not weary yourself to gain wealth, cease from your consideration of it. When you set your eyes on it, it is gone. For wealth certainly makes itself wings, like an eagle that flies toward the heavens.*" I believe that a lot of people are involved in get-rich-quick schemes, not legitimate stock market investing.

In general, when you invest in the stock market you're buying equity in companies like IBM, Xerox, General Motors, Microsoft, and Cisco. What you should be doing is buying their stock in anticipation that the company will grow and make a profit in which you will share.

But when speculators buy stocks whose price-to-earnings ratios (price versus earnings) are in the thousands of percent—in other words, the price they pay for the stock is hundreds or thousands of times higher than the annual earnings of the company—they're not buying that stock for the value of the company. They're buying it for the speculative potential of the stock. Literally, they're speculating (gambling) that the price will go up.

"*Do not boast about tomorrow, for you do not know what a day may bring forth*" (Proverbs 27:1).

Many people did guess right when the market was going up, but they guessed wrong when the market went down. A great many amateur speculators lost money they couldn't afford to lose.

If you're buying stock for the long term and for the earnings the company can generate, in my opinion, that's investing in the stock market. If you're buying it simply because you think the price will go up and you can sell your inflated stock to someone else at a higher price, that's known as the greater-sucker theory.

So, in large part, it's not *where* you invest your money, it's the *attitude* you have about the investment.

QUESTION:

How do you feel about gold and silver as investments?

I'm thinking about investing in some precious metals right now. They've been down for a long time. A friend of mine says that he thinks they're going to go up if the economy takes a major dive.

ANSWER:

I believe that people, Christians included, can invest in any area, if they understand the potential risk and return and if they don't risk money they can't afford to lose.

Gold, as a metal, has been used as a standard of value for thousands of years, primarily because it is easily storable, easily divisible, and a limited resource that can't be counterfeited.

Silver also serves as a base commodity for currency, to a lesser degree for the same reasons, although the price of silver has been artificially depressed for many years. Over the past millennium, gold (to a high degree) and silver (to a lesser degree) have been hedges against economic turmoil—both in economic depressions and runaway inflation. But over the last decade or so both gold and silver have been declining in value, as our society has shifted to more regulated economic systems.

If you're looking at precious metals as investments, you probably could have done better in almost anything else that you might have chosen—even a savings account at your local bank. Will they go up in the future? Probably. Does anybody know when? I doubt it.

If you're going to invest in gold or silver, I counsel you to risk only a small percentage of your assets. Pray about this before you do it and make sure you have the peace of the Lord in your investment program.

"'The silver is Mine, and the gold is Mine,' declares the LORD *of hosts"* (Haggai 2:8).

QUESTION:

What do you think about mutual fund companies that engage in questionable and objectionable areas?

I have begun to do some reading about some mutual fund companies and I realize that many engage in areas that might be questionable and objectionable to a Christian. I wouldn't like to put my money with a mutual fund company that does this.

ANSWER:

I'm always mindful of what the apostle Paul says: *"Whatever you do in word or deed, do all in the name of the Lord Jesus, giving thanks through Him to God the Father"* (Colossians 3:17). Everything we do is a witness of what we believe. Therefore, there are going to be some investments that are unacceptable to Christians.

I recommend that you do some research and then make up your own mind. Obviously it's very difficult to choose a mutual fund that does not invest in something that is objectionable to somebody. You'd have to make a decision whether it is objectionable to you as a Christian.

All Christians should be concerned about how their money is going to be invested. If you invest in a mutual fund company, get a copy of their prospectus. That will tell you where their money is invested. There are many mutual fund companies that publish data to assure shareholders that they don't invest in objectionable areas. But you have to read their prospectus to see what they call questionable.

For some it's making war planes; for others it's not investing in tobacco; and for others it's avoiding alcohol. So what you and I might consider objectionable may not be to the fund's investors.

You have to make up your own mind. The information is available if you're willing to do a little work. If you see questionable areas that a mutual fund is investing in on your list, write the mutual fund company directly and ask for details. I've done that before and found that some of the companies were investing in activities like pornography and abortion, so you do have to be careful.

Obviously, you can't possibly decide how a company uses every dollar. Some buy and sell hundreds or thousands of stocks every single day. But you can do your best to find out if they consciously invest in things that you know would be contrary to your personal values. Every Christian should do some investigating. Some practical resources to help you are listed in item 15.4 in the Appendix.

QUESTION:

What to you think about the no-money-down, guaranteed profits real estate advertising on television?

This sounds too good to be true. Can you give me some advice?

Answer:

This much I can tell you: The advocates of the no-money-down real estate philosophy make their money by selling books or information, not by buying and selling real estate. I've talked to dozens of people across this country who've tried doing what was recommended on one of these television programs and everyone I know lost money.

There are very few people who can profit from no-money-down real estate—for a couple of reasons. First, the properties that are offered and discussed are run-down properties, generally located in run-down areas, where there are few qualified buyers. The best buys in the no-money-down homes are in depressed areas of our country. Therefore, you need to have the skills to fix them up, and you need to have a tough hide to collect your rent.

I believe there are homes available, but they're not going to be profitable for the majority of people. Most people who are enticed to buy no-money-down properties find they can neither rent them nor resell them, and they end up frustrated. Ultimately, most just give up and give the houses back.

I recommend you avoid these no-money-down speculators. If you're going to buy real estate, look for good properties and remember that in real estate there are three basic things you have to look for: location, location, location. Consider what God's Word says: *"My son, if sinners entice you, do not consent"* (Proverbs 1:10).

Question:

Is it better to pay off the car or invest?

We've paid down a lot of our debts and now I find that, with a raise, we have $500 a month extra. Do you think that we should put it all on our car payment until we pay it off, which would take only about two years, or should we start doing some investing as well?

ANSWER:

Generally speaking, I encourage you not to do one thing to the exclusion of everything else. My recommendation is, rather than trying to put all your surplus on the automobile, that you spread it over your budget a little bit. Maybe allocate $100 to $150 a month to pay off the car, even if it stretches the payoff to three years rather than two.

Allocate some of the money into your Entertainment/ Recreation budget and perhaps some into your Clothing budget. After your budget is working well, then use some of the surplus to invest.

You and your wife should pray about your budget and do what's best for both of you. It may be that she's been feeling too confined; this is an opportunity to loosen up a little bit. Remember, being the best steward does not necessarily mean being the most frugal. *"It is the blessing of the LORD that makes rich, and He adds no sorrow to it"* (Proverbs 10:22).

QUESTION:

How can you give people advice to invest when in fact it is unscriptural?

I've listened to your radio program for a long time, and I've heard you talk to Christians and give them advice about investing. I believe that Christians should not invest or be involved in the investment world, because this promotes greed and covetousness and money is lost that could otherwise be put back into the kingdom.

Answer:

I disagree. If Christians are giving what they believe God wants them to give and they still have a surplus of money, then I believe the Scripture tells us that some of it is to be put aside for future needs. Otherwise, how would the money be available for the projects that God wants done in the future if we don't save for them?

Proverbs 6:6–11 tells us that ants store food during the summer, knowing that the time will come when they will need those resources. The same thing applies to God's people. We also see in the parable of the talents (Matthew 25:14–30) that God wants us to use our mental and financial assets to further the kingdom of God.

But if all God's Word said about investing is to just make it and store it—in other words, "Make all you can and can all you make"—then many of the rich people of the world would be right on target. However, there is a balance, as found in the parable of the rich fool (Luke 12:16–21).

A farmer is an investor. He takes a portion of his crops and he puts it in the ground, caring for it and trusting that it is going to grow into a large harvest. In the story of the rich fool, he had a large harvest, but instead of looking for how he could share his harvest, he decided he would tear down his barns and build larger ones, and God called him a fool.

So somewhere between the ant who stores and the rich fool is the balance that God wants us to have. That does not preclude God's people from being involved with investing. The scriptural justification for investing is to provide for future needs by multiplying surpluses. Some of the legitimate needs for the future are spontaneous giving, education of your children, getting debt free, and retirement—at least slowing down in your older years. That does not make investing wrong; it makes it a balanced part of God's plan for a Christian.

12
RETIREMENT

RETIREMENT, AS WE KNOW IT TODAY, IS A relatively new idea. Very few people in the nineteenth and early twentieth centuries retired from their vocational activities. There were several reasons for this.

First, few average-income people made enough money to set aside the necessary funds.

Second, the government played only a minor role in their society and lacked the resources, or the authority, to take the citizens' money and hold it for retirement.

Third, retirement just wasn't a popular concept in a Bible-dominated/influenced society. We're told today that the reason was because people didn't live as long. Not true. The average death age was younger than today but only because of the high infant mortality rate.

Retirement is an affluent society's invention. The hard laborers have always had to slow down with age. But the phenomenon of young, healthy people kicking back and enjoying the fruits of their labor is only the evidence of a non-biblically based society.

God intends for us to stay active and involved. If you happen to be fortunate enough to have surplus resources, God expects much of them to be put back into His work. If you have the financial wherewithal to retire, then volunteer with a ministry.

QUESTION:

What advice can you give us about retiring?

We are getting ready for retirement next year but don't know exactly what retirement means, and I'm not sure that we can afford to retire.

ANSWER:

First, it's important to decide whether you should retire. Second, it's very important for you to assess whether or not you can afford to retire. The best way to do that is to get on the budget that you anticipate you'll be living on after retirement.

Let's assume that you're earning $50,000 a year currently and that after retirement, including all sources of anticipated income, you're going to be making $30,000 a year. Then you need to adjust immediately to a $30,000-a-year annual budget to see if you can live on it, because if you can't there are some pretty drastic adjustments that need to be made.

> The man least dependent upon the morrow goes to meet the morrow most cheerfully.
>
> EPICURUS

Either you'll have to make the decision to continue to work, at least part-time, or you'll have to reduce some of your overhead. I've seen many couples who have cycled into retirement without anticipating the decline in income, and it takes an emotional and financial toll on them.

Many people think that after retirement it's going to be a lot cheaper for them to live because they don't have to go in to work, but generally that's not true. Because you have more free time (unless you're involved with volunteer work—as you should be), you tend to spend more money.

QUESTION:

Should we stretch our budget and join a retirement plan right now?

Our budget is very tight, but my husband's company offers a retirement plan that matches 10 percent of any money we put in it per year.

ANSWER:

I suggest that you start with about 5 percent of your income and take advantage of this retirement plan. It may stretch your budget; but you can do it if you make it a priority. For example, do you know how people are able to pay taxes? They are deducted from their checks before they get them, and the same principle applies here. You make whatever adjustments you have to. Pay yourself first and put money into a long-term investment account—in your case, the investment account is your company retirement plan. It's a very good idea for most families.

Another point to emphasize: Don't treat your retirement account like a savings account and continually dip into it for the things you want. This is a long-term savings—for retirement or, at the very least, for the education of your children.

You should monitor the results of your retirement account each year and determine whether the money is invested properly. Don't take the approach that someone else is smart enough to know how to invest your money. Nobody cares more about your money than you do, and if you ignore it you can lose some or all of it.

"Without faith it is impossible to please Him, for he who comes to God must believe that He is and that He is a rewarder of those who seek Him" (Hebrews 11:6).

QUESTION:

Should my husband and I keep our retirement accounts separate?

We both have worked all our lives, and we're going into retirement in a couple of years. If I choose a single payout annuity with my company I will receive more money, and if he chooses a single-payout annuity with his company he would receive more money per month.

ANSWER:

You need to be very careful, because single payout means that if you die he won't get your retirement, and if he dies you won't get his retirement. If you have developed a budget based on both your incomes, that's going to create a major problem if one of you dies. So I would not choose that option unless you know that neither of you will need the other's income. With a two-life payout, if you die your pension would go to him (and vice versa).

Don't make a hasty decision based on a bribe from your retirement plans (they make money on single-life annuities). You need to be very certain that you can live on your income and he can live on his; otherwise one of you will have a financial crisis when the other one dies.

QUESTION:

Where's the best place to invest for retirement?

My husband and I are just beginning our working careers, but we are looking for places to invest our retirement income. Over the last couple of years we have put it in the stock market, but now the stock market has taken a significant drop and we have lost nearly half of what we put in our accounts. Should we even worry about something as long-term as retirement?

ANSWER:

Yes, you do need to invest for the long term. If you're a couple in your mid- to late twenties, you need to look at the long term, and the long term for most people in this country is the stock market. Of course, the market goes up and the market goes down, but overall it has gone up for more than one hundred years now.

If I were you, I would start my investing program by choosing a good-quality mutual fund, or perhaps more than one, and put my money there. I like mutual funds primarily because they have professional management and they invest in a great variety of companies, so you automatically have diversity. Granted, you may get in at the wrong time and the market will drop, but it will come back as long as the country is prospering, and we are a very prosperous country.

The concept is called *dollar cost averaging*. This means that you put money in when it is high and you put money in when it is low, and overall you are going to get the average value of the stock market. So I encourage you to use mutual funds to start your investment program. And, because of your ages, I would suggest that you look at growth mutual funds. They are a little more volatile, but since you have many years to invest you should do quite well over the long term.

In item 15.0 in the Appendix you'll find resource information on retirement. Read it and then make your own choices.

QUESTION:

How much money is enough for retirement?

We are in our seventies, and my husband has been thinking about retiring for a long time, but he's still working pretty much full-time. He says he just doesn't have enough money saved for retirement.

Answer:

Many people love what they do and choose to continue working—even at seventy and beyond. When this is true, most will never retire, regardless of the reasons. However, if your husband is working only for the money and is waiting until he has "enough" money saved, probably he will never have enough. This is because he may well be living in the fear cycle, which means "I always need a little bit more."

Seriously, the way to tell when you have enough money for retirement is very simple. Look at how much you're living on right now, which would be your income less taxes and whatever you're saving and giving. And then, when your total retirement account has enough money to provide you that amount of money per year, you'll be financially qualified for retirement. But that still may not be God's plan for your lives.

Not everybody should retire, and that may be true of your husband. I remember a study of sixty-five- to seventy-five-year-old men done at Harvard University many years ago. The study showed that the men

> Whoever, in middle age, attempts to realize the wishes and hopes of his early youth, invariably deceives himself. Each ten years of a man's life has its own fortunes, its own hopes, its own desires.
>
> JOHANN WOLFGANG VON GOETHE

who continued to work lived longer. In fact, only 6 out of the 100 had died by age seventy-five.

Many of the men who retired at sixty-five lost their sense of worth, as many people do when they stop working, and almost half of them had died by age seventy-five. Your husband may be dealing with an emotional situation instead of a financial situation.

QUESTION:

How would our church set up a retirement plan for our pastor?

ANSWER:

As a church body or a church committee, you need to meet and vote on the retirement plan for your pastor. He is self-employed, as all pastors are; therefore, you can set up what is called the SEP-IRA for him. Basically, it's money you designate for retirement, but he must choose to set up the SEP-IRA because it is his money.

He can elect to have any financial organization manage the money for him. It could be a bank, an insurance company, a mutual fund company, or a stock company. Have a good planner in the church help him choose the option that would best suit him. You'll find more information on investing in item 15.0 in the Appendix.

QUESTION:

How does early retirement affect Social Security?

I'm almost sixty-two and I'm thinking about retiring. Would I be better off financially to work until I am sixty-five, or should I retire at sixty-two?

ANSWER:

According to Social Security rules, if you retire at sixty-five, you'll gain more money at retirement but you'll lose the potential income you would have had at sixty-two, sixty-three, and sixty-four. By my calculations, it takes approximately fifteen years of Social Security retirement income, beyond age sixty-five, to make up for the money that would have been earned in those first three years. So financially speaking you're better off retiring at age sixty-two than you are at sixty-five. However, that's not the primary decision that must be made, because there are many other factors that go into deciding whether you should retire—the most important of which is God's plan for your life.

QUESTION:

How would I calculate what I have saved for retirement?

I have my money in a variety of places: in cash that we've saved, in IRAs, and in 401(k)s. I have no way to know exactly how much we're going to make when I retire.

ANSWER:

In regard to your invested assets, you simply need to go to a financial adviser and have him help you put together an investment plan that might include shifting some of your assets around so they would generate income for you at retirement. Then you will be able to do a calculation based on that amount, but I recommend that you get professional help. You'll find resources listed in item 15.1 in the Appendix.

Question:

Since I elected to be exempt from Social Security as a pastor, could I now work part-time long enough to qualify for the minimum Social Security benefits?

A friend said that if I would do that I could draw Social Security in addition to my denominational pension.

Answer:

As a pastor, you had the option of being exempt from the Social Security income tax on your wages earned as a pastor only. If you work in any other occupation, you are subject to the Social Security tax. Consequently, your friend is correct.

If you work at another job, and let's say that you went to work at J.C. Penney store as a salesperson, that money would be subject to Social Security withholding. If you worked a minimum of forty quarters, which is necessary to qualify, you would draw some Social Security. The amount you would draw depends on your contributions.

It's important to keep in mind that the amount of money you can draw from Social Security is dependent on the amount of money you paid in, so you probably would be drawing the minimum amount, but you would be qualified under the Social Security retirement plan, and you also would qualify for Medicare benefits.

The fact that you can avoid all Social Security taxes in your salary as a pastor and then later qualify for Social Security by working at a secular job is called *double-dipping*. Many people who retire, such as federal and state employees, do qualify for Social Security benefits later by doing this.

Even though it is legal, be sure you're comfortable with the ethics of it. Your being exempt from Social Security tax required you to sign an affidavit that you object to government-provided social welfare, which Social Security is.

QUESTION:

With all the publicity about how underfunded the Social Security system is, how secure is our Social Security income for when we retire?

My wife and I are both approaching retirement in the next ten years and our primary income is going to be Social Security.

ANSWER:

The best anyone can do is give you an opinion about the solvency of Social Security. In my opinion, I believe that those who are already qualified for benefits will be protected no matter what. However, the potential financial difficulties of Social Security are pretty significant.

First, if the economy once again suffered the ravages of inflation, it could easily destroy the stability of those living on Social Security. I encourage you to continue to work, at least some part-time job, to help offset that potential. Currently, inflation is very low, but there is no way to tell about

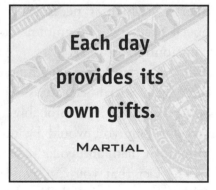

Each day provides its own gifts.

MARTIAL

the future. Social Security does have a built-in cost-of-living adjustment, but any prolonged inflationary period could undermine the value of your income.

Second, although I do believe Social Security will be protected for those who currently qualify, it's going to be a pretty skimpy living, so a part-time job can help to supplement your income. An extra $100 or $200 a month can go a long way toward making retirement a lot more enjoyable for you and your wife.

In my opinion, for younger workers entering the system, I don't believe the future of Social Security looks very good. Fewer new workers are contributing to the system, and the recipients are living a lot longer, which causes an acute actuarial problem. Almost certainly, we are going to push the retirement ages back and reduce the benefits once we get well into the twenty-first century. By about 2020 or so, I believe we are going to see the retirement age increased to about seventy and the benefits decreased dramatically. Otherwise, the system is going to run out of money.

So a young couple, even though they are qualified for Social Security, would be wise to build their own retirement account. Common sense tells me that an alternative retirement would be very prudent for anybody entering the system today. God's Word says, *"The mind of the prudent acquires knowledge, and the ear of the wise seeks knowledge"* (Proverbs 18:15).

ACKNOWLEDGMENTS

I WOULD LIKE TO SINCERELY THANK MY editor, Adeline Griffith, for her time and talents devoted to this and to many other projects.

And I would be remiss if I didn't thank Harvey Nowland for his help in developing the Appendix for this book and for his writing expertise.

Many thanks to you both.

Larry Burkett

APPENDIX

THIS APPENDIX HAS BEEN ORGANIZED topically for easy use. Each general topic listed below has its own section in the Appendix:

1.0 Automobiles

2.0 Budgeting

3.0 Budgeting Help for Married or Engaged Couples

4.0 Business

5.0 Career Direct Guidance System

6.0 Credit Counseling

7.0 Crown Financial Ministries

8.0 Debt Elimination

9.0 Educational and Vocational Decisions

10.0 Fair Debt Collection Practices Act

11.0 Family Money Issues

12.0 Giving

13.0 Housing

14.0 Insurance

15.0 Investing

16.0 Mortgage Prepayment

17.0 Tools

Each subtopic has been assigned an item number. For example, the general topic "Budgeting" is listed as 2.0; its subtopic, Consumer Credit Counseling Service, is listed as item 2.3. When Appendix items are referenced in the book, you will be able to go straight to the specific information you need.

1.0
AUTOMOBILES

1.1 See the Percentage Guide for Family Income form on pages 336–37 of this Appendix.

1.2 Many resources are available that can help you determine the quality, economy, dependability, and affordability of automobiles. Review new and used car values before making a purchase at Consumer Reports, www.consumerreports.org; Kelly Blue Book auto buyers guide, www.kbb.com; Edmunds, www.edmunds.com; and Cars Direct, www.carsdirect.com.

You also can research a car's vehicle identification number (VIN) on-line at CarFax, www.carfax.com.

1.3 Two Internet sites that can help make it easier to research and evaluate automobile insurance are Yahoo! Auto Insurance, www.yahoo.com/auto.html; and Excite Auto Insurance, www.excite.com/money/insurance/auto_insurance.

2.0
BUDGETING

2.1 The Savings Account Allocation form is one example of the many types of useful resources available to help you develop a Crown Financial Ministries budget. See pages 338–39 of this Appendix.

2.2 Budgeting helps available from Crown Financial Ministries and your local Christian bookstore include the following:

- *Money Matters Deluxe* software with Larry Burkett's time-proven guidelines for successful budgeting, biblical counsel on related financial topics, expense tracking by budget category, and *SnapShot Gold* software.

- If you don't use a computer, Crown has many other helpful resources for you. Check our Web site, www.crown.org, or call toll-free (800) 722-1976 for more information.

- The budget counseling referral service is a lay ministry of volunteer budget counselors, the local church, and Crown Financial Ministries. There is no fee for this service (you have the option of purchasing workbooks that will enhance your study of godly stewardship, but you are under no obligation to purchase any item).

Counselors have completed *The Counselor's Self-Study Course,* and they help God's people set up budgets and learn how to honor the Lord with their finances.

To receive an application for a referral counselor by e-mail, just send a blank e-mail to counselor@crown.org (we do not read messages sent to this address). You will receive an auto-response with further directions. You may call (800) 722-1976 or write to Crown Financial Ministries, 601 Broad St. SE, Gainesville, GA 30501-3790.

2.3   If you need the assistance of a mediator with creditors, often organizations such as Consumer Credit Counseling Service can help. You may contact Consumer Credit Counseling Service at (800) 251-CCCS or www.cccsatl.org.

3.0
BUDGETING HELP FOR MARRIED OR ENGAGED COUPLES

3.1   Engaged or married couples of any age can benefit from the wisdom and practicality of the *Money in Marriage* CD-ROM software. It can be used by an individual couple or in a group setting with a group leader or counselor. *Money in Marriage* will help identify root causes of money problems or those that may be encountered in the future. The CD-ROM includes four independent modules:

- Individual personality assessments for two individuals
- "Hoarder/Spender" assessments for two individuals
- An interactive first budget
- An interactive Q&A (question and answer) session with Larry Burkett.

Two workbooks, one for each individual; an audiotape, "Honey, Let's Talk," that encourages open communication; and a second tape, "Taking Charge of Your Credit Card," complement the CD-ROM assessments.

3.2   *Women Leaving the Workplace* is a book that looks at stay-at-home situations from every woman's viewpoint, including those who may not want to stay at home or have tried it and failed, as well as practical counsel on how to survive the cutback from two incomes to one. To order, go to our Web site, www.crown.org, call (800) 722-1976, or contact your local Christian bookstore.

4.0
BUSINESS

4.1 The following companies provide business bookkeeping and accounting resources:

- Safeguard Business Systems
  455 Maryland Dr.
  Ft. Washington, PA 19034
  (800) 523-6660

- McBee Systems
  299 Cherry Hill Rd.
  Parsippany, NJ 07054-1175
  (800) 256-1272

4.2 Practical business accounting programs for the computer, such as *Quick Books Pro*, can be found at the www.quicken.com Web site. This information is not an endorsement. Resources you choose should provide services and counsel that are compatible with your own convictions and needs.

4.3 The Service Corps of Retired Executives (SCORE) is a resource partner with the U.S. Small Business Administration (SBA), involved with aiding in the formation, growth, and success of small businesses nationwide. You can get help on-line from one of more than 800 volunteer SCORE business counselors. Their interactive Web site allows you to enter questions, or search for answers using key words, at www.score.org.

4.4 *Business by the Book* (Thomas Nelson), a seminar by the same name, and the audiotape series God's Principles for Operating a Business, are some of Crown Financial Ministries' many resources designed to help business owners.

5.0
CAREER DIRECT
GUIDANCE SYSTEM

IN TODAY'S SOCIETY, THERE ARE MORE than 30,000 jobs from which to choose; yet most people don't have a plan to find the right career.

The *Career Direct® Guidance System* on CD-ROM is a complete assessment tool, suitable for adults and older teens. It contains assessment instruments that profile a person's personality, interests, skills, and work values, and it instantly generates more than thirty pages of individualized reports.

Separate systems for educational decision making and new career-matching features, accompanied by a series of audiotapes and other tools, will help you make educational or occupational decisions to manage your career. See www.crown.org for details.

There is also a paper version of *Career Direct®*.

6.0
CREDIT COUNSELING

6.1   If you want to investigate working through a credit management organization, we recommend one like Consumer Credit Counseling Services at (800) 251-CCCS or Web site www.cccsatl.org.

6.2   For more data on church-related indebtedness, see the Barna Research Web site, www.barna.org, or www.emptytomb.org. Empty tomb®, inc. serves the church by providing financial discipleship strategy and information about church giving patterns.

6.3   The Federal government has laws designed to protect consumers. For information about the Consumer Credit Protection Act, go to their Web site, www.ftc.gov/bcp/menu-credit.htm.

6.4   For information about any of the three credit reporting agencies and your credit report, you can contact them at:

- Equifax
  P.O. Box 740241
  Atlanta, GA 30374-0241
  (800) 685-1111; www.equifax.com

- Experian (formerly TRW)
  P.O. Box 949
  Allen, TX 75013
  (888) EXPERIAN (397-3742); www.experian.com

- Trans Union
  760 West Sproul Rd.
  P.O. Box 390
  Springfield, PA 19064-0390
  (800) 916-8800; www.tuc.com

7.0
CROWN FINANCIAL MINISTRIES

CROWN FINANCIAL MINISTRIES WANTS TO help you become financially free so you'll be able to know Christ more intimately and be free to serve Him. Crown has an extensive range of resources, including volunteer budget counselors, seminars, small-group Bible studies, software, and books. To aid you in your educational and occupational decision making, we have an assessment tool that profiles personality, interests, skills, and work values.

You may contact Crown Financial Ministries through our Web site, www.crown.org; by telephone, (800) 722-1976, or write to us at 601 Broad St. SE, Gainesville, GA 30501-3790.

8.0
DEBT ELIMINATION

THE FOLLOWING METHOD CAN BE USED for eliminating debt, including credit card payoff. Of course, any plan for reducing debt requires that no more debt be incurred.

DEBT ELIMINATION STRATEGY (EXAMPLE)

Acct Name	Monthly Payment	Interest Rate	Balance Due
#1	$50	18.2 %	$1,500
#2	$50	18.6 %	$ 860
#3	$50	21.8 %	$ 475
#4	$100	23.2 %	$ 690

Organize the list (as much as possible) with largest balances toward the top (#1) and smallest balances toward the bottom (#4). Do your best to list accounts with the highest interest rates toward the bottom of the list. Concentrate on paying off the account at the bottom of the list first, and systematically work your way to the top. When a debt is paid, apply the amount you had been paying for that one to the next higher debt.

9.0
EDUCATIONAL AND VOCATIONAL DECISIONS

9.1   You can find information on subjects such as mutual funds and the index funds by looking in financial magazines such as *Cheapskate Monthly, Consumer Reports, Family Money, Frugal Living Newsletter, Kiplinger* (which has several specialized magazines), and *Money*. Many of these magazines, including *Barron's Online*, also can be accessed on the Internet for a fee. We also recommend the *Sound Mind Investing* newsletter and book of the same name. See www.soundmindinvesting.com.

9.2   Education trusts, called Section 529 Prepaid Tuition Plans, are state-operated trusts that offer residents a way to "lock-in" on lower tuition rates. Parents make contributions on college tuition that they expect to be paid in the future. More information is available on the Internet at www.about.com. Search under *education* and *financial aid.*

9.3   Educational financial aid information.

   The following Internet sites provide helpful financial aid information:

- www.collegeboard.org
- www.collegenet.com
- www.embark.com
- www.salliemae.com
- www.collegequest.com

For college financial planning help, visit the Web site of the College Savings Plans Network, www.collegesavings.org, an affiliate of the National Association of State Treasurers.

For a copy of the U.S. Department of Education's FAFSA form (Free Application for Federal Student Aid), go to their Internet site, www.fafsa.ed.gov, or call (800) 4-FEDAID.

Gordon Wadsworth's book, *Cost Effective College*, www.costeffectivecollege.com, has strategies and resources to help students and parents pay for the high cost of college whether it's tomorrow or years from now. It has hands-on advice on things such as lists of Internet sites that offer free scholarship services, samples of Free Application for Federal Student Aid (FAFSA) forms, ways to maximize your acceptance at the colleges of your choice, and how to turn college loans into grants upon graduation.

Murray Baker is the author of *The Debt-Free Graduate: How to Survive College Without Going Broke*, www.debtfreegrad.com. Melissa Morgan and Judith Allee are the authors of *Home Schooling on a Shoestring*. To order a copy of the book, call Crown Financial Ministries at (800) 722-1976 or visit your local Christian bookstore.

Dan Cassidy is the author of *Last Minute College Financing*, *Dan Cassidy's Worldwide College Scholarship Directory*, and *The Scholarship Book 2001*. Contact (800) HEADSTART to reach his fee-based search organization, National Scholarship Research Service.

10.0
FAIR DEBT COLLECTION PRACTICES ACT

THE FAIR DEBT COLLECTION PRACTICES Act (TFDCPA) was passed by Congress in 1977. The law does not erase any legitimate debt you owe; however, the act prohibits certain debt collection practices, some of which follow.

Harassment. Debt collectors may not harass, oppress, or abuse any person. For example, debt collectors may not

- use threats of violence or harm to the person, property, or reputation.
- publish a list of consumers who refuse to pay their debts (except to a credit bureau).
- use obscene or profane language.
- repeatedly use the telephone to annoy someone.
- telephone people without identifying themselves.
- advertise your debt.

False statements. Debt collectors may not

- falsely imply that they are attorneys or government representatives.
- falsely imply that you have committed a crime.
- falsely represent that they operate or work for a credit bureau.
- misrepresent the amount of the debt.
- indicate that papers being sent are legal forms when they are not.

Debt collectors may not say that

- you will be arrested if you do not pay your debt or that they will seize, garnish, attach, or sell your property or wages, unless the collection agency or the creditor intends to do so, and it is legal.
- actions will be taken against you that legally may not be taken.

Debt collectors may not

- give false credit information about you to anyone.
- send you anything that looks like an official document from a court or government agency when it is not.
- use a false name.
- collect any amount greater than your debt, unless allowed by law.
- deposit a post-dated check before the date on the check.
- make you accept collect calls or pay for telegrams.
- take or threaten to take your property unless this can be done legally.
- contact you by postcard.

For a more detailed description of the TFDCPA, get a copy of *Debt-Free Living* at your local Christian bookstore or by calling (800) 722-1976. Also, go to www.ftc.gov/os/statutes/fdcpajump.htm.

11.0
FAMILY MONEY ISSUES

11.1 *Financial Parenting* contains solid, practical advice to parents on teaching their children biblical financial management. Topics include stewardship, giving, financial contentment, diligence and the work ethic, long-term financial planning, borrowing and lending, saving and investing, and budgeting.

11.2 *Cost Effective College*, www.costeffectivecollege.com, has strategies and resources to help students and parents pay for the high cost of college, whether it's tomorrow or years from now. The cost of attending a public college for one year now equals the cost of buying a new car. If you attend a private college, double that amount. *Cost Effective College* offers hands-on advice on things such as lists of Internet sites that offer free scholarship services, samples of Free Application for Federal Student Aid (FAFSA) forms, ways to maximize your acceptance at the colleges of your choice, and how to turn college loans into grants upon graduation.

Money Management for College Students helps students understand the monetary aspect of college plans and provides the counsel they need to avoid financial pitfalls: managing finances, balancing a checkbook, obtaining college loans, using credit cards wisely, choosing a college major, and much more.

For more information or to order any of these resources, visit www.crown.org or call toll-free, (800) 722-1976.

11.3 The *Crown Financial Study for Teens Workbook* helps teens learn what God says about money and has practical financial exercises designed to help teens create habits that will set them on a lifelong journey of responsible money handling. For more information, visit Crown's Web site at www.crown.org or call toll-free, (800) 722-1976.

11.4 You can find a full range of resources on the Crown Web site to help your children and young people learn about God's way of handling money. Go to www.crown.org or call (800) 722-1976. There are helps for parents too.

12.0
GIVING

12.1 The National Christian Foundation focuses on providing an opportunity, vehicle, and procedure for people to give, in the areas that God has encouraged and equipped them to give, through donor-advised funds.

> National Christian Foundation
> 1100 Johnson Ferry Rd. NE, Ste. 900
> Atlanta, GA 30342
> Phone: (404) 252-0100
> Fax: (404) 252-5277

The Foundation Center has libraries in several cities around the U.S. and provides many publications and services that can help you find a Christian or community foundation through which you may give donor-advised gifts.

> The Foundation Center
> 79 Fifth Ave. at 16th St.
> New York, NY 10003-3076
> Tel: (212) 620-4230 *or* (800) 424-9836
> Fax: (212) 807-3677
> Internet: www.fdncenter.org

12.2 Crown has a series of manuals and videos to help churches establish a ministry to single parents and a helpful book for benevolence committees called *Business Management in the Local Church.*

13.0
Housing

Visit the Crown Financial Ministries Web site at www.crown.org for some beneficial on-line tools. One of Crown's software resources, called *SnapShot Gold,* can handle any of the debts you already have, or it can deal with a debt you might be considering. *SnapShot Gold* is an ideal tool for answering your "What if?" questions about loans or investments.

14.0
INSURANCE

14.1 There are Christian medical cost-sharing plans that offer an alternative to traditional health insurance. Some of them advertise in Christian magazines, and you may be able to find contact information in those sources. Crown Financial Ministries does not endorse these plans, but they may offer reasonable "coverage" for some individuals or families who cannot afford traditional health insurance. You need to investigate thoroughly what the plans cover and what they do not, any waiting period for preexisting conditions, the monthly cost, and *especially* the average length of time it takes to receive benefits.

14.2 A Medi-Gap health insurance policy helps pay for some nursing home costs, including the "gaps," or co-insurance left by Medicare, such as the co-pay owed for days 21 through 100 of a Medicare Benefit period. Premiums for Medi-Gap policies vary between companies. Some of the companies providing Medi-Gap insurance:

American Republic	Golden Rule
Sixth and Keo Sts.	712 11th St.
Des Moines, IA 50334	Lawrenceville, IL 62439
(800) 247-2190	(800) 937-4740

This information is not offered as an endorsement. You must determine that any resource you choose provides services and counsel that are compatible with your own convictions and needs.

14.3 The Memorial Society is a nonprofit organization that helps reduce burial costs through a funeral home near you.

> Continental Association of Funeral
> and Memorial Societies
> 6900 Lost Lake Rd.
> Egg Harbor, WI 54209
> (800) 458-5563

This information is not offered as an endorsement. You must determine that any resource you choose provides services and counsel that are compatible with your own convictions and needs.

15.0
INVESTING

15.1 The Christian Financial Planning Institute is an independent, nonprofit organization that provides comprehensive financial advice from highly qualified professionals. For more information visit their Web site, www.christianfpi.org.

15.2 A number of resources are available for the young and not-so-young to assess a person's personality profile, such as *Personality I.D.®, Your Child Wonderfully Made, The Pathfinder,* and *Career Direct-YES!* For more information visit Crown's Web site at www.crown.org.

15.3 Larry's *Investing for the Future* and mutual fund adviser Austin Pryor's *Sound Mind Investing* are two user-friendly tools, worded in everyday language and presented in easy-to-digest portions. Go to Crown's Web site at www.crown.org for more investing information.

15.4 You may check the www.soundmindinvesting.com and www.crosswalk.com Web sites for assistance. Crown Financial Ministries offers this as information and not as an endorsement.

16.0
MORTGAGE PREPAYMENT

MORTGAGE PREPAYMENT. DRAMATIC SAVINGS result when you pay $50 extra each month on a 30-year, $100,000 mortgage at 7 percent interest.

	Original Mortgage	With Extra $50 Payment
Interest Paid	$139,511.00	$107,855.81
Term	30 years	24 years 3 months
Total Payments	360	291
Interest Saved		$31,655.19
Total Time Saved		5 years 9 months
Payments Eliminated		69

Increase the extra payment amount to $100 and you'll save $50,508.27 in interest and eliminate a total of 114 payments (that's 9½ years). The benefit of paying any extra amount has a powerful leveraging effect on savings returned to you.

17.0
Tools

Use the tools in this section to help you with your budgeting and savings plans:

- Percentage Guide for Family Income
- Savings Account Allocations

PERCENTAGE GUIDE FOR FAMILY INCOME

Family of Four

(The Net Spendable percentages also are applicable to Head of Household family of three.)

Gross Household Income	$25,000 or less	$35,000	$45,000	$55,000	$65,000	$85,000	$115,000
1. Tithe	10%	10%	10%	10%	10%	10%	10%
2. Tax	5.1%	14.9%	17.9%	19.9%	21.8%	25.8%	28.1%
Net Spendable Income	$21,225	$26,285	$32,445	$38,555	$44,330	$54,570	$71,185
Net Spendable Income percentages below total 100%							
3. Housing	38%	36%	32%	30%	30%	30%	29%
4. Food	14%	12%	13%	12%	11%	11%	11%
5. Auto	14%	12%	13%	14%	14%	13%	13%
6. Insurance	5%	5%	5%	5%	5%	5%	5%

Category							
7. Debts	5%	5%	5%	5%	5%	5%	5%
8. Enter./Recreation	4%	6%	6%	7%	7%	7%	8%
9. Clothing	5%	5%	5%	6%	6%	7%	7%
10. Savings	5%	5%	5%	5%	5%	5%	5%
11. Medical	5%	4%	4%	4%	4%	4%	4%
12. Miscellaneous	5%	5%	7%	8%	8%	8%	8%
13. Investments[1]	—	5%	5%	5%	5%	5%	5%

If you have this expense below, the percentage shown must be deducted from other budget categories.

Category							
14. School/Child Care[2]	8%	6%	5%	5%	5%	5%	5%

Category							
15. Unallocated Surplus Income[3]	—	—	—	—	—	—	—

1. This category is used for long-term investment planning, such as caring for elderly parents or retirement.
2. This category is added as a guide only. If you have this expense, the percentage shown must be deducted from other budget categories.
3. This category is used when surplus income is received.

SAVINGS ACCOUNT

Date	Deposit	With-drawal	Balance	Housing	Food	Auto Insur.	Auto Maint.

ALLOCATIONS

Insur-ance	Clothing	Medical	Debts				

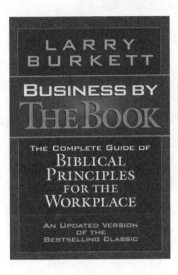
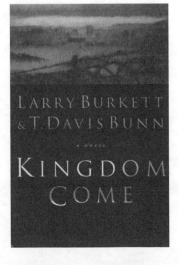